CHILD DEVELOPMENT WITHIN CULTURALLY STRUCTURED ENVIRONMENTS

Parental Cognition and Adult–Child Interaction

Volume 1

Edited by

Jaan Valsiner
University of North Carolina at Chapel Hill

ABLEX PUBLISHING CORPORATION
NORWOOD, NEW JERSEY

LIBRARY OF CONGRESS
Library of Congress Cataloging-in-Publication Data

Parental cognition and adult–child interaction / edited by Jaan Valsiner.
     p.   cm. — (Child development within culturally structured
environments ; v. 1)
   Bibliography: p.
   Includes index.
   ISBN 0-89391-487-8
   1. Children and adults. 2. Social interaction in children.
3. Parent and child. 4. Cognition. I. Valsiner, Jaan.
II. Series.
BF723.A33C48 vol. 1
303.3'2 s—dc19
[303.3'23]   88-6361
                                                              CIP

Ablex Publishing Corporation
355 Chestnut Street
Norwood, New Jersey 07648

Contents

List of Contributors

Anita Gärling, Department of Psychology, Umea University, S-90187 Umea, Sweden.

Tommy Gärling, Environmental Psychology Unit, Umea University, S-90187 Umea, Sweden.

Paula E. Hill, Developmental Psychology Program, University of Michigan, Ann Arbor, Mi. 48109.

George W. Holden, Department of Psychology, University of Texas at Austin, Austin, Tx. 78713.

Nada Ignjatović Savić, Institute of Psychology, Faculty of Philosophy, University of Belgrade, Cika Ljubina 18-20, 11000 Belgrade, Yugoslavia.

Tünde Kovač-Cerović, Institute of Psychology, Faculty of Philosophy, University of Belgrade, Cika Ljubina 18-20, 11000 Belgrade, Yugoslavia.

Ana Pešikan, Institute of Psychology, Faculty of Philosophy, University of Belgrade, Cika Ljubina 18-20, 11000 Belgrade, Yugoslavia.

Dijana Plut, Institute of Psychology, Faculty of Philosophy, University of Belgrade, Cika Ljubina 18-20, 11000 Belgrade, Yugoslavia.

Kathy L. Ritchie, Department of Psychology, University of Texas at Austin, Austin, Tx. 78713.

Peter Stratton, Department of Psychology, University of Leeds, Leeds, England.

Jaan Valsiner, Developmental Psychology Program, Department of Psychology, University of North Carolina at Chapel Hill, Chapel Hill, N.C. 27514.

Marinus H. van IJzendoorn, Department of Theoretical Pedagogics, Leiden University, 2312 AK Leiden, The Netherlands.

René van der Veer, Department of Theoretical Pedagogics, Leiden University, 2312 AK Leiden, The Netherlands.

GENERAL INTRODUCTION

Children's Social Development Within Culturally Structured Environments

Jaan Valsiner

Department of Psychology
University of North Carolina

The reader of the two-volume series that bears the title *Child development within culturally structured environments* is entering a realm of somewhat untraditional directions in research in developmental psychology. Most of the traditional emphases in child psychology can be characterized in terms of narrowing down the focus of research into strictly defined content domains. Therefore, for example, we can evidence research on domains like "social development" that is usually kept separate from the domain of "cognitive development," whereas the proponents of the latter may keep their research equally strictly separated from the former. On the rare occasions where a synthesis between the narrow research perspectives emerges (e.g., in the case of "social cognition"), it very often takes the form of annexation of one perspective by the other (e.g., "social cognition," viewed as cognition, applied to content material that is loosely classified as "social"). Alternatively, it may become an eclectic mixture of theoretical ideas and methodologies that are haphazardly borrowed from both fields, but which never become united into an integrated theoretical perspective.

In contrast, the various contributions to the present two volumes are put together with the aim that an integrated perspective could emerge as a result. That perspective entails interdependence of the developing child with his or her structured and culturally meaningful environments. The child is an active agent within these environments and changes those by acting upon it. On the other hand, the existing structure of the environment constrains the activity of the child, both in terms of physical possibilities and by cultural meanings that are embedded in the child's environment. In the present context, "social" and "cognitive" development are not two separate or haphazardly intermingled domains, but are united into one: all cognitive development is social in its nature (as it is guided, although not determined, by the cultural environment), and all social development involves psychological processes that are cognitive in their nature.

The approach that characterizes the contributions to the present two volumes strives to overcome impasses that are outgrowths of two traditional themes in psychology. These themes have been of interest to psychologists at least over the whole independent history of that discipline. First of those is the fundamental general-biological issue of the contributions of the organism and its environment to the development of the former. This question has recurred with remarkable consistency in psychologists' thinking. At times, of course, the issue of "nature-or-nurture" has been declared "dead"—only to be resurrected by a further generation of psychologists who may be little eager to inquire into the intellectual pitfalls of the previous efforts to solve that complicated problem. The second theme has been almost as pervasive— how can we understand social development in human ontogeny, and in which ways (if any) human social development differs from that of other species?

Both of these questions can be viewed as metatheoretical paradoxes (Valsiner, 1987) that may be more productively bypassed by devising more adequate theoretical systems, than "solved" by any empirical research. One of the possible metatheoretical strategies that can be used is the shift from exclusive separation of the organism and its environment, to viewing the two as separate but interdependent parts of the system that organizes development (see Gottlieb, 1976, 1985; Johnston, 1981). The organism, from that perspective, does not "confront" the pressures of environment as an "opponent," and the latter does not function as the impartial judge of organisms to determine which of them are the "fittest." Instead, the organism makes use of the environmental conditions in the process of active adaptation, which leads to changes in the environment and in the organism itself (Lewontin, 1981).

The issue of specificity of human social development, as it is ordinarily construed in child psychology in terms of child socialization as superimposition of "the social" on "the biological" (nurture vs. nature), can be reformulated along similar lines. The processes of human social development are unique in the sense of integration of biological organismic basis of development (largely shared with other primate species) with specifically human culture—a product of *specifically hu-*

man cultural history which is shared with no other species. Similarly to the epigenetic perspective on biological development, in human social development the developing person is interdependent with the cultural environment, which serves as the resource for the development of the person (Valsiner & Benigni, 1986).

The shared metatheoretical basis of the variety of contributions that are united within the covers of this two-volume series is the interdependence of the developing child and its cultural environment. That interdependence is not an individual affair, but relates to the ways in which child development is organized by cooperative effort of multiple social agents, and in conjunction with the structured nature of the environment. The first volume is devoted to issues of parental cognition and its linkages with the conduct of parents and children in the process of interaction. The second volume deals with the issues of cooperative construction (co-construction) that are involved in children's development. That development takes place *within* environments that are *socially* organized by people who surround them. These people are not passive and neutral bystanders who observe the unfolding of children's "natural" psychological functions in an "objective" way. Instead, they are interested—sometimes in an obsessive way—in guiding children's development in directions that they feel and think are "appropriate" or "desirable"—only rarely meditating about what determines the appropriateness or desirability of these directions. The latter, of course, is the result of their own cultural development, and of their inescapable interdependence with their current cultural environments, which guide children's caregivers towards adopting child-rearing ideas and action strategies in accordance with communally shared folk models.

Despite the active role of the "social others" of the developing child, the social development of the latter is not an one-sided affair of being "forced" to accept externally superimposed "culture" in the course of development. The developing child is an *active participant* in his or her own social development. He or she is one of the agents in the social framework that organizes his or her own social development.

These core theoretical ideas are brought together within a frame of reference that the present author has labelled *individual-socioecological* (Valsiner, 1987, chap. 3). That reference frame constitutes the metatheoretical background for the present volume. In the present two volumes, different contributors address the issues of how environments of children and adults are structured for the purposes of assisting children's development in culturally appropriate directions, and how both children and adults are collective participants in one another's psychological development that takes place in culturally structured environments.

The emphasis on the *culturally structured* environments is crucial for understanding development. It is mainly due to the historical role of Gestalt psychology that psychologists' thinking at times has retained the structural nature of the phenomena they study. However, understanding of the *cultural* nature of the structure of environments has been rare. Only infrequently has that aspect of environment given direct attention in contemporary research literature (e.g., Csikszentmihalyi & Rochberg-Halton, 1981). Interestingly, the idea of cultural organization of children's growth environments has been in general terms recognized as the cornerstone of a number of progressive theoretical systems of human development of this century (Basov, 1931; Vygotski, 1929). "Cultural organization" in the context of the present volumes entails the structuring of children's developmental environments differentially by meanings shared by a suprapersonal collective social unit—social group or ethnic population. Such cultural structuring of environments guides children's development both directly (as children act with objects within such environment on their own), and via the social mediation of persons who are interdependent with the cultural meaning system, on the one hand, and give care to the developing child, on the other. Hence the emphasis in these volumes on children's *social* development within culturally structured environments.

Individual contributions to the volumes cover a vast ground, ranging from more traditionally oriented approaches to child development from the perspectives of environmental and developmental psychologies to specific topics of anthropology and education. Such interdisciplinary coverage is a necessary background for a synthetic theoretical view on children's development (see Epilogue, in Volume 2), since it broadens the world view of child psychology and cuts across boundaries between different disciplines. The existence of such boundaries is another example of how cultural structuring, this time that of science, guides researchers towards specific research activities that may easily lead to artificial limits to solutions of rather comprehensive problems. The science of child development itself develops within culturally organized environments which selectively guide researchers to some (rather than other) questions for inquiry and prescribe certain methods for such investigation. Hopefully, the contributions to the present volumes help the reader to transcend some of the socially instituted structural limits on how we study child development, and replace those by some general suggestions with the help of which new structure of the research process might emerge.

REFERENCES

Basov, M.Ia. (1931). *Obshchie osnovy pedologii* [General foundations of pedology]. Moscow-Leningrad: Gosizdat (in Russian).

Csikszentmihalyi, M., & Rochberg-Halton, E. (1981). *The meaning of things: Domestic symbols and the self.* Cambridge, England: Cambridge University Press.

Gottlieb, G. (1976). The roles of experience in the development of behavior and the nervous system. In G. Gottlieb (Ed.), *Neural and behavioral specificity* (pp. 25–54). New York: Academic Press.

Gottlieb, G. (1985). Anagenesis: Theoretical basis for the ecological void in comparative psychology. In T.D. Johnson & A.T. Pietrewicz (Eds.), *Issues in the ecological study of learning* (pp. 59–72). Hillsdale, NJ: Erlbaum.

Johnston, T. (1981). Contrasting approaches to a theory of learning. *Behavioral and Brain Sciences, 4,* 125–173.

Lewontin, R.L. (1981). On constraints and adaptation. *Behavioral and Brain Sciences, 4,* 244–245.

Valsiner, J. (1987). *Culture and the development of children's action.* Chichester, England: Wiley.

Valsiner, J., & Benigni, L. (1986). Naturalistic research and ecological thinking in the study of child development. *Developmental Review, 6,* 203–223.

Vygotski, L.S. (1929). The problem of the cultural development of the child. *Journal of Genetic Psychology, 36,* 415–434.

PART ONE

Parental Thinking and Action: Mediators of Culture in Child Development

INTRODUCTION

The contributions to Part One deal with the parental cognition as a link between developing children and their environments. Caregivers' thinking about child–environment relationships constitutes the psychological foundation for adults' purposeful guidance of child development. At the same time, parental thinking about children is closely connected with the cultural texture of the adults, as it feeds into the maintenance and innovation of cultural folk models about children and their rearing.

In Chapter 1, Peter Stratton outlines a systemic view of family relationships that is relevant for organizing child development. His perspective of *transactional adaptation* within families, and an emphasis on the reflexivity of family members' thinking about the thinking by other members of their selves (nested cognitive models) is a significant contribution towards capturing the cognitive complexity of the child socialization process. Reflexivity of cognitive processes has only rarely been subjected to explicit study (see Lefebvre, 1977, 1982). Its analysis in the context of family relationships provides novel opportunities for understanding the relationships between culture, parental thinking, and children's actions.

The concept of "culture" in Stratton's paper appears in two senses. First, it denotes the context (and product) of families' functioning, along the lines of analysis of complex phenomena in terms of systemic causality that Stratton advocates. Secondly, it appears in the sense of cross-cultural comparisons of parental thinking which have revealed the fact that families of different ethnic backgrounds think about (and bring up) their children in different ways. That second way of looking at culture is also overviewed in Chapter 2 (George Holden and Kathy

Ritchie), whose comparison of American and Japanese parental thinking supports Stratton's claim for the relevance of cultural structuring of family life as the environment in which child development takes place. However, in the cross-cultural comparisons present in empirical research literature, "culture" usually ceases to be a systemic entity and becomes an "index variable" (see Epilogue for further discussion of that issue).

Holden and Ritchie provide an extensive overview of different aspects of parental thinking and acting in their caregiving role that have found coverage in pertinent research literature. However, as is often the case with empirical research in child psychology, the corpus of published studies covers a vast area of phenomenology and shares little in terms of theoretically substantiated foundations for the empirical research efforts. To remedy the dominance of empiricistic philosophies that are widespread in contemporary child psychology, Holden and Ritchie proceed to give an analysis of parental reasoning along the lines of dialectical thinking. For many contemporary readers, the meaning of "dialectics" may be rather vague, and perhaps often flavored by instances of the use of that way of thinking in imprecise ways in social-political discourse. Therefore, it seems appropriate to note that the philosophical foundation of "dialectics" has nothing in common with the overly active use of that term in some branches of sociology or political ideologies. Instead, it constitutes a philosophical world view that emphasizes the inevitable interdependence of opposite parts within the same whole (system), and a refusal to reduce complex (systemic) phenomena to isolated elementary constituents. Furthermore, dialectical world view, differently from its nondialectical counterparts, is eminently suitable for capturing the processes of development of systemic phenomena. It fits particularly well for the needs of developmental psychologists, and—as Holden and Ritchie demonstrate—is an indispensable tool for the analysis of parental cognitive processes. Caregivers' reasoning process always operates under conditions where opposite states of affairs, pertaining to child's interests, potential dangers inherent in child–environment relationships, and caregivers' own needs, are to be integrated to result in concrete solutions to practical problems. Furthermore, Holden and Ritchie recognize the *process* nature of caregivers' reasoning and acting—"parental intelligence" is not an entity residing in the minds of parents, but a cognitive process that unfolds over time, being provided with a constant flow of information about the problem situation the parent is experiencing in relation with the child and his or her environment. That parental problem solving is necessarily time-dependent should be no surprise. Nevertheless, it is curious that the process orientation carefully described by Holden and Ritchie is so rare in contemporary child psychology, despite its prominence in the past (Werner, 1937, 1957), and in the subfields of decision-making and problem-solving research in the cognitive psychology of our present time (Simon, 1983; Toda, 1980, 1983a,b).

Finally, Part One of the present book ends with an analysis of parental reasoning about child–environment relationships in conjunction with accident prevention tasks. Tommy and Anita Gärling (Chapter 3) address the question of how *potential* events of definitely negative value (children's accidents within dangerous environmental settings) can be prevented by parental actions. These actions towards accident prevention are closely intertwined with attributional thinking by the caregivers about the child *and* the environmental settings the child is in. The Gärlings make use of the line of reasoning on contemporary cognitive theory that analyzes complex decision processes into the "heuristics" (see Kahneman, Slovic, & Tversky, 1982). However, the authors demonstrate that parental reasoning about children's accident prevention is more complex than any direct application of explanatory "heuristics" may explain.

Taken together, the three chapters of Part One complement one another in pointing to the need of developing more sophisticated theoretical tools and empirical methodologies for understanding the complexity of the parental reasoning processes. These processes cannot be studied as an object of investigation in themselves, since they reflect the open-ended nature of child-environment relationships. Parental reasoning serves as the foundation on which caregivers' social assistance to children in their interaction with environments is based.

REFERENCES

Kahneman, D., Slovic, P., & Tversky, A. (Eds.). (1982). *Judgement under uncertainty: Heuristics and biases.* Cambridge, England: Cambridge University Press.

Lefebvre, V.A. (1977). *The structure of awareness.* Beverly Hills, CA: Sage.

Lefebvre, V.A. (1982). *Algebra of conscience.* Dordrecht, The Netherlands: Reidel.

Simon, H.A. (1983). Search and reasoning in problem solving. *Artificial Intelligence, 21,* 7–29.

Toda, M. (1980). Emotion and decision making. *Acta Psychologica, 45,* 133–155.

Toda, M. (1983a). Future time perspective and human cognition: An evolutional view. *International Journal of Psychology, 18,* 351–365.

Toda, M. (1983b). What happens at the moment of decision? Meta-decisions, emotions, and volitions. In L. Sjöerg, T. Tyszka, & J.A. Wise (Eds.), *Human decision models* (pp. 257–283). Bodafors, Sweden: Doxa.

Werner, H. (1937). Process and achievement—A basic problem of education and developmental psychology. *Harvard Educational Review, 7,* 358–368.

Werner, H. (1957). The concept of development from a comparative and organismic point of view. In D.B. Harris (Ed.), *The concept of development: An issue in the study of human behavior* (pp. 125–148). Minneapolis, MN: University of Minnesota Press.

CHAPTER 1

Parents' Conceptualization of Children as the Organizer of Culturally Structured Environments

Peter Stratton

Department of Psychology
University of Leeds
Leeds, Great Britain

From the beginning of life it is overwhelmingly the family that mediates cultural and social values and presents them to the child. As the child grows, other sources of influence come to be important, but it is arguable that the family remains as the single, dominant, most powerful source of cultural values. There is a substantial empirical literature which deals with the ways that cultural values, as represented in parental behaviors, influence children within families. However, there has been little coordinated study of the family within developmental psychology, and certainly the transmission of cultural influence to the child has not been a major focus of attention. Handel (1985), introducing the third edition of *The Psychosocial Interior of the Family,* states that "families are not simple reflections of the society to which they belong and the culture in which they participate. Rather, families exert effects at their own level of organization." However, he also points out "a glaring omission. It is an astonishing fact that no social science concerns itself with studying how families function. . . . For the most part, the field of . . . family therapy has taken on this task, and the social sciences have apparently been content to allow this to occur" (pp. xi–xiii). These statements are a warning that information about the forms in which cultural values are incorporated in family functioning, and the effects on the child, is widely scattered through the literature of a number of disciplines and subdisciplines.

5

Cultural values within families have in fact been extensively investigated within developmental psychology in the massive studies of child rearing that flourished around the mid-century (Becker, 1964; Martin, 1975). It may not have been entirely apparent to these scientists that the major dimensions chosen for study—love versus hostility, control versus autonomy, etc.—represented major cultural preoccupations of the time. In fact it seems that little consideration was given to the source of parental beliefs about child rearing, and the field at that time almost entirely ignored the role of children in shaping their parents' behavior. We now know that the accumulation of statistical relationships between parental behaviors or attitudes and the characteristics of children was largely unproductive. I would propose that a major reason for this was the lack of a theoretical basis for interpreting the relationships between the two classes of variables in a realistic way. This in turn is attributable to the lack of detailed theoretical frameworks which would help researchers to conceptualize the processes by which families function. It is to be hoped that the neglect of the family by psychology is coming to an end, and there are signs that this might be so. Introducing a special issue of *Child Development* devoted to family development, Kaye (1985) considered that "the awareness of developing children as interacting members of developing family systems is already entrenched in so many investigators' minds as to constitute an irreversible paradigm shift" (p. 280). However, Kaye also points out that all of the articles in the issue offer questions, not answers.

This chapter will review some representative examples of recent studies which provide information about how parents' beliefs about children are a channel for cultural influences in their families, but a comprehensive survey will not be attempted for two reasons. First, there is an enormous quantity of material that could be interpreted under the heading of transmission of cultural values within the family, which it is far beyond the scope of a single chapter to summarize. Secondly, a listing of cultural influences within a simple model, in which the parents are viewed as a kind of filter through which cultural values are transmitted to the children, would be unproductive. There is in fact a major difficulty in knowing how something as abstract as a cultural value can have an effect on behavior. Family theorists have concentrated much more on the ways that families create their own reality (Reiss, 1981), and parts of this reality may relate only indirectly, or not at all, to values in the wider culture.

Stein (1985) proposes that values only affect people when they are used, as in the processes of family adaptation. In fact Stein argues that it is a mistake to see the family as the "agent of the internalisation of the (impersonal, external) culture . . . instead, culture is a result of the externalisation and re-creation of family" (p. 219). The proposal is that families over the generations solve the problems posed by their biological inheritance and by society, by inventing a culture which enables the relationships, the sources of difficulty, the rules, and the unacceptable desires, to be treated as existing outside the family. Culture is therefore not something that exists separately from the family and which has a causal influence on what goes on inside families. Rather, it is a creation arising from the need to externalize family processes, but which in turn has an effect of legitimating those processes and, so, of stabilizing family functioning.

Stein's analysis suggests that a search for correlations between cultural values and children's behavior will be unproductive. Not that relationships will not be found. If cultural beliefs are an externalization of family processes, then important parts of these processes will have clear parallels in society. A public form of this process, as Stein points out, is the ambivalent attitude to such figures as the outlaw and the lunatic, who are needed to portray essential but unacceptable aspects of the family. But his formulation fundamentally questions the assumption that, if we know how cultural values are transmitted to children, we will have a route to understanding their behavior. Instead it directs us to examining beliefs within families as the primary phenomenon. Cultural beliefs are useful in this process, because they provide a public form of what may be inaccessibly private within the family. The focus of this chapter will therefore be to explore belief systems within families, particularly those that can be expected to directly affect the children, but will attempt to conceptualize the relationship between family belief systems and wider cultural values. Because of the impoverished state of our psychology of the family, it will be necessary first to establish a way of conceptualizing family processes. The next two sections therefore summarize two formulations which are fundamental to the psychology of the family being developed by the Leeds Family Research Centre. The presentation is restricted to those aspects that relate to parental beliefs about children and their development, having been extracted from a more general account (Stratton & Hanks, in preparation). Parental beliefs about children, which are clearly reflected in cultural values, seem to be the most central to an understanding of how families set up the sociocultural environment within which children function.

TRANSACTIONAL ADAPTATION

A productive process within developmental psychology has been to coordinate the two concepts of transaction and adaptation. The significance of a transactional view (Sameroff & Chandler, 1975; Stratton, 1977) has been to provide a conceptual framework within which it is possible to recognize the reciprocal nature of influence between parents and children. Until now, the concept of transaction has been applied almost exclusively to dyads, and it is proposed that it will be fruitful to broaden the concept for application to full family functioning. First however, the current status of the two concepts is summarized. The transactional model explicitly works in terms of sequences in time in which the action of one partner establishes the environment within which the response of the second partner is made. That response in turn changes the situation, so that the environment for the first partner is now different, and the response can be expected to be a function of this new environment. The concept of transaction has been very effective in allowing the study particularly of mother–infant dyads to recognize that whatever influences may be operating on the mother from outside the relationship, the behavior, dispositions, and past history of the infant will also exert a considerable influence on her. The influence of the infant on its caregiver (Lewis & Rosenblum, 1974) has come to be widely recognized since Bell (1968) drew attention to this direction of effects. From this perspective it follows that, to a large extent, children create their own environments, though this is not to ignore the other influences on both participants.

The concept of adaptation (Stratton 1982a, 1985) is most clearly defined in terms of the individual. At its simplest, it proposes that individuals will always adopt the best solution they can to the demands of any situation as they perceive them. In most cases, and almost invariably for children, individual adaptations are as short sighted as are evolutionary adaptations. That is to say, the solution is defined in terms of the immediate resources and constraints, and with little or no reference to longer-term consequences. One important implication of this perspective is that it is the responsibility of the child-rearing environment to set up demands which will in turn provoke functional adaptations. That is to say, the caregivers need to pose challenges to the child such that, by meeting these challenges, the child will develop competences and behavioral dispositions which will enhance future adaptations (Stratton, 1985).

The two concepts of *transaction* and *adaptation* underlie the discussions throughout this chapter, but the brief descriptions given here provide an adequate basis for the first development, which is to comment on the relationship between them. Stratton (1982a) has argued that any specific adaptation is likely to have potential benefits and potential losses in terms of future functioning. That is, a particular adaptation will produce competences and dispositions which will equip the individual to function well in certain future environments, but less well in others. Subsequently (Stratton 1982b), the term *transactional adaptation* was coined to refer to the interdependence of the two concepts. In terms very similar to Piaget's concepts of *assimilation* and *accommodation,* it was recognized that adaptations may be achieved either by modifying the individual to cope with the demands, or by modifying the environment so that the demand is coped with in a different way. For infants the latter strategy invariably means having an effect on the caregiver which brings about the desired result. For example, a hungry infant may solve the problem by modifying the behavior of the caregiver so that food is provided. It is clear that this class of adaptations is one that involves a transaction, and reflecting on the transactional nature of the adaptation makes it clear that the apparently simple situation of a baby eliciting food from a caregiver has very extensive implications. The particular technique employed by the baby, for example a particular form of crying, will not only mobilize appropriate action to deal with the hunger but will also influence the caregivers' perception of the baby, and so may have consequences far into the future. So we come to the point that adaptations will frequently involve influencing other people, usually members of the family, and because of the transactional nature of this process, the whole context in which future adaptations will have to be made may be modified by the particular processes that have already gone before.

THE FAMILY AS AN ENTITY

Much of the literature on the family readily comes to deal with families as if they were independent entities with their own existence. The approach of treating families as having the same dynamic processes and life cycles as individuals, which was particularly associated with the psychoanalytic approach, is now generally regarded as inappropriate. However, abandoning this perspective has left the field without any very clear way of conceptualizing the family as an entity. On the other hand, those working with families, particularly in therapy, have no doubt that the family is not just a collection of individuals who influence each other. I would propose that a significant advance in conceptualizing the emergent properties of the family can be achieved by considering the complex conceptual processes that are fundamental to family interaction. I will therefore briefly describe a formulation of these processes which will then be a basis for interpreting some empirical evidence about the ways parents conceptualize their children.

There are several conceptualizations within psychology of the processes I wish to describe, but most of them carry a considerable number of implications from the theories with which they are associated. I have therefore chosen to formulate my ideas in terms of models. Taking, as an example, the model of a bridge that an engineer might construct: The general characteristic of a model is that it is a representation, in different materials, of those aspects of a complex reality which are of major concern. Our starting point is that each human being carries in his or her brain a model of their world. In common with other models, this is a simplified representation in different materials, and it is highly selective, modelling only those aspects which are important to the functioning of the individual. There is a reflexive element here, as it is the cognitive system, i.e., the model, which evaluates information and decides what is significant. Only one aspect of the reflexivity of these models concerns us here.

A unique feature of the models that we operate is that they include as an important component a model of ourselves. This aspect has been extensively covered within psychology under the headings of body schema and self image. Another important feature of our models is that they include models of other people, but not only this: They also simulate other peoples' models of their world. For example, I have some estimation of how my students see their worlds, and I can adjust my teaching to take account of that information. I have a much more elaborate estimation of the model of reality that my own children have developed, and many of the decisions I take about them are influenced by that knowledge. Proceeding from here, one aspect of the world that these other people have to model is myself—a relatively unimportant part of the world of my students, but a much more significant part of the world of my children. In either case they will have a model of me, and I have some idea (whether accurate or not) of what that model may be. This everyday phenomenon, that two people will each have an idea of what the other one thinks of them, will occur whenever there is a relationship, and the elaborateness of the conceptualization will increase as the relationship increases in significance and complexity. It is therefore axiomatic that the process will reach its most complex forms within families, where there is an enormous amount of information about, and investment in, the other members. Let us suppose that John thinks that his sister Jane sees him as insensitive, self-confident, brave, but not too bright. This is our core phenomenon of Johns' model of Jane's model of John.

It can be seen that, within a small family, say, John, Jane, and their two parents, the scope for a complex network of beliefs is already very great. Extending our core phenomenon to all four people, each member of the family will have his or her own image of himself or herself, an image of each of the other three family members, and models of the image that each of those three people have of him or her. More than this, there is a circular process, because the image that people have of themselves is almost certainly derived from the interpretations of their characteristics and behavior that they are offered by other members of the family. It is necessary to say "almost certainly," because we have in fact very little empirical evidence, but the issue is discussed further below. However, it is a basic contention of this chapter that this is a fundamental part of the process of the development of the individual within the family, and to some extent what follows is an argument in support of this assumption. If the family hold beliefs about the kind of person that I am, and if my beliefs about myself have grown up influenced by the other members of my family, it is clear that my behavior is likely to be strongly constrained by these expectations. It is a commonplace that it is very difficult to act "out of character" in the presence of one's own family, even if that character has been discarded in all other environments. Rather more concretely, Darley and Fazio (1980) discuss the conditions in which normal social inter-actions are subjected to expectancy confirmation processes and so produce self-fulfilling prophecies.

The web of interlocking beliefs within which the individual is held in the family goes beyond what has already been described in at least two ways; the perception of relationships, and the nesting of beliefs. In our small family, John not only perceives and models the other individuals, but he perceives the relationships between them. For example, John conceptualizes the relationship between his parents, the differences in that relationship when he or his sister are present, and the way his relationship with either of his parents is modified when the other one is present. This potentially allows the nesting of models within models for relationships, so, for example, John is aware that his parents know he has an antagonistic relationship with Jane. This is the first level of his model of his parents' model of the relationship between himself and his sister. This second form of complexity relates to the fact that modelling of other peoples' models is readily, and quite naturally, taken to several levels of nesting within families. These nested models can be described as operating either horizontally or vertically. Consider the following two perfectly ordinary statements that John might make:

1. Jane reckons that mother thinks I'm modest.
2. Jane knows I think she's unfair when I see her avoiding me.

The first of these I would call a horizontal nesting. Being modest is an evaluation of oneself. Mother thinking that John is modest is mother's model of John's evaluation of himself. Jane reckoning that mother thinks that John is modest is Jane's model of mother's model of John's evaluation of himself. And we have to remember that this statement was made by John, and so we have John's model of Jane's model of mother's model of John's model of himself. Horizontal nesting is therefore a sequence in which each step consists of one member of the family having a representation of the beliefs of another member of the family. The second sentence can be charted as follows:

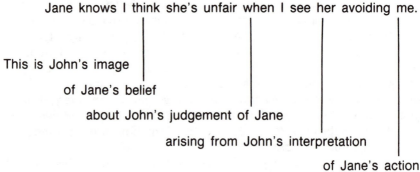

Jane knows I think she's unfair when I see her avoiding me.

This is John's image

of Jane's belief

about John's judgement of Jane

arising from John's interpretation

of Jane's action

as implying an evaluation of John.

Such a sequence differs from a horizontal nesting because perceptions are embedded within each person's models. John's model of Jane incorporates a knowledge (or at least a belief) about Jane's perception of an aspect of his model "Jane knows I think". This perception by Jane is seen by John as contingent on her further knowledge of his perception "I see her", of her action "avoiding me"; an action which itself implies an evaluation of John. We have called such examples vertical nesting because of the progressive relationship within each person's models. One of the major differences between the two kinds of nesting is that horizontal sequences entail that successive models become progressively simpler and inevitably less accurate. The inaccuracy arises because the later models are entirely incorporated within earlier ones and are less open to direct experience. In vertical nesting one is dealing with a progression of different aspects of the same person's model, each of which may be open to direct evidence.

Now, the reason why these nested beliefs are so powerful within families is that they are the basis on which family members interact with each other. Any meaningful interpersonal interaction is based on each participant conceptualizing the other person's view of the situation and both sending messages and interpreting the other's reactions in the light of that knowledge. So how John treats Jane on a particular occasion will reflect his image of himself and his evaluation of Jane; also his knowledge of how she will perceive this treatment, the effects of it on her perception of him, and what her perception of his action will tell her about his perception of her. Obviously, the list could go on for a long time before it exhausted the degrees of nesting that are easily and naturally operated by all family members. Furthermore, we have not got beyond John's initial action and so have not started to consider Jane's response, we have not considered any perceptions of relationships, and we have only been taking account of two participants. It is quite clear that this conceptualization opens up the possibility of an enormously complex analysis of family function which we do not yet have the techniques to specify in a manageable form. However, I hope that, from this very preliminary presentation, it is possible to progress from seeing a family as a group of interacting individuals, to seeing the mutual conceptualizations as so richly interdependent that the family emerges with its own existence and identity.

This section has attempted to show how the belief systems of family members, particularly their beliefs about each other, can form an extremely complex network. This network was referred to above as a web, and it seems that, in practice, a spider's web is quite an appropriate model. It is a complex structure which provides support, a framework within which movement can be directed, and a structure by which basic resources can be provided. However, for the unwary, it may also be an invisible trap with unknown dangers, and the characteristic that, unless you are strong enough to break free, the harder you struggle the more firmly you are held. All models have their limitations, and I do not want to pursue this one too far. Instead, I wish to take the two concepts, of transactional adaptation and of mutual conceptualization, as a background for interpreting a representative sample of the available evidence about parents' conceptualizations of children.

PARENTS' BELIEFS AND CHILDREN'S ENVIRONMENTS

Having described the two sets of concepts of transactional adaptation and mutual conceptualizing, it is now possible to provide a more explicit formulation of the hypothesis of this chapter. It is proposed that all parents have both a general conceptualization of what children of any given age, sex, etc. are like, and a specific set of beliefs about each of their own children. Considering a specific child, the beliefs of a parent will determine how the child is treated. Treatment here includes the information the child is given about the kind of person he or she is, as well as more practical arrangements. From this treatment the child will build up models both of what kind of person he or she is and of how he or she is perceived by the parents, as well as models of the parents. These models will provide the basis for the child to choose particular modes of behavior, which will feed back to the parents' perceptions. This circular process can be charted as follows:

It must be recognized that this is only one cycle, taken out of the interlocking cycles which make up the full family process, but it is the part of that process which is most important for our present purposes. An effective investigation of the hypothesis propounded at the beginning of this section would require a study which followed all of the stages of this cycle. Because the discipline of psychology has only recently, and gradually, been working towards such formulations, it is inevitable that evidence, where it exists, will apply to only a limited segment of the cycle. I shall therefore review the kinds of evidence we have about each stage of the cycle of Figure 1, and attempt to indicate why it needs to be interpreted within the full circular framework. In many areas there are an enormous number of relevant studies, so that any choice is rather arbitrary. I have tried to select examples which are contemporary and representative, and which are particularly relevant

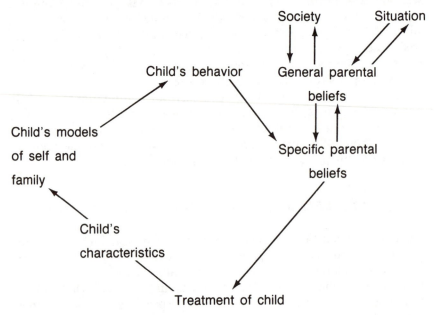

Figure 1. Cycle through which cultural beliefs are related to the behavior of a child in a family.

to the issue of cultural beliefs. Following this review, a case will be described which illustrates the circular process of Figure 1. The first stage of the review deals with parents' cultural beliefs, first about children in general, and then about their specific child.

PARENTS' CULTURAL BELIEFS

The two levels at which parents' cultural beliefs are incorporated into their family will be labeled *general* and *specific*. Examples of the former are beliefs about gender role, moral values, political and religious views, and beliefs about the nature of child development. These views are held about people or types of person in general, so, while they will be applied to a particular child, they relate to a broader belief system of the parent. Specific beliefs may also be held about individual children. A particular child may be regarded as especially bright, shy, stubborn, robust, or selfish. While there have been some studies of specific beliefs, mostly within the framework of temperament studies, there has been much more research on general parental beliefs.

General Parental Beliefs

Parents from different cultures can be expected to have marked differences in their beliefs which should be reflected in the family. Many studies have used this fact as a basis for exploring parental beliefs. In an instructive study Goodnow, Cashmore, Cotton, and Knight (1984) investigated mothers' beliefs about child development in samples with Australian and Lebanese backgrounds. They found that ethnicity was a better predictor of beliefs about developmental timetables than were socioeconomic status, gender, or birth order, but feel that the implications go beyond a simple model of age expectations fitting the values of the culture. It is argued that more fundamental values underlie the differences. Thus it is suggested that in Western culture it is assumed that "earlier is better," and that learning must not be left too late. In contrast is the belief in Lebanese culture that children should not be pressured because they will be able to acquire the necessary skills when the time comes that they need them. DeVries and Sameroff (1984) studied three East African cultures and found consistent relationships between cultural beliefs about children, and both the treatment the children received and their temperamental characteristics.

Differences can also be found between parents within one culture. Ispa, Gray, and Thornburg (1984) found that, when compared to parents in "thing-oriented" jobs, parents in person-oriented jobs reported less need to be in control when interacting with their children, more receptivity of their children's bids for attention, more willingness to encourage and be involved in their children's play, and a greater willingness to let their children direct their interactions. These studies are representative of a large number which indicate that parents' expectations about children tend to be in accordance with more general cultural beliefs. Other origins of parents' general expectations are less well studied, though we know that, at least for women, many beliefs about children and child rearing are derived from their own mothers (Cohler & Grunebaum, 1981). The available studies also indicate that parental beliefs translate rather directly into ways of treating the children. Our provisional model supposes that the process works by general beliefs affecting specific beliefs, which in turn determine the treatment of the child. It may be that this assumption will have to be questioned, but it will be provisionally accepted for the present as being the most likely route for most of the important effects.

Specific Parental Beliefs

A very large body of research has been based on the analysis of child temperament that was first reported by Thomas, Chess, Birch, Herzig, and Korn (1963). Many of these studies have relied on parental reports for their information about children and, in so doing, assume that these reports are at least reasonably accurate. This assumption has been increasingly shown to be unjustified by research which has also studied the children directly (St. James-Roberts & Wolke, 1983; Zeanah, Keener, & Anders, 1986). Also, in the East African study (DeVries & Sameroff, 1984) quoted above, the temperament ratings of children by their mothers were found to owe more to cultural values and expectations than they did to the actual characteristics of the children. It seems that parents' perceptions of their young children cannot be regarded as being simply determined by the characteristics of the children. Most of the studies have concentrated on the pattern of temperament identified as the "difficult child," and it is easy to recognize in this case that parental beliefs about the child, whether or not accurate, are likely to be important.

A measure of maternal perception of the infant has been reported by Broussard (1978), who reports a number of studies which show that scores on the "Neonatal Perception Inventory" (NPI) predict aspects of maternal behavior, the mother–child relationship, and the quality of functioning of the child for up to 10 years subsequently (Broussard 1976, 1979). However, the NPI is a very simple scale of six items, and is completely uninformative about the forms that maternal perceptions of babies may take. One conclusion that could be drawn from these studies is that, if such a crude measure of maternal perception is such a powerful predictor, then a detailed knowledge of how mothers perceive their babies would open the way to major advances in our understanding.

A series of studies is under way in the Leeds Family Research Centre (LFRC) which is designed to investigate the significance of parental perceptions. One interest is in how the initial perceptions that parents have of their babies affect the early transactions, and what kinds of long-standing patterns are set up as a result. The first stages, reported by Stratton (1987) involved the development of a checklist of 78 items that could be applied to a baby, and presenting these to 88 primiparous mothers 12 days after the birth. Mothers had first to judge whether each term could meaningfully be applied to a 12-day-old baby, then to rate their own, and an "ideal," baby on the applicable items. Some of the major findings were as follows:

The judgement of whether an item was applicable or not was based on judgements about the kinds of capacities that babies have. So a factor analysis generated a first factor composed of items that describe negative emotions (*inactive, unhappy, tense, hostile*, etc.). Some mothers felt that these kinds of terms could be applied to a baby, while others did not. Subsequent factors were labelled *social assertiveness, responsiveness, positive emotional openness*, etc. The beliefs about which items were applicable were most consistently associated with characteristics of the mothers, in particular social class, maternal age, and the type of feeding adopted.

In the factor analysis of the mothers' ratings of their own babies, the first factor was labelled *positiveness*, being composed of items like *aggressive, tough, confident, vigorous, strong, learns fast, socially responsive*, etc. This factor was positively associated with the time for which the mother had held her baby during the hour following birth. The factors from these scores reflected qualities of the baby: *positiveness, easygoing, demanding, attractive/pleasant*, etc. In general these items correlated most consistently with various measures of the amount of contact that mothers had been able to have with their babies following the birth.

Looking at individual items, the amount of separation of mother from baby during the first 2 days correlated with higher ratings of *distrustful, lazy,* and *shy*, and lower ratings of *enjoys food, happy, expressive,* and *good*.

When there had been a longer delay after the birth before the mother was able to hold her baby, she was more likely (at 12 days) to rate the baby as higher than an ideal baby on *active, stubborn, restless,* and *noisy,* and lower than the ideal on *passive, attractive,* and *happy.*

In a subsequent (unpublished) study, Kryshna Singh and I followed up a sample of 25 mothers and found that maternal perceptions postnatally predicted several measures of the quality of the mother–infant relationship at 10 weeks.

A number of conclusions can be drawn from this research that have a bearing on understanding how parental perceptions of their children mediate external influences and provide the cultural context within which the children will develop. It seems that mothers approach their first baby with a coherent set of expectations about the nature of babies, and they very quickly also acquire a specific perception of their own baby. These perceptions are influenced by the circumstance of the mother and by her experiences at the birth of the baby. The tendencies in mothers' perceptions that were identified are of a kind that would be expected to significantly influence the kinds of interactions that would be set up. To take just one example from Stratton (1987), some mothers do not feel it is meaningful to think in terms of a baby having negative emotions, as indicated by their rating items like *inactive, unhappy, tense,* and *hostile* as inapplicable. Such mothers would have to interpret the behavior of a stiffly unhappy baby differently from a mother who feels that a baby can be thought of as having negative emotions. Whichever mother is "right," there can be little doubt that their babies will be treated differently, and so are likely to become different. The consistency with which measures of early contact correlated with mothers' perceptions is also notable (altogether, 28 measures of obstetric experience were tested). It was concluded that maternal perceptions of babies are an important route by which perinatal and broader cultural influences on the mother can affect her relationship with the baby.

Effects of Parental Cultural Beliefs on Their Children

Few people, from Freud and Watson to Laing (1971), have doubted that parental beliefs have an effect on children within the family. However, as with many areas of psychology, the empirical evidence is less clear than what is "obviously" true. Studying American families of Japanese and Caucasian origin, McDermott, Char, Robillard, Hsu, Tseng, and Ashton (1983) found differences of cultural attitude towards children which are at least as substantial as those of Goodnow et al. (1984). In this case Japanese parents placed a higher value on collective action, an orientation to practical tasks, and a concentration on cognitive approaches, as in the sharing of ones deepest thoughts. In contrast, the

Caucasian parents valued individuality and the expression of emotions, with a belief that children should be exposed to the reality of difficulties of relationships within the family. However, this research group has also studied the attitudes of adolescents within the same sample of families and has not found differences to parallel the differences between their parents (McDermott, Robillard, Char, Hsu, Tseng, & Ashton, 1983). At least during adolescence, internal needs and the common external culture shared by these two groups seem to have overridden parental influence.

At the other end of the age scale, one focus for research has been the treatment of children according to gender expectations, and there seems little doubt that parents do treat their children differentially. Immediately after birth, it seems that mothers will treat the sexes differently, talking and offering *en face* stimulation more to girls and giving boys more vestibular stimulation (Thoman, Liederman, & Olson, 1972; Hwang, 1978). The earliest indications of an awareness of sexual identity seem to appear during play (Cairns, 1979), and a number of studies have demonstrated parental bias in the kinds of play encouraged. Weitzman, Birns, and Friend (1985) found significant differences in five out of eight measures of mothers' language to their (2.5- to 3.5-year-old) sons and daughters, in ways that would be likely to facilitate cognitive development more in the males. These differences were still present, though not as strongly, in a group of mothers identified as holding nontraditional views of sex roles. Weitzman et al. did not relate the maternal measures to the children's behavior, but O'Brien and Huston (1985) reported such data for a younger sample. They found substantial differences in the ways parents treated their male and female toddlers, but the expectations of parents were not clearly reflected in the children's play. It must, however, be said that the play choices of the children, particularly the boys, were so strongly sex-typed that some findings were likely to have been obscured by ceiling effects.

The clearest expression of parental attitudes to sex roles is likely to be in their own choices of activities both in the home and with respect to employment. Specifically, the participation of the father in domestic activities, and the participation of the mother in employment outside the home, should be expected both to indicate an important aspect of their perceptions of appropriate sex roles and to convey this information to their children. Paternal participation in domestic activity has been assumed to be rising over the last few years, but we have little evidence of the effects, if any, on the children. In fact Beail (1985) reports data which suggest that the actual degree of participation by fathers may have been greatly overestimated, particularly by the fathers themselves.

The effects of maternal employment have been much more intensively studied, and in general it has been found to be associated with positive effects on daughters, particularly in their attitude to femininity, but some negative consequences for boys (Hoffman, 1983). There are several possible explanations of such findings, but Alvarez (1985) has conducted a detailed analysis which proposed that the effects of maternal employment on the child are mediated by the ways that mothers think about their children. The study found little direct relationship between the factors influencing whether the mother worked and her attitude to her children (Bronfenbrenner, Alvarez, & Henderson, 1984). However, the kind of work combined with the sex of the child constituted a powerful predictor of how positively the mother viewed her children. More specifically, mothers who worked from choice and who experienced less role conflict over working were more likely to view their children positively. However the most important factor in perception of the male children seems to have been the type of work. All mothers tended to see boys as more active, but this was construed positively by mothers working part time, but negatively, with the sons being reported as being demanding and noncompliant, by full-time workers.

With studies such as that of Alvarez we are beginning to tackle the interplay of influence in a meaningful way. It seems that, at least in this case, the factors responsible for the parents' choices in their own lives did not directly affect their perceptions of their children. These perceptions seem to have resulted from an interaction between the nature of the adaptation that working represented, and the characteristics of the child. Having said this, the limitations of the study must be recognized. The measure of maternal attitude related only to positive perception of the child, and so is very restricted. Also, although the focus of the study was on maternal perception as mediating between employment and the effects on the child, no information was obtained about the children. So, while other studies leave little doubt about the fact of a link between maternal employment and child characteristics, the nature of the link is still speculative. Indeed, Alvarez points out that an important factor in shaping maternal attitudes may be the characteristics of the child, but accepts that his study provided no way of assessing this possibility. The child's contribution to the process is discussed next by viewing the child as a mediator of the effects of specific parental beliefs.

Children's Characteristics Mediating Parental Influence

In the model propounded in Figure 1, the treatment of the child is mediated both by the characteristics of the child and then by the models held by the child of itself, other family members, and family relationships. Family beliefs are also represented within the child's model, and these will eventually come to be the general beliefs with which the grown-up child starts a new phase of family formation and parenting.

We have evidence from a variety of sources that a particular form of treatment will have different effects depending on the child to whom it is applied. The finding by Schaffer (1966) that active children do better in a less stimulating environment while inactive children thrive on greater stimulation is a specific instance based on temperament. More generally, the follow-up of the infants in the New York study (Thomas, Chess, & Birch, 1968) was interpreted as indicating that the effects of temperamental dispositions are mediated by parental attitudes and treatment of the child. It could equally well be cited as evidence that the effects of parental treatment are mediated by the temperament of the child. Cultural values may operate in such a way that the effect of a specific kind of treatment will have different outcomes. For example Rohner and Pettengill (1985) found that the evaluation that children make of parental behaviors may differ according to cultural values. While American youths treated a high level of parental control as indicating hostility and rejection, Korean youths associated control with warmth and low ratings of neglect. Such examples are very much in keeping with what would be predicted by the concept of transactional adaptation. A finding with similar implications, but related to the age of the child, is reported by Karniol and Ross (1975). They examined the effect of parental instructions to play with a toy on the judgement of subjects about whether the child really wanted to play with the toy. Kindergarten children regarded a parental instruction as increasing the likelihood that playing with the toy was internally motivated, whereas parental instruction reduced the perception of internal motivation for older children. This example was chosen from the many that are available because it introduces a major component of family belief systems, that is, beliefs about the causes of events, including the behavior of family members, issues that are returned to below.

The Child's Models

The ways that the child's experiences affect the formation of models about the self and other members of the family is not so directly amenable to empirical study. The process has, however, been assumed in a wide range of approaches to development, particularly those with therapeutic implications. In the most general sense, theories of self-image and identity formation, of which Erikson's (1968) is representative, assume that the sense of self derives from experiences of how one is treated and how ones behavior is responded to, and early in life these experiences will be mostly within the family. Personal construct theory (Kelly, 1955; Bannister & Fransella, 1985) and the associated techniques of repertory grids are based entirely on the claim that the most important source of individuals' world views, and of their behavioral choices, is their perception of the significant relationships they experienced during development. The whole family therapy movement is based on a fundamental assumption that symptomatic behavior of an individual child is an expression of an unresolved conflict within the family (Hoffman, 1981). However, a concomitant of this view is that children adopt the definition of themselves that is provided by their family, and in disturbed families this means accepting that they are either mad or bad (Laing, 1971). A final example, for which some evidence has already been cited, is the finding that parents' beliefs about children derive from the way they were treated in childhood, which is itself evidence that children internalize representations of parents based on the ways they perceive the treatment they have received during childhood.

In a sense the whole of developmental psychology consists of the attempt to draw links between each of the earlier stages of Figure 1 and the child's behavior. No claim is being made here that the particular route mapped in this chapter is the only possible one, but it is suggested that the frequent failure to find strong direct connections, for example the large-scale failure of the child-rearing studies, indicates the need for a more systemic approach.

FULL CIRCLE

In exploring the proposed sequences of Figure 1, evidence has been quoted from studies that are representative of the ways that separate links have been tackled. In summary, there is evidence for each of the stages. Many studies have shown that parents bring to their role beliefs and expectations about children, and these beliefs have diverse origins though their own experiences as children seem likely to be particularly powerful. Whatever their source, these general beliefs will reflect the values of the broader culture, remembering Stein's (1985) point that the general cultural beliefs are (to an unknown extent) derived from the ways that families function within the culture. Many studies point to the fact that these general beliefs have a considerable influence on the ways that parents will perceive their own children, while there is much less evidence that children modify their parents beliefs about the nature of children in general. Examples have been cited to indicate that the beliefs held by parents do affect the ways they treat their children, but in several cases there seemed to be little direct consequence in the behavior of the children. In itself this suggests that parental treatment is not directly linked to child behavior but is mediated through other processes. Evidence is then provided to support the claim that the consequences of treating a child in a particular way will depend on characteristics of the child. The link to the various models held by the child is less easy to establish, partly because empirical work has not been couched in these terms and partly because we are dealing with unobservable constructs. Nevertheless, the idea that the child's view of self and of the roles of others derives from the kind of treatment provided within the family is widely supported in the literature.

While there is an increasing recognition that developmental psychology must progress to interpreting child behavior as part of a wider system, such perspectives are much more complex than those of simple linear causality, and correspondingly difficult to translate into practical understanding. In such circumstances a specific example may be particularly helpful. I have taken the case of a family in which the child had a minor degree of congenital handicap; she could be designated as "clumsy," as a specific example through which the circle of Figure 1 can be explored. Children who are handicapped offer particular challenges in cultures which place a high value on competitiveness and achievement. They also challenge a developmental psychology which tends to view childhood primarily as a preparation for adulthood, and to evaluate the characteristics of children and the caring practices of their parents in terms of their consequences for the adult that the child will become.

Before offering the illustrative case, there are two particular aspects that may be present in families with a handicapped child that should be mentioned. Brinker and Lewis (1982) discuss five reasons why handicapped infants are likely to experience fewer environmental contingencies. They then point out that the parents will also experience less contingent responding from these infants, which will in turn further reduce the contingent experiences offered to the child. Pollner and McDonald-Wikler (1985) report a case in which a severely retarded child was perceived by her whole family as being highly competent. The behavior of the child was shaped, and persistently misinterpreted, in ways that would sustain the belief. External agencies, which universally assessed the child as severely retarded, came to be seen by the family as having been fooled by the child: further proof of her intelligence. This is an extreme case by any standards, but it indicates the extent to which it is possible for parents' interpretations of a child's behavior to be filtered by their general needs and expectations.

I will take as my illustrative example a case of a mildly handicapped child which has already been described in another context (Stratton, 1985). The characteristics of the case can be listed as follows:

- Having been born following a disastrous obstetric history, and destined to be an only child, Lucy was very precious to her parents, and they knew how vulnerable infants are having had six previous miscarriages or neonatal deaths.
- They recognized early that she was slow, but had to make substantial and continued efforts, during which they came to exaggerate Lucy's disability, to obtain medical recognition and help.
- The parents came to believe that Lucy needed protection, especially from experiences of failure.
- They therefore protected her from challenges and never indicated to her that they expected successful performance from her.
- If Lucy waited long enough, the parents would always perform any task for her.
- Lucy developed low self-esteem and had no expectation of being able to improve her abilities in any area. It seemed to be important to her that her parents should do things for her. We suspected that she believed that interaction between her parents was dangerous and that they should be kept busy worrying about her.
- Lucy displayed very little competence and would not persist in any tasks she found difficult. In fact she showed considerable competence at being incompetent; for example, however her nightdress was given to her, she would invariably get it on inside-out so that her parents "had to" take it off and put it back on properly.
- When Lucy was 12, the parents brought her to our family therapy clinic to recruit our help in getting her moved from an ordinary school into a more protected environment. They felt that the educational and medical agencies, who had judged that Lucy was capable of participating in ordinary school life, were uncaring and unwilling to recognize Lucy's disabilities.

The specific form of Figure 1 applied to this family is portrayed in Figure 2.

CONCLUSION

It has been a fundamental assumption of this chapter that the family is the major socioculturally structured environment inhabited by children, and that it is through the family that the influence of cultural values on children is mediated. However, it is also clear that the family can no longer continue to be treated as a kind of invisible screen

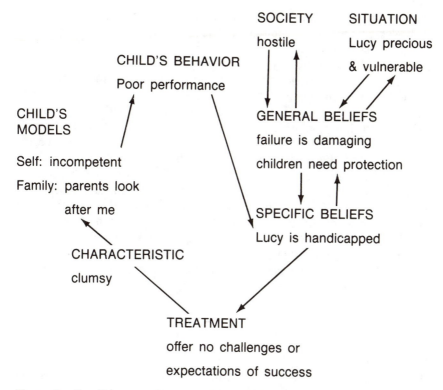

Figure 2. Specific example of a cycle in which parental beliefs have operated in particular circumstances to produce incompetence in their child.

through which cultural influences pass. The material reviewed indicates that the family is not a microcosm of society, faithfully reproducing within the home the beliefs, values, and attitudes of the wider culture. Each family is an independent entity with its own laws, and while the need to interface effectively with the outside world imposes constraints on the forms that families can take, it is certainly the case that, in our own culture (perhaps to an extreme extent), families may work very differently from any organizations in the outside world. There are in fact values of our culture which ensure that this will happen; for example, the value placed on family privacy, the rights of parents to treat their children as they judge fit, the sanctity of the home, and the acceptance that behavior and relationships within the family may be very different to those outside.

The objective of this chapter has not been to describe the many forms of cultural environment offered by families, but to develop an understanding of the processes within families by which cultural values come to have an influence on children. Because the family has been so neglected within psychology, it has been necessary to develop or import most of the concepts needed for this analysis, but it has then been possible to locate empirical findings within the framework constructed. It has to be accepted that the conceptual framework is extremely limited in relation to the complexity and diversity of family functioning. The version presented here was derived from a more elaborate formulation which attempts to offer a much more comprehensive account of family functioning (Stratton & Hanks, in preparation). But even the limited model that it has been possible to present within this chapter gives some indication of why direct relationships between cultural factors as expressed in society, and children's behavior will be very rare. The limitations of the account offered merely indicate the need for a much more comprehensive account of the family than any that is available at present, but subsequent chapters take up specific aspects of the major themes discussed here, particularly the role of parental beliefs and the need to understand relationships in terms of systemic rather than linear causality.

REFERENCES

Alvarez, W.F. (1985). The meaning of maternal employment for mothers and their perceptions of their three-year-old children. *Child Development, 56,* 350–360.

Bannister, D., & Fransella, F. (1985). *Inquiring man.* London: Croom Helm.

Becker, W.C. (1964). Consequences of different kinds of parental discipline. In M.L. Hoffman & L.W. Hoffman (Eds.), *Review of child development research* (Vol 1). New York: Russell Sage Foundation.

Bell, R.Q. (1968). A reinterpretation of the direction of effects in studies of socialization. *Psychological Review, 75,* 81–95.

Beail, N. (1985). Fathers and infant caretaking. *Journal of Reproductive and Infant Psychology, 3,* 54–63.

Brinker, R.P., & Lewis, M. (1982). Discovering the competent handicapped infant: A process of approach to assessment and intervention. *Topics in Early Childhood Special Education, 2,* 1–6.

Bronfenbrenner, U., Alvarez, W.F., & Henderson, C.R. Jr. (1984). Working and watching: Maternal employment status and parents' perceptions of their three-year old children. *Child Development, 55,* 1362–1378.

Broussard, E.R. (1976). Neonatal prediction and outcome at 10/11 years. *Child Psychiatry and Human Development, 7,* 85–93.

Broussard, E.R. (1978). Psychosocial disorders in children: early assessment of infants at risk. *Continuing Education, 18,* 44–57.

Broussard, E.R. (1979). Assessment of the adaptive potential of the mother infant system: The neonatal perception inventories. *Seminars in Perinatology, 3.*

Cairns, R.B. (1979). *Social development: The origins and plasticity of interchanges.* San Francisco, CA: W.H. Freeman.

Cashmore, J.A., & Goodnow, J.J. (1985). Agreement between generations: A two-process approach. *Child Development, 56,* 493–501.

Cohler, B., & Grunebaum, H. (1981). *Mothers, grandmothers, and daughters: Personality and child-care in three generation families.* New York: Wiley.

Darley, J.M., & Fazio, R.H. (1980). Expectancy confirmation processes arising in the social interaction sequence. *American Psychologist, 35,* 867–881.

De Vries, M.W., & Sameroff, A.J. (1984). Culture and temperament: Influences on infant temperament in three East African societies. *American Journal of Orthopsychiatry, 54,* 83–96.

Erikson, E.H. (1968). *Identity: Youth and Crisis.* New York: Norton.

Goodnow, J.J., Cashmore, J., Cotton, S., & Knight, R. (1984). Mothers' developmental timetables in two cultural groups. *International Journal of Psychology, 19,* 193–205.

Handel, G. (1985). *The psychosocial interior of the family* (G. Handel, Ed.). New York: Aldine.

Hoffman, L. (1981). *Foundations of family therapy.* New York: Basic Books.

Hoffman, L.W. (1983). Work, family and the socialization of the child. In R.D. Parke (Ed.), *Review of child development research: Vol. 7. The family.* Chicago, IL: University of Chicago Press.

Hwang, C.P. (1978). Mother–infant interaction: Effects of sex of infant on feeding behaviour. *Early Human Development, 2,* 341–349.

Ispa, J.M., Gray, M., McPhail & Thornburg, K.R. (1984). Childrearing attitudes of parents in person-orientated and thing-orientated occupations: A comparison. *The Journal of Psychology, 117,* 245–250.

Karniol, R., & Ross, M. (1975). The development of causal attributions in social perception. *Journal of Personality and Social Psychology, 34* (3), 455–464.

Kaye, K. (1985). Family development. *Child Development, 56,* 279–280.

Kelly, G.A. (1955). *The psychology of personal constructs* (Vols. 1 & 2). New York: Norton.

Laing, R.D. (1971). *The politics of the family and other essays.* London: Tavistock Publications.

Lewis, M., & Rosenblum, L.A. (1974). *The effect of the infant on its caregiver.* Wiley: New York.

McDermott, J.F., Char, W.F., Robillard, A.B., Hsu, J., Tseng, W.S., & Ashton, G.C. (1983). Cultural variations in family attitudes and their implications for therapy. *Journal of the American Academy of Child Psychiatry, 22,* 454–458.

McDermott, J.F., Robillard, A.B., Char, W.F., Hsu, J., Tseng, W.S., & Ashton, G.C. (1983). Re-examining the concept of adolescence: Differences between boys and girls in the context of their families. *American Journal of Psychiatry, 140,* 1318–1322.

Martin, B. (1975). Parent–child relations. In F.D. Horowitz (Ed.), *Review of child development research* (Vol. 4). Chicago, IL: University of Chicago Press.

O'Brien, M., & Huston, A.C. (1985). Development of sex-typed play behaviour in toddlers. *Development Psychology, 21* (5), 866–871.

Pollner, M., & McDonald-Wikler, L. (1985). The social construction of unreality: A case study of a family's attribution of competence to a severely retarded child. *Family Process, Inc., 24*(2), 241–254.

Reiss, D. (1981). *The family's construction of reality,* Cambridge, MA: Harvard University Press.

Rohner, R.P., & Pettengill, S.M. (1985). Perceived parental acceptance-rejection and parental control among Korean adolescents. *Child Development, 56,* 524–528.

Sameroff, A.J., & Chandler, M. (1975). Reproductive risk and the continuum of caretaking casualty. In F.D. Horowitz, M. Hetherington, S. Scarr-Salapatek, & G. Siegel (Eds.), *Review of child development research* (Vol. 4). Chicago, IL: University of Chicago Press.

Schaffer, H.R. (1966). Activity level as a constitutional determinant of infantile reaction to deprivation. *Child Development, 37,* 596–602.

Stein, H.F. (1985). Values and family therapy. In J. Schwartzman (Ed.), *Families and other systems,* New York: Guilford Press.

Stratton, P. (1977). Criteria for assessing the influence of obstetric circumstances on later development. In T. Chard & M. Richards (Eds.), *Benefits and hazards of the new obsterics.* London: SIMP.

Stratton, P. (1982a). Emerging themes of neonatal psychobiology. In P. Stratton (Ed.), *Psychobiology of the human newborn.* Chichester: Wiley.

Stratton, P. (1982b). Significance of the psychobiology of the human newborn. In P. Stratton (Ed.), *Psychobiology of the human newborn.* Chichester: Wiley.

Stratton, P. (1985). The role of the family in childhood risk: The origins of competence. In T. Garling & J. Valsiner (Eds.), *Children within environments.* New York: Plenum.

Stratton, P. (1987). Maternal attribution of characteristics to the newborn: A mediator of the effects of early contact on attachment. (Submitted for publication).

Stratton, P., & Hanks, H.G.I. (in preparation). *A psychology of the family: concepts and applications.* London: Methuen.

St. James-Roberts, I., & Wolke, D. (1983). Differences between maternal and objective ratings of "difficult" neonatal behavioural style: Implications for temperament research and clinical perspectives. *Journal of Reproductive and Infant Psychology, 1,* 53–60.

Thomas, E.B., Leiderman, P.H., & Olson, J.P. (1972). Neonate–mother interaction during breast feeding. *Development Psychology, 6,* 110–118.

Thomas, A., Chess, S., Birch, H.G., Hertzig, M.R., & Korn, S. (1963). *Behavioural individuality in early childhood.* New York: University Press.

Thomas, A., Chess, S., & Birch, H.G. (1968). *Temperament and behaviour disorders in children.* New York: New York University Press.

Weitzman, N., Birns, B., & Friend, R. (1985). Traditional and nontraditional mothers' communication with their daughters and sons. *Child Development, 56,* 894–898.

Zeanah, C.H., Keener, M.A., & Anders, T.F. (1986). Developing perceptions of temperament and their relation to mother and infant behaviour, *Journal of Child Psychology and Psychiatry, 27,* 499–512.

CHAPTER 2

Child Rearing and the Dialectics of Parental Intelligence*

George W. Holden and Kathy L. Ritchie

Department of Psychology
University of Texas

"The oldest profession of the race is facing failure. This profession is parenthood . . . the rearing of children is the most difficult of all professions, more difficult than engineering, than law, or even than medicine itself" (Watson, 1928, pp. 11–12).

John B. Watson was not the first psychologist to recognize that child rearing, beginning with the provision of care to the neonate and continuing on through the socialization of the child into a competent adult, is an arduous task. Yet, he was a provocative advocate for the need for parents to attend to their own child-rearing behavior and its effects on their offspring. Ironically, the solution to the father of behaviorism's quote printed above is not a behavioral one; rather, it lies in the cognitive activity of parents. Mary Weeks, an early parent educator in this country, would have agreed as she once wrote,

> Experts are writing, experienced mothers are talking, everywhere are movements looking toward the more sensible rearing of children. There is no excuse for not trying to do our mothering in a more rational way. The good mother is the thinking mother, always on the lookout for suggestions to better her methods; learning from everything she reads in

* We thank Judith Langlois, John Meacham, William Swann, and Jaan Valsiner for their helpful comments on an earlier draft of this chapter. This work was supported, in part, by a grant from the University Research Institute, University of Texas, and an equipment grant from IBM's Project Quest to the first author.

papers and books, and from the school and about the life about her what to do and what not to do with her children. (Weeks, 1914, p. 197)

Unfortunately, all too little has been written about the cognitive activity of the effective or "good" parent. This chapter begins to redress that neglect by seeking to define the nature of parental intelligence. In this chapter, we will begin by discussing criteria for parental intelligence. That discussion will lead into a review of the research associating certain parental actions with positive outcomes in children in North America. To illustrate the cultural relativity of some of these acts, a review of parental characteristics from Japan will also be presented. Based on these reviews, a new conceptualization of the meaning of parental intelligence will then be proposed. We will argue that intelligent parental behavior is a consequence of the dialectic process rather than any amalgam of specific parental characteristics.

RESEARCH INTO PARENT-CHILD RELATIONS

It is true that cognitive aspects of parental behavior—or, more accurately, parental social cognition—has seen a resurgence of interest in recent years. Following the early work on parental attitudes (Schaefer, 1959) and values (Stolz, 1967), investigators are now delving into parents' expectations, attributions (Dix, Ruble, Grusec, & Nixon, 1986), perceptions, stereotypes, and beliefs (Goodnow, 1984; Sigel, 1985) in an effort to understand what parents are thinking about their children and how those thoughts influence parental action. Little, though, has been written about what are the parental cognitive requirements needed to be effective and successful parents. What actions constitute intelligent parental behavior? What are the parental characteristics associated with positive child outcome? Why are some parents more successful at child rearing than others? In what ways does effective parental behavior differ across cultures? These questions can be reduced to one basic query: What is parental intelligence?

It was over 60 years ago that the proceedings of a conference on parent education were published under the title *Intelligent Parenthood* (Lawton, 1926). Intelligence, in that volume as well as at least one more recent book employing the name (Tudor-Hart, 1966), has been used synonymously with knowledge. An intelligent parent has been viewed as one who is knowledgeable about child development. Such a characteristic is obviously one requisite, but what about others?

As Kail and Pellegrino (1985) have pointed out, the term *intelligence* can be used to refer to intelligent acts—in this case, appropriate parental behavior—or to mental processes, including the underlying cognitive abilities that lead to intelligent behavior. Because no recent research exists on the mental processes that contribute to parental intelligence, we will examine what have been considered to be intelligent acts in parents.

A Short Review of "Intelligent Acts" by Parents

The research literature that has described parental behavior and the consequences of differing behavior patterns on child outcome is a vast and unwieldy body of research. Therefore, this review will by necessity be modest. A great number of parental characteristics have been associated with positive child outcome. In order to review these, we focused our review on parental characteristics associated with child outcome during the first decade of a child's life. To do this, we began by reviewing secondary sources, some of which were directed toward introductory students of behavior (e.g., Hetherington & Parke, 1986; Shaver, 1985) and others designed for advanced students (Maccoby & Martin, 1983; Wachs & Gruen, 1982). Efforts were made to select representative examples from the research literature; we did not attempt to be exhaustive. A second tactic we employed to simplify the task was to omit distinctions of parental behavior based on the age of the child. When we discuss the use of reasoning, for instance, the reader can assume we are not referring to the use of that behavior with 3-month-old infants!

In compiling lists of parental behaviors, we organized the characteristics around three basic roles that parents adopt when rearing their offspring. These roles are often overlapping and interconnected, but are heuristically useful as they provide conceptual categories for organizing parental behavior. The three roles are all operating, at times simultaneously, by the later half of the first year of life. The three parental roles are caregiving, managing, and nurturing. The parental characteristics associated with positive outcomes in children will be summarized below. For each role, a corresponding table provides citations of representative primary and some secondary research sources concerning that characteristic.

The Caregiving Role

The *caregiving role* refers to how parents must provide the child with the appropriate social and physical resources for the child's physical and emotional short-term needs. Thus, the caregivers' goal within this role is to create an environment where infants and young children feel secure and where their basic needs are being met. The most important parental characteristics in creating this environment appear to be responsivity and sensitivity, consistency, and warmth.

Parental *responsivity, sensitivity,* and, to a lesser extent, *consistency,* are terms that are often used interchangeably and therefore are frequently associated with similar outcomes. For example, sensitivity has been defined as the provision of "contingent, appropriate and consistent responses to an infant's signals or needs" (Lamb & Easterbrooks, 1981, p. 127). The most commonly cited effects of these positive parental characteristics include such outcomes as a secure attachment, enhanced feelings of self-efficacy, and advanced cognitive development.

Parental *warmth* has also been frequently associated with positive child outcomes. The development of self-esteem, prosocial behavior, and cognitive development have each been related to parental warmth. Furthermore, parental warmth, along with emotional involvement, has been related to attachment, intelligence quotients, and self-esteem. Positive child outcomes and the associated parental characteristics from the caregiving role are summarized in Table 1.

The Child Management Role

A second basic role parents adopt is that of managers of their children's behavior, in specific, and the context of the children's development, in general. This role includes much more than discipline. General management decisions include mundane organizational tasks such as how the child will spend the day, and executive management decisions including what role the child will play in the decision-making process. Within this parental role, five types of parental characteristics have been reported to be associated with positive outcomes in children. These include *flexibility, consistency, affection, firmness,* and the use of certain *control methods* (such as inductive reasoning) over others. These characteristics have been associated with positive child outcomes in the areas of compliance and self-control, self-esteem, and prosocial behavior (see Table 2).

The Nurturing Role

Parents not only provide care and management, but also must promote children's development so they can become competent adults. Fogel, Melson, and Mistry (1986) have called this role *nurturance,* which they define as "the provision of guidance, protection and care for the purpose of fostering developmental change congruent with the expected potential for change of the object of nurturance" (p. 55).

Table 1. Child Outcomes Associated with Characteristics of Parents in the Caregiving Role

Child Outcome	Parent Characteristic
Secure Attachment	Sensitive and Responsive (Ainsworth, Bell, & Stayton, 1971; Belsky, Rovine, & Taylor, 1984; Crockenberg, 1981; Clarke-Stewart, 1973)
	Accessible (Ainsworth et al., 1971)
	Warm and affectionate (Clarke-Stewart, 1973)
	Emotionally involved (Clarke-Stewart & Hevey, 1981)
Compliance/Cooperation	Responsive—boys (Martin, 1981)
	Sensitive (Schaffer & Crook, 1980; Stayton, Hogan, & Ainsworth, 1971)
	Consistent—boys (Lytton, 1977, 1980)
Sense of Control Over Environment	Consistent (Lewis & Brooks-Gunn, 1979; Watson, 1972)
Self-Esteem	Consistent—boys (Coopersmith, 1967)
	Warm—boys (Coopersmith, 1967)
	Emotionally involved—boys (Coopersmith, 1967)
Moral and Prosocial Development	Consistent (Aronfreed, 1976; Parke, 1974, 1977)
	Warmth (Hoffman & Saltzstein, 1967)
	Emotionally involved (Johnson, 1962)
Cognitive and Language Development	Responsive (Baumrind, 1967; Elardo, Bradley, & Caldwell, 1977; Honzik, 1967; Radin, 1971; Seegmiller & King, 1975; Wulbert, Ingles, Kreigsmann, & Mills, 1975; Yarrow, Rubenstein, & Pederson, 1975)
	Warm (Kelly & Worrell, 1977)
	Emotionally involved (Bayley & Schaefer, 1964; Bradley & Caldwell, 1976; Honzik, 1967)
Miscellaneous	
Socially Responsible	Responsive (Baumrind, 1967, 1978; Baumrind & Black, 1967)
Socially Assertive	Responsive (Baumrind, 1967; Baumrind & Black, 1967)

Investigations into the consequences of the parental nurturance role have spanned the areas of cognitive development, prosocial behavior, self, and moral development. In general, the findings indicate consistently that parents can help their children develop in these areas by being *supportive, encouraging,* and *involved* with the child; *respecting the child* and *allowing some freedom;* having *high yet appropriate expectations;* and *modeling the desired behavior.*

In summary, a number of parental characteristics have been found by investigators to be associated with various kinds of positive child outcomes. Within the caregiving role, the major characteristics include being responsive, sensitive, consistent, and warm. In the managing role,

Table 2. Child Outcomes Associated with Characteristics of Parents in the Child-Management Role

Child Outcome	Parent Characteristic
Compliance/Cooperation	Uses multiple strategies (Chapman, 1979)
	Consistent—boys (Lytton, 1977, 1980)
	Uses reasoning (Baumrind & Black, 1967; Lytton, 1979; Minton, Kagan, & Levine, 1971)
	Uses psychological rewards (Lytton, 1977)
	Sensitive (Schaffer & Crook, 1980)
	Affectionate (Feshbach, 1978)
Self Control/ Internalization	Gives child choices—boys (Lytton, 1980)
	Consistent—boys (Kuczynski, 1983; Parke, 1974, 1977)
	Uses reasoning (Kuczynski, 1983; Minton, et al., 1971; Parke, 1974)
	Warm and involved (Gordon, Nowicki, & Wichern, 1981)
Prosocial Development	Flexible, gives choices (Eisenberg-Berg & Mussen, 1978; Mussen, Harris, Rutherford, & Keasey, 1970)
	Affectionate (Mussen, et al., 1970)
	Firm (Hoffman, 1970)
	Sets high standards (Hoffman, 1970; Mussen et al., 1970)
	Uses reasoning (Hoffman & Saltzstein, 1967; Zahn-Waxler, Radke-Yarrow, & King, 1979)
	Empathetic (Zahn-Waxler et al., 1979)
Self-Esteem	Gives child choices (Coopersmith, 1967)
	Affectionate—boys (Coopersmith, 1967)
	Firm (Coopersmith, 1967)
	Sets high standards—boys (Coopersmith, 1967)
	Uses reasoning—boys (Coopersmith, 1967)
Cognitive and Language Development	Gives child choices (Elardo et al., 1977; Bradley & Caldwell, 1976)
	Uses reasoning (Hess & Shipman, 1967)
	Uses psychological rewards (Feshback, 1973)
	Sets high standards (Radin, 1973; Seegmiller & King, 1975)
Moral Development	Consistent (Aronfreed, 1976; Parke, 1974, 1977)
	Uses reasoning (Aronfreed, 1976; Hoffman, 1970; Hoffman & Saltzstein, 1967; Parke, 1974, 1977)

being flexible and affectionate but firm while using inductive methods of management were the key parental characteristics. Finally, those parental characteristics associated with the nurturing role include being supportive and involved, allowing the child some freedom, setting high standards, respecting the child, and modeling the desired behavior.

Table 3. Child Outcomes Associated with Characteristics of Parents in the Nurturing Role

Child Outcome	Parent Characteristic
Compliance/Cooperation	Involved (Lytton, 1977, 1980; Martin, 1981)
	Respects the child (Stayton et al., 1971)
	Sensitive, accepting (Stayton et al., 1971)
Self-Control/ Internalization	Encourages mature behavior—boys (Lytton, 1980)
	Involved (Gordon et al., 1981)
	Encourages discussion of child's feelings (Block, 1971)
	Allows child freedom—boys (Lytton, 1980)
Altruism/Empathy	Appropriate expectations (Mussen et al., 1970)
	Allows child freedom (Eisenberg-Berg & Mussen, 1978; Mussen et al., 1970)
Self-Esteem	Encourages mature behavior; allows freedom—boys (Coopersmith, 1967)
	Involved (Coopersmith, 1967; Loeb, Horst, & Horton, 1980)
	Respects the child—boys (Coopersmith, 1967)
Cognitive and Language Development	Supportive (Kelly & Worrell, 1977)
	Sets high standards (Baumrind & Black, 1967; Greenberg & Davidson, 1972; Holloway & Hess, 1982; Radin, 1973)
	Involved (Bradley & Caldwell, 1976; Elardo et al., 1977; Honzik, 1967; Seegmiller & King, 1975; Wulbert et al., 1975)
	Shows interest in child's context (Greenberg & Davidson, 1972; Radin, 1973)
	Allows child freedom (Kelly & Worrell, 1977)
	Interacts at appropriate level (Hoff-Ginsberg & Shatz, 1982)
Moral Development	Encourages discussion of child's feelings (Block, 1971; Hoffman, 1984)
	Involved (Johnson, 1962)
	Models appropriate behavior (Brody & Shaffer, 1982)
Miscellaneous Socially Responsible	Sets high standards—boys (Baumrind, 1971; Baumrind, 1978)
Social Assertiveness	Sets high standards—girls (Baumrind, 1967; Baumrind & Black, 1967)

Qualifying Comments

This review provides a representative sample of findings which have been reported in the literature on those parental characteristics associated with various types of positive outcomes in children. However, there are serious limitations with this body of research. Many of the studies are dated, have small sample sizes, omitted or failed to control for important subject characteristics (e.g., age, gender), sampled only middle-class Caucasian families, and failed to include possible mediating ~iables such as child characteristics (see Grusec & Kuczynski, 1980). direction of effects are therefore confounded (Bell & Harper, 1977). example, it is plausible that some parents are less directive and ᴜse more reasoning *because* their children are more mature, rather than the other way around. As investigators have become increasingly cognizant of the multiple influences on parent–child behavior, there has been a parallel decline in the number of studies trying to identify causal relations. More problematic is the fact that many of the findings are not robust either within the study or across studies. Take, for example, sensitivity. That characteristic is generally considered to be a critical maternal behavior, yet it has not been consistently defined or adequately operationalized and thereby has resulted in somewhat conflicting results (Wachs & Gruen, 1982).

A number of investigators have identified sex differences with some parental variables (see Tables 1–3). It is not clear, though, whether these are simply inconsistent findings or are real differences. For example, Bayley and Schaefer (1964) found that maternal emotional involvement is positively related with girls' cognitive development but not boys' development. Honzik (1967), however, found this relationship for boys but not girls.

Another issue which is unclear is whether there are "sensitive" periods for certain parental behaviors, or if continuity of the behavior is more important. For instance, involvement has inconsistent relationships with children's cognitive development until after the child is 2 years old (Wachs & Gruen, 1982). Also, how does the parental behavior change in response to the changes in the child? A reviewer readily realizes that the research evidence to date for parental characteristics affecting child outcome is less than conclusive.

Having tempered the findings of the review, it is clear that more thorough work needs to be done on the relationship between parental characteristics and child outcome. In some ways, it is an unfortunate trend that researchers have become more likely to avoid tackling the question of what effects parents have on children. Although that research question is fraught with pitfalls, the answers remain essential. We await new evidence to provide additional support. In the mean time, we will have to settle for the results that we reviewed; these characteristics of parents identified as "intelligent acts" do have intuitive and logical appeal.

Child Rearing in Japan

To better understand the nature of parental intelligence as well as parental behavior in general, it is useful to examine parents in another culture. How do the "intelligent acts" of American parents compare with the beneficial characteristics of parents in another culture? Are there universal characteristics that are common to "intelligent" parents in any culture—similarities created by parents adapting to the same tasks of child rearing (Levine, 1977)—or are the characteristics largely particular to specific cultures? An analysis into cross-cultural differences as well as parallels would provide a better perspective on understanding the nature of the parental task in general. In order to provide sufficient contrast, information about parent–child relations from a non-Western country was sought. Japan was the comparison country selected on the basis of the availability of information about the parent–child relationship.

The Japanese have been the focus of a considerable amount of cross-cultural research, ever since Ruth Benedict (1946) and William Caudill (1952) published their studies on the Japanese personality. Caudill pursued his work with investigations of mother–child relations. His studies (e.g., Caudill & Schooler, 1973; Caudill & Weinstein, 1969) have been influential—both in terms of stimulating interest and affecting subsequent studies (see Chen & Miyake, 1986, for a critique of his work). Since the time of Caudill's early work, a number of anthropological and psychological studies of the parent–child relationship have been conducted in Japan. Compared with cross-cultural research in other non-Western societies, there is a relatively large and current body of descriptive data concerning the parent–child relationship (e.g., Lebra, 1976, 1984; Stevenson, Azuma, & Hakuta, 1986). From these studies, inferences can be made about parental characteristics that are associated with positive outcome in Japanese children. The parental qualities will be organized around the three basic roles of parents that were presented earlier.

In their role as caregivers, Japanese mothers (most fathers play only a minimal role in child rearing), above all else, promote close physical contact—called "skinship"—at every opportunity. From breastfeeding to sleeping and bathing with their infants, mothers are literally rarely out of touch with their offspring. In fact, mothers seldom leave their children with another adult. In one study, the mothers of 12-month-old infants reported that they left their children alone an average of 2.5 times per month—and even then the children were left with a father or a grandmother (Miyake, Chen, & Campos, 1985). In another study, only two out of 24 mothers of 2-year-olds had left their children with another adult at least once over a 1-month period (Takahashi, 1982). Because infants and young children are viewed as sacred (Takahashi, 1986), mothers believe that they should be reared in a permissive and indulgent environment. Holding the view that childhood should be free from frustrations and tensions, mothers therefore try to appease their children's emotional needs immediately (Lebra, 1976). At the same time, this responsivity is accompanied by a message of need, as the children are socialized into *amae* relations, a term which has been traditionally defined as "the feeling of dependency coupled with the expectation of indulgence" (Azuma, 1986, pp. 7–8). (To foreshadow a later point, Kumagai & Kumagai, 1986, have argued that *amae* would be better defined as a feeling of interdependence.)

The permissiveness of the child-centered environment is, at times, mediated by the parents' role of child management. When disciplining a child becomes necessary, Japanese mothers encourage the child to take the adult's perspective with appeals to feelings and consequences (Conroy, Hess, Azuma, & Kashiwagi, 1980). Given the emphasis on close mother–child proximity, it should come as no surprise that Japanese parents punish their children by locking them *out* of the house (Lebra, 1976).

The third parental role, nurturing a child's development, is carried out by encouraging feelings of interdependence, so that the children are socialized into maintaining harmonious and positive interactions. Self-discipline, politeness, conformity, attentiveness to others, and a strong sense of group identity are valued and encouraged.

Clearly, Japanese mothers' approach to child rearing differs markedly from that employed by American mothers. Effective mothering in Japan is characterized by promoting interdependence through indulgence, permissiveness, and close physical contact, in contrast to the encouragement of independence in young children in the United States. In America, the mother is the authority figure and the child is expected to obey, whereas in Japan, the children are expected to behave appropriately or perform the correct act *before* they are told (Azuma, 1982). Japanese mothers promote conformity, fitting into the existing situation, and feeling a sense of group identity, while American mothers are pushing autonomy and individualism, uniqueness, and obedience. As Weisz, Rothbaum, and Blackburn (1984) have persuasively argued, these differences in child rearing techniques help to create a different orientation toward feelings of control than in Western countries. Americans gain rewards and exert control by influencing existing realities, while Japanese tend to fit into the existing world and gain a sense of control through adapting themselves to the environment.

Japanese parents do indeed have some very different socialization goals and approaches than American middle-class families. These goals reflect how one is socialized to adapt to a culture (Levine, 1977). But, even within a larger culture, multiple socialization goals can be found (Ogbu, 1981). In a recent discussion of child rearing in some of the ethnic groups in the United States, Harrison, Serafica, and McAdoo (1984) remind us that "the socialization message differs for ethnic families as a reflection of ethnic values and goals, and of the social status of the family system within the larger system" (pp. 346–347). For example, one overriding goal of Black families in America is bicultural adaptation. Black children are taught different types of appropriate behavior, as determined by the ethnic context. Those divergent socialization goals may help to account for some of the observed differences in parental behavior between individuals of different ethnic groups (e.g., Hess & Shipman, 1967). Thus, in assessing parental behavior, or defining intelligent acts, one must account for the cultural basis of the parental action.

A NEW MODEL: THE DIALECTICS OF PARENTAL INTELLIGENCE

At this point, the reader may suspect that we subscribe to a "vessel" model of an intelligent parent: An intelligent parent is similar to an appropriately shaped container which contains the traits or abilities which lead to "intelligent acts." In different cultures or ethnic groups, the vessel may be shaped somewhat differently. For middle-class American families, the parent of a preschooler should "contain" a lot of warmth and some firmness. A Japanese parent, on the other hand, need not contain the firmness characteristic. By and large, the available research supports such a model. Yet, upon closer examination, the analogy of the container cannot function. How can a parent be simultaneously gentle and firm, consistent and flexible, or empathetic while expecting mature behavior? At any one moment, a parent might be a paragon of one characteristic while being a parody of another! This observation compels us to seek a model of parental intelligence that accepts conflicts and contrasts and allows for a more dynamic nature of the competing characteristics.

The dialectic approach provides a convenient model with which to understand parental intelligence. *Dialectics* as a term has been used in various ways, including a dialogue or a method for discovering truth (Reese, 1982). Based on the philosopher Hegel's writings (e.g., 1967), the most common usage of the term concerns a way of representing knowledge and the generation of knowledge through thesis, antithesis, and subsequent synthesis. That synthesis then becomes a new thesis and the process is repeated, albeit at a different level. This notion is at the heart of Piaget's well-known view of the complementary and interdependent yet oppositional processes of assimilation and accommodation. A primer on dialectics can be found in Salkind (1985); more advanced discussions and applications appear in Engels (1940) and Basseches (1984).

Klaus Riegel (1975, 1976) and others have seized upon dialectics to provide an improved model of human development. Such a model assumes that individuals are changing in a changing social world. Thus, the focus of study is altered. Instead of looking for traits or abilities, attention is directed to "interactive changes in common activities and everyday situations" (Riegel, 1976, p. 691). Individuals face conflicts and crises which motivate change. Out of the conflict comes a temporary synthesis or harmony before more conflict arises. Individuals experience two types of dialectics: "Outer" dialectics, or conflicts with other individuals or situations; and "inner" ones, or internal cognitive debates within an individual (Riegel, 1975).

The notion of dialectics is especially appropriate for parents for at least two reasons. The task of parents is, by definition, to rear a rapidly changing organism; change rather than stability is the *modus operandi*. As a result, parental behavior must be adaptive. Parents must modify their behavior in response to their offspring; the process of adaptation is inherent in the task of parenting. Second, competing or conflicting thoughts and feelings are a common attribute of parents. This parental "disequilibrium" need not operate at the level of conscious thought or decisions. For example, "outer" dialectics—those concerning different individuals—can appear in many guises. A common one all parents face is balancing the child's needs with the parent's needs. A second type of dialectic involves deciding between competing sources of child-rearing beliefs or advice—such as differences in child-rearing beliefs between the mother and father or whom to believe, a veteran multiparous women or a novice male pediatrician. Scarr (1984) has recently written a book about the relatively recent yet profound parental dilemma in American society: Whether a working woman should continue to work outside the home after parturition. Concomitant with that dilemma come others: What kind of child care setting is best for the child? For how many hours a day? What to do if the child gets sick? How does one "make up" for the lost time? etc.

Another type of dialectic perpetually dogs parents. In contrast to the external dilemmas, this second type involves inner conflicts residing within the parent's thoughts. A hint that such dialectics existed can be found in the work of the early investigators into the nature of parent behavior, such as Schaefer (1959), who employed attitude questionnaires to classify parental child-rearing views on two bipolar dimensions— warmth vs. hostility and autonomy vs. control. These dichotomies between parents also suggest the potential for these differing feelings or beliefs to converge *within* an individual parent as well. More recently, Bell (Bell & Harper, 1977; Bell & Chapman, 1986) has proposed a "control theory" of parental reactions to child behavior. Parents have upper and lower limits of tolerance for behavior, and, so long as the child behaves within the expected limits, the system is in equilibrium. However, "disequilibrium results when one participant contributes too much or too little too soon or too late, thus violating the expectations of the other person in the system" (Bell & Chapman, 1986, p. 595).

In our review of the characteristics of parents associated with positive outcomes in children, it was clear that different investigators advocated opposing characteristics. Some researchers suggested that parents should be warm; other investigators highlighted the benefits of firmness. Similarly, some psychologists supported the benefits of parental flexibility when their peers were advocating consistency. Parent observers, such as Belsky, Lerner, and Spanier (1984), have recognized the complex nature of parenting. They described the parental characteristics associated with cognitive development as "In summary, the most effective pattern of parenting for facilitating children's success in school as well as their general intellectual development seems to involve being nurturant without being too restrictive, responsive but not overly controlling, and stimulating but not directive" (p. 66). How can parents do that? The answer to the paradox lies in the dialectic approach. Parents do indeed, as the research indicates, have to juggle opposing characteristics in rearing their children.

Out of the mouths of parents and parent educators comes additional support for the view that parents must combine competing characteristics. In 1926, the organizer of a conference on parent education, in her welcoming address, advised that "The guiding hand must be gentle and loving, but it must be firm and wise as well" (Lawton, 1926, p. 2). Conversations with parents are replete with examples. For example, in Bettleheim's (1962) book *Dialogues with Mothers,* one mother is quoted as explaining: "Yes, but the other thing I thought about—at this two-and-a-half-year-old stage when they're so domineering, I thought they should be humored as much as they can. So I was torn between two things" (p. 34). Another mother admitted "I know one thing . . . that when I correct [him] with intense inner disapproval, or shout at him, or get angry with him . . . I'm immediately overwhelmed with guilt feelings" (p. 63). A third mother worries about whether the use of "bribery," which she knows is effective, is an acceptable technique in order to get her child to do something.

These statements illustrate child-rearing dialectics. In Hegelian terms, the parent has a thesis or idea about how to respond or deal with the child. But in response to that idea, maybe due to changes in the child, situation, or parental awareness, an antithesis or contradictory thought occurs to the parent. A synthesis or resolution of the two opposing views is the result of the dialectic process. The synthesis represents the progression to a qualitatively different state or way of thinking. In time, a new thesis emerges from the previous synthesis and the cycle repeats itself, fostering change and development.

A few examples of these dialectics will illustrate their pervasive nature within the three basic parental roles. First, there can be conflict or disequilibrium *between* the three parental roles identified earlier. Which role should dominate in any given situation? When a child has misbehaved and is aware of it, should a parent manage the child or use the situation to promote the child's development? When and in what situations should a parent abandon the managing role in order to nurture the child's development?

Within the three roles there is the potential for a considerable amount of conflict. The caregiver role has the least amount of within-parent discord. Even so, one can identify examples. Some mothers fear that being highly responsive to their infant will result in a spoiled personality. Does a nurturant environment mean creating a completely safe setting, or one that allows the child freedom to explore—and thus exposure to some risk? Is a "better" environment for the child one that is child-centered and revolves around the child's needs at the expense of the family's needs? Warmth has long been associated as an important characteristic of nurturant parents, but how much warmth is enough? When does maternal warmth become seductive, as Sroufe and Ward (1980) have begun to explore? Japanese parents face the conflict of encouraging close physical contact with their daughters but, at the same time, teaching them to be modest while sleeping or bathing with a sibling or parent. Examples of child-rearing dialectics, for many North American parents, can be found in Table 4.

The role of child management raises the potential of more within-parent conflicts. Parents know that they need to be firm in enforcing their rules, but what parent does not show flexibility by taking into account situational factors? Which characteristic is more important? Similarly, being firm yet warm can be a difficult behavioral combination to exhibit simultaneously. Should parents tell children the truth—such as why a child should not be friendly toward unfamiliar persons—or is it better to protect them from the anxieties caused by harsh realities?

Table 4.   Examples of Child-Rearing Dialectics within the Three Basic Parent Roles

Thesis	Antithesis	Synthesis
In the Caregiving Role		
Allows exploration	Guards against dangers	
Adapts to child's needs	Maintains own or family's needs	
Open, flexible for child	Provides structure	
Shows warmth	Becomes seductive	
Is responsive	Spoils the child	
In the Managing Role		
Seeks obedience, respect	Question rules and authority	
Is firm/consistent	Is flexible/warm	
Is honest with child	Protects child from harsh realities	
Changes the environment	Changes the child	
Is present oriented	Is future oriented	
In the Nurturing Role		
Provides autonomy	Is uninvolved	
Shows interest	Is over-involved	
Gives independence	Maintains dependence	
Encourages sociability	Encourages wariness of unfamiliar	
Encourages mature behavior	Allows child to be child	
Provides novelty	Maintains consistency	
Teaches	Allows child to discover on own	
Develops one talent	Encourages all around development	
Seeks to change child	Accepts child's shortcomings	
Gives freedom	Controls external influences	
Guides	Responsive to child's needs	
Follows child's preference	Follows social norms	

Which approach is better: To child-proof a home by locking up appealing electronic equipment and thereby modifying the environment, or try to teach the child not to touch certain objects? For older children, does one seek compliance but, in the next breath, encourage them to question authority? A final example of conflict within the child management role concerns one's temporal orientation. Should one be present- or future-oriented in responding to a child's behavior. Although some parental responses can be highly effective (e.g., diverting the child's attention) they are not useful for teaching the child to self-regulate. Kuczynski (1984) experimentally induced mothers to use either power assertive responses or reasoning—depending on their perception of how long their children needed to perform a task.

The third role is the most demanding and complex: nurturing a child's healthy development. It also involves the greatest number of dialectics. Should parents encourage free choice—such as in areas of television watching, book reading, or friendship selection—or try to control external sources of potentially negative influence? A number of dialectics are related to intellectual development: Is it better to directly teach children or let them discover on their own? How much novelty in contrast to consistency should be provided? When does maternal interest in a child become overinvolvement? Should a parent capitalize on a child's apparent talent detected early or, instead, encourage a child's development in many domains? In Japan, parents face the "educational dilemma" of whether to prepare their children for college entrance examinations or to promote well-rounded personalities (Lebra, 1984). If a child does not perform at the expected level, is this due to unrealistic expectations or inadequate effort by the child? Does a father swallow his pride and accept the shortcomings of his offspring or seek to change the child's behavior? Another example of a conflict in the nurturing role concerns the highly touted parental behavior of promoting mature behavior. When is this action occurring at the expense of empathizing with the child or letting a child act like the child he or she is (cf. Elkind, 1981)? In Japan, mothers promote interdependence in their infants and young children, but, eventually, the mothers must alter their behavior to teach independence. The mothers must make decisions about how and when to change their behavior to avoid infantile tyranny and "insatiable dependency and the mutual entrapment" (Lebra, 1984, p. 177).

Having raised all these parental cognitive dilemmas, we should be quick to point out that there are, of course, no "answers" to these questions. That is, no set answers exist to any of these or the countless other similar ones that parents must deal with in child rearing. The thesis and antithesis are not the mirror images they appear to be; rather, they are interconnected, and together they form parts of the whole. The dichotomies or halves are interrelated and cannot be dealt with as simple opposites.

One can expect, though, that the ways in which parents resolve the conflicts have multiple repercussions. For parents, their level of stress, anxiety, and self-esteem as a parent may be tied to how well they deal with the resolution of these dialectics. Children, we hypothesize, reap the benefits of parents who can skillfully manuever their way through the conflicts to arrive at appropriate syntheses. Take the problem of sociability, for example. Suppose a mother encourages her infant to be sociable to others by inviting friends to handle and spend time with the infant. As the infant grows into a toddler, he becomes exceedingly gregarious. At this point, the mother starts to worry. In addition to the toddler's ease with unfamiliar people, the child is now capable of locomotion. These two basic changes, along with newspaper reports, have now introduced a fear into the mother: My child is not wary of strangers—he might get abducted. To that antithesis, the mother has to alter her behavior. For a sociable 9-month-old child, this might mean engaging in more careful monitoring of his whereabouts. For older children, this might mean teaching them under what situations they need to be careful. Both of these responses represent temporary solutions—or transient syntheses to the thesis and antithesis.

Parental Intelligence as a Process

A dialectical approach necessitates a view of parental intelligence that differs from the psychometric approach of trying to tap fixed abilities, capacities, or skills. Parental behavior is not a constant or a set of constants. As Cantor and Kilhstrom (1985) wrote about social intelligence: "Intelligent action, as contrasted with the instinctual or the reflexive, is flexible rather than rigidly stereotyped, discriminative rather than indiscriminate, and optional rather than obligatory" (p. 13). Parents alter their behavior in response to changes in the child, themselves, the context, or the culture. Therefore, a static-trait approach to parental behavior or intelligence misses a basic characteristic of parents—the ability to alter their child-rearing behavior in response to anticipated or actual changes.

Investigators into the nature of intelligence have also expressed a dissatisfaction with the psychometric approach to human intelligence (e.g., Frederiksen, 1986; Gardner, 1983; Sternberg, 1984; Valsiner, 1984). Intelligence does not operate except in a person–environment relationship, and, therefore, it should be viewed as a process which is context-bound (Valsiner, 1984). Sternberg has recently proposed that a more accurate definition of intelligence should be the "purposive adaptation to, shaping of, and selection of real-world environments relative to one's life" (Sternberg, 1984, p. 271). Efforts are now being made, on a variety of fronts, to understand the nature of practical intelligence (Rogoff & Lave, 1984; Sternberg & Wagner, 1986). The appropriate question, as is being recognized increasingly, is "How are people intelligent," *not* "How intelligent are people" (Valsiner, 1984).

Parental intelligence, we propose, is manifested in the ways in which parents deal with and respond to the task of rearing children. Often, the task involves use of the dialectical process to solve a problem. Problem, here, refers to goal-seeking or problem-solving behavior in general. Parents are intelligent by making the appropriate decision or arriving at the proper synthesis of the thesis and antithesis under the specific circumstances and then implementing that decision in a suitable fashion. Multiple cognitive components are required for intelligent acts, including knowledge about children in general as well as one's own child, accurate perceptions and attributions about the situation and individuals involved, the differential weighing of the factors involved, and the awareness of as well as ability to use various strategies or plans of action. Finally, intelligent parents must have the capacity to adapt and modify to the changing nature of their offspring.

The Study of Parents and Parental Intelligence

What does this dialectical view of parental behavior mean for the study of parents and parental intelligence? Such a view holds a number of implications, both explicit and implicit. Foremost, the dialectic view assumes that parents, like children, are ever-changing. Instead of trying to detect the traits inherent in a parent, those adopting the dialectical approach would recognize that parental behavior is multiply determined and would instead direct their attention to understanding the influences on thinking and behavior and the interaction between the influences and the characteristics of the parent. Simple classification systems designed to categorize parents (e.g., Baumrind, 1971; Maccoby & Martin, 1983) may be useful for quantitative analyses but fail to capture the nature of the phenomenon.

A second implication is that the dialectical view highlights the cognitive determinants of parental behavior. In doing so, it emphasizes the importance of focusing on parental decision making and problem solving behavior. Static measures of parental attitudes, beliefs, or knowledge can address certain questions, but the "action" in parental cognition lies in how they solve problems, resolve conflicts, and make decisions. For example, the decision to place an only child in daycare in order to provide the child with exposure to peers is a significant one for that child and may well be indicative of the parents' thinking and action in creating what they see as an optimal environment for their child's development.

Thus, a third implication of this approach is that it highlights the importance of understanding the type of social and physical niche that parents create (Holden, 1985b; Scarr & McCarthy, 1983). For it is these conditions or situations that are the parents' solutions to the "problems of living." These problems include, not just concerns or complaints about a child (e.g., noncompliance), but also parental expectations or long-term goals for the child. The problems run the gamut from realistic to fantastic, transient to chronic.

Regardless of how they are classified, the problems provoke some kind of "solution"—a cognitive and/or behavioral response. These solutions may be arrived at either proactively or reactively, carefully thought out or otherwise (Holden, 1985b). Two questions then are of interest: What solutions have been developed, and how were they arrived at? Answers to problems about the physical environment (such as the presence of toxic substances in the home) are easier to assess than the solutions to the social environment. But, given the fact that the vast majority of the task of child rearing lies in the dynamic nature of social interactions, a more extensive focus on family interaction processes is needed. The work of Gerald Patterson (1986) in understanding the interactions of aggressive boys and their families is exemplary.

A final implication of the dialectical approach to understanding parents is that it necessitates a more complex and sophisticated model of parental behavior. Parental behavior occurs within contexts; it must be examined within contexts. These contexts are defined by differing locations, actors, histories, and goals. The danger of collapsing across these distinctions is that the essential nature of the parent may well become obscured. By failing to differentiate between these many types of contexts, the fact that parents think, react, and anticipate during their interactions with their offspring has been lost.

Having argued that psychologists need to employ more complex models to study the complex phenomenon of parental behavior, how do we propose to study parents and parental intelligence? There are two parts to our answer. The first addresses the question of what should be studied. One pressing need is to have more phenomenological information about parents' behavior and thinking toward their offspring. How consistent is parental behavior across contexts and time? How does previous parenting experience influence subsequent interactions with a second child? What types of short- and long-term goals do parents hold and seek for their children? What influences one parent's definition of what constitutes a problem? Are parents aware of the dialectical nature of child rearing? In what ways do parents synthesize dilemmas? Although psychologists have acknowledged that parents are thinking beings (e.g., Parke, 1978), developmental models and research into parents have yet to make that concession. For example, how parents think and adjust their thinking as well as consequent action to differing social contexts needs to be investigated.

The second part of our answer to how should we study parents concerns methodology. For the study of behavior, we consider naturalistic studies of parent–child interactions which maintain the integrity of the context for the parents and children (e.g., Holden, 1983) to provide considerably more meaningful data than acontextual research. Similarly, laboratory analogues which maintain a contextual relevance but add control are worthwhile approaches (e.g., Zussman, 1980).

The study of parental social cognitions, including problem solving, is more problematic, for it can be a methodologically messy business. Questionnaires are too constrained by the printed word to provide a useful method to tap anything but simple, static cognitions. Interviews provide a considerable improvement over questionnaires with regard to flexibility, but they too have substantial limitations. For example, the presence of an interviewer precipitates biases (e.g., Yarrow, 1963), as does the reflective thinking that is common in interviews. Reliably reducing interview data is often a time-consuming and difficult task. So how does one study parental thinking and reasoning?

A novel approach has been developed by the first author to study parental thinking (Holden, 1985a). Labelled Computer-Presented Social Situations (CPSS), this technique assesses parental social cognition and reported behavior by eliciting responses to social interaction situations that are presented on a microcomputer. Thus, assessments of cognitive processes related to social interactions can be made. Furthermore, the technique is a promising tool with which to investigate the nature of parental intelligence. As Frederiksen (1986) has argued, human intelligence needs to be investigated through the presentation of realistic simulations of real-life problem situations. In doing so, responses would more accurately reflect the nature of intelligence and allow it to be studied more comprehensively. Frederiksen predicts: "The structure of intelligence of the future may not be a static model, but one that varies as subjects change and as circumstances are altered" (p. 445).

There are a number of advantages with the CPSS technique. The major benefits of this approach include: (a) the experimenter or apparent evaluator is removed from the setting, allowing the subject to work confidentially and answer questions anonymously; (b) because of the interactive nature of the programs, the technique traces "thinking in action"; (c) simulations of situations can be presented in an appealing and engaging way; (d) use of the computer helps to create a "closed system" or "microworld" which serves to limit misinterpretations and provides boundaries for examining cognitive processes; (e) based on the input, the CPSS approach is capable of branching as well as rejecting missing data; and (f) the data can be rapidly and automatically reduced. Currently, two of the most serious limitations involve the expense of purchasing a microcomputer and the literacy requirement. As research developments and manufacturing improvements lower the price and the accessibility of hardware and machine generated voice communications, these problems will be overcome.

Two directions for the study of parents are afforded by this technique. The CPSS approach can be used to investigate basic processes of parental social cognition, or it can be used to assess parental reports of behavior. The first study (Holden, 1985c) to test this technique was designed to determine whether the effects of differing amounts of child-rearing experience influenced how individuals solved a child-rearing problem. A total of 192 mothers, fathers, nonmothers, and nonfathers operated two CPSSs. The target problem, labelled the Cry Problem, presented the situation of a baby crying in her home. The instructions were to collect only the fewest and most important information units out of the 25 units available in order to correctly diagnose the cause of the crying. The information was organized into five categories (Information about . . . the Baby, . . . the Parents; . . . the Time; . . . the Situation; and . . . the Cry itself). There were five units per category (e.g., the baby's age; how long since the baby was last fed). Nine competing hypotheses (e.g., the baby was . . . hungry, . . . wet, . . . tired, . . . teething) were provided, but the information units led to only one correct cause. In order to control for differences in problem-solving approaches, all subjects also operated a control problem which was structured identically but involved diagnosing why an adult was experiencing insomnia.

The Cry Problem began with the instructions and information stem ("A baby was crying at 10:30 a.m., in her room, in her parents' home"). The subjects then began selecting information units. After each unit was selected, and the content of the unit displayed on the monitor (e.g., "The baby is 6 months and 2 days old"), the subjects decided whether they were ready to select a hypothesis. Typically, subjects remained in the information acquisition loop until they had collected about eight information units. Then they would make a guess as to the cause. After selecting one hypothesis, the subjects then rated their confidence in that hypothesis. At that point, the subjects were told whether they had chosen the correct hypothesis. If they were right, the problem was solved. If not, they could select another hypothesis or return to the information-acquisition loop.

All the subjects reported that the technique was easy to use—even for those who had never touched a computer before. There were no effects for the order of problem presentation (Cry or Insomnia Problem first), but there were effects for both gender and parental status as determined by an analysis of covariance. As expected, when using performance on the Insomnia Problem as a covariate, the nonparents needed more information than parents to solve the Cry Problem, and men used more information than women. The adjusted means indicated the average number of units acquired was 9.3 for mothers, 10.4 for fathers, 11.3 for nonmothers, and 13.0 for nonfathers. When it came to selecting the hypothesis, the male nonparents differed from the other three groups in making more incorrect guesses. These nonfathers averaged about one more incorrect hypothesis than the other subjects.

The results indicated that, when accounting for performance on the Insomnia Problem, parents and women were more efficient in solving the Cry Problem than nonparents and men, respectively. In addition, parents and nonparent women were more accurate in determining the correct cause than were the nonparent men.

Similar results were found when looking at some of the process data. About 75% of the mothers, 60% of the fathers, 30% of the nonmothers, and only 15% of the nonfathers acquired the information unit about the baby's age within their first five information choices. Overall, the study indicated that this approach was a useful heuristic device to explicate how individuals reason about common problems. The study also provided useful new information about how individuals with differing amounts of experience with infants solved a common care-giving task—identifying the cause of crying.

The second research direction afforded by the technique lies in its ability to collect parental reports of their behavior. Because the experimenter is removed from the interaction and parents interactively respond to ongoing child-rearing situations, it is expected that parental reports will provide a more veridical yet cost-effective way to assess parental behavior. One study currently in progress to test this proposition involves observing and tape recording mothers as they interact with their 2-year-old children in the supermarket. One week later, the mothers come to the research laboratory to operate a CPSS which simulates the experience of taking a child to the supermarket. The correspondence between how mothers actually behaved in the market and how the mothers "acted" in the simulation is being investigated.

Additional studies are being planned to examine other aspects of parental social cognition and its relationship to behavior. For example, in order to examine the dialectical view of parental thinking, child-rearing dilemmas (Table 4) are being translated into software to explore the ways parents arrive at solutions to those problems. The program will assess the variables that parents take into account, the solutions they arrive at, and some of the influences and correlates of that process. It is expected that, through these studies, a more complete understanding of the nature of parents, the relationship between parental cognition and behavior, and, eventually, how parents influence the development of their offspring will be realized.

CONCLUSION

Taken together, this new conception of parents and the work described here is beginning to provide a more accurate and comprehensive understanding of the complex cognitive requirements needed for intelligent parenting. This view is in sharp contrast to that held about 60 years ago by John Watson, who believed that familiarity with behavioral principles was the most important information to aid parents in their "most difficult" task. His advocating the use of conditioning as a halcyon child-rearing technique was, of course, naive and simplistic, yet many authors of child-rearing manuals have followed in his path (e.g., Fromme, 1956; Schaefer, 1978). Such efforts are misguided; there will never be a satisfactory "cookbook" approach for effective parenting, because of the nature of the task. The reason that psychologists don't know the recipes for the optimal rearing of children is that there are no set recipes. What is available, based on the research literature, are the ingredients. But knowledge about the ingredients is not enough. Successful rearing of children—and thus the outcome of parental intelligence—involves a series of unique recipes accounting for the specific characteristics of the parent and child, given the particular time, situation, and cultural context. And, those recipes, in their rich and infinite variety, are created through the dialectical process.

REFERENCES

Ainsworth, M.D.S., Bell, S.M., & Stayton, D.J. (1971). Individual differences in strange situation behavior of one-year-olds. In H.R. Schaffer (Ed.), *The origins of human social relations.* London: Academic Press.

Aronfreed, J. (1976). Moral development from the standpoint of a general psychological theory. In T. Lickona (Ed.), *Moral development and behavior.* New York: Holt.

Azuma, H. (1982). Current trends in studies of behavioral development in Japan. *International Journal of Behavioral Development, 5,* 153–169.

Azuma, H. (1986). Why study child development in Japan? In H. Stevenson, H. Azuma, & K. Hakuta (Eds.), *Child Development and Education in Japan* (pp. 3–12). New York: Freeman.

Basseches, M. (1984). *Dialectic thinking and adult development.* Norwood, NJ: Ablex.

Baumrind, D. (1967). Child care practices anteceding three patterns of preschool behavior. *Genetic Psychology Monographs, 75,* 43–88.

Baumrind, D. (1971). Current patterns of parental authority. *Developmental Psychology Monograph, 4* (1, Pt. 2).

Baumrind, D. (1978). Parental disciplinary patterns and social competence in children. *Youth and Society, 9,* 239–276.

Baumrind, D., & Black, A.E. (1967). Socialization practices associated with dimensions of competence in preschool boys and girls. *Child Development, 38,* 291–327.

Bayley, N., & Schaefer, E. (1964). Correlations of maternal and child behaviors with the development of mental abilities: Data from the Berkeley Growth Study. *Monographs of the Society for Research in Child Development, 29.*

Bell, R.Q., & Chapman, M. (1986). Child effects in studies using experimental or brief longitudinal approaches to socialization. *Developmental Psychology, 22,* 595–603.

Bell, R.Q., & Harper, L.V. (1977). *Child effects on adults.* Hillsdale, NJ: Erlbaum.

Belsky, J., Lerner, R.M., & Spanier, G.B. (1984). *The child in the family.* Reading, MA: Addison-Wesley.

Belsky, J., Rovine, M., & Taylor, D. (1984). The Pennsylvania Infant and Family Development Project, III: The origins of individual differences in infant-mother attachment: Maternal and infant contributions. *Child Development, 55,* 718–728.

Benedict, R. (1946). *The chrysanthemum and the sword: Patterns of Japanese culture.* New York: Meridian.

Bettelheim, B. (1962). *Dialogues with mothers.* New York: Free Press.

Block, J. (1971). *Lives through time.* Berkeley, CA: Bancroft Books.

Bradley, R., & Caldwell, B. (1976). Early home environment and changes in mental test performance in children from 6–36 months. *Developmental Psychology, 12,* 93–97.

Brody, G.H., & Shaffer, D.R. (1982). Contributions of parents and peers to children's moral development. *Development Review, 2,* 31–75.

Cantor, N., & Kihlstrom, J.F. (1985). Social intelligence: The cognitive basis of personality. In P. Shaver (Ed.), *Self, situations and social behavior: Review of personality and social psychology, Vol. 6* (pp. 15–33). Beverly Hills, CA: Sage.

Caudill, W. (1952). Japanese-American personality and acculturation. *Genetic Psychological Monographs, 45,* 3–102.

Caudill, W., & Schooler, C. (1973). Child behavior and child rearing in Japan and the United States: An interim report. *Journal of Nervous and Mental Disease, 157,* 323–338.

Caudill, W., & Weinstein, H. (1969). Maternal care and infant behavior in Japan and America. *Psychiatry, 32,* 12–43.

Chapman, M. (1979). Listening to reason: Children's attentiveness and parental discipline. *Merrill-Palmer Quarterly, 25,* 251–263.

Chen, S., & Miyake, K. (1986). Japanese studies of infant development. In H. Stevenson, H. Azuma, & K. Hakuta (Eds.), *Child development and education in Japan.* New York: Freeman.

Clarke-Stewart, K.A. (1973). Interactions between mothers and their young children: Characteristics and consequences. *Monographs of the Society for Research in Child Development, 38,* (6 & 7, Serial No. 153).

Clarke-Stewart, K.A., & Hevey, C.M. (1981). Longitudinal relations in repeated observations of mother-child interactions from 1 to 2 1/2 years. *Developmental Psychology, 17,* 127–145.

Conroy, M., Hess, R.D., Azuma, H., & Kashiwagi, K. (1980). Maternal strategies for regulating children's behavior: Japanese and American families. *Journal of Cross Cultural Psychology, 11,* 153–172.

Coopersmith, S. (1967). *The antecedents of self-esteem.* San Francisco, CA: Freeman.

Crockenberg, S.B. (1981). Infant irritability, mother responsiveness, and social support influences on the security of infant–mother attachment. *Child Development, 52,* 857–865.

Dix, T., Ruble, D.N., Grusec, J.E., & Nixon, S. (1986). Social cognition in parents: Inferential and affective reactions to children of three age levels. *Child Development, 57,* 879–894.

Eisenberg-Berg, N., & Mussen, P.H. (1978). Empathy and moral development in adolescence. *Developmental Psychology, 14,* 185–186.

Elardo, R., Bradley, R., & Caldwell, B. (1977). A longitudinal study of the relation of infant home environment to language development at age 3. *Child Development, 48,* 595–603.

Elkind, D. (1981). *The hurried child: Growing up too fast.* Reading, MA: Addison-Wesley.

Engels, F. (1940). *Dialectics of nature.* New York: International Publishers.

Feshbach, N.D. (1973). Cross-cultural studies of teaching styles in four-year-olds and their mothers. In A. Pick (Ed.), *Minnesota symposia in child psychology* (Vol. 7). Minneapolis, MN: University of Minnesota Press.

Feshbach, N.D. (1978). Studies of empathic behavior in children. In B.A. Mager (Ed.), *Progress in experimental personality research* (Vol. 8, pp. 1–47). New York: Academic.

Fogel, A., Melson, G.F., & Mistry, J. (1986). Conceptualizing the determinants of nurturance: A reassessment of sex differences. In A. Fogel & G.F. Melson (Eds.), *Origins of Nurturance* (pp. 53–67). Hillsdale, NJ: Erlbaum.

Frederiksen, N. (1986). Toward a broader conception of human intelligence. *American Psychologist, 41,* 445–452.

Fromme, A. (1956). *The ABC of Child Care.* New York: Doubleday.

Gardner, H. (1983). *Frames of mind: The theory of multiple intelligences.* New York: Basic.

Goodnow, J. (1984). Parents' ideas about parenting and development: A review of issues and recent work. In M.E. Lamb, A.L. Brown, & B. Rogoff (Eds.), *Advances in developmental psychology,* (Vol. 3, pp. 193–242). Hillsdale, NJ: Erlbaum.

Gordon, D., Nowicki, S., & Wichern, F. (1981). Observed maternal and child behavior in a dependency-producing task as a function of children's locus of control orientation. *Merrill-Palmer Quarterly, 27,* 43–51.

Greenberg, J.W., & Davidson, H.H. (1972). Home background and school achievement in black urban ghetto children. *American Journal of Orthopsychiatry, 42,* 803–810.

Grusec, J., & Kucynski, L. (1980). Direction of effect in socialization: A comparison of the parent's versus the child's behavior as determinants of disciplinary techniques. *Developmental Psychology, 16,* 1–9.

Harrison, A., Serafica, F., & McAdoo, H. (1984). Ethnic families of color. In

R.D. Parke (Ed.), *Review of child development research, Vol. II, The family* (pp. 329-371). Chicago, IL: University of Chicago.

Hegel, G.W.F. (1967). *The phenomenology of mind.* New York: Harper and Row.

Hess, R., & Shipman, V. (1967). Cognitive elements in maternal behavior. In J. Hill (Ed.), *Minnesota Symposium on Child Psychology* (pp. 57-81). Minneapolis, MN: University of Minnesota.

Hetherington, E.M., & Parke, R.D. (1986). *Child psychology: A contemporary viewpoint* (3rd ed.). New York: McGraw-Hill.

Hoff-Ginsberg, E., & Shatz, M. (1982). Linguistic input and the child's acquisition of language. *Psychological Bulletin, 92,* 3-26.

Hoffman, L.W. (1984). Work, family and the socialization of the child. In R.D. Parke (Ed.), *Review of child development research, Vol. II, The family* (pp. 223-282). Chicago, IL: University of Chicago.

Hoffman, M.L. (1970). Moral development. In P.G. Mussen (Ed.), *Carmichael's manual of child psychology* (Vol. 2, pp. 261-360). New York: Wiley.

Hoffman, M.L., & Saltzstein, H.D. (1967). Parent discipline and the child's moral development. *Journal of Personality and Social Psychology, 5,* 45-57.

Holden, G.W. (1983). Avoiding conflict: Mothers as tacticians in the supermarket. *Child Development, 54,* 233-240.

Holden, G.W. (1985a). Analyzing parental reasoning with micro-computer presented problems. *Simulation and Games, 16,* 203-210.

Holden, G.W. (1985b). How parents create a social environment via proactive behavior. In T. Garling & J. Valsiner (Eds.), *Children within environments: Towards a psychology of accident prevention* (pp. 193-215). New York: Plenum.

Holden, G.W. (1985c, April). *Diagnosing why a baby is crying: The effect of caregiving experience.* Paper presented at the biennial meeting of the Society for Research in Child Development, Toronto, Canada.

Holloway, S.D., & Hess, R.D. (1982). Causal explanations for school performance: Contrasts between mothers and children. *Journal of Applied Developmental Psychology, 3,* 319-327.

Honzik, M. (1967). Environmental correlates of mental growth: Predictions from the family setting at 21 months. *Child Development, 38,* 337-364.

Johnson, R.C. (1962). A study of children's moral judgments. *Child Development, 33,* 327-354.

Kail, R., & Pellegrino, J.W. (1985). *Human intelligence: Perspectives and prospects.* New York: Freeman.

Kelly, J.A., & Worrell, L. (1977). The joint and differential perceived contribution of parents to adolescents' cognitive functioning. *Developmental Psychology, 13,* 282-283.

Kuczynski, L. (1983). Reasoning, prohibitions, and motivations for compliance. *Developmental Psychology, 19,* 126-134.

Kuczynski, L. (1984). Socialization goals and mother–child interaction: Strategies for long-term and short-term compliance. *Developmental Psychology, 20,* 1061–1073.

Kumagai, H.A., & Kumagai, A.K. (1986). The hidden "I" in Amae: Passive love and Japanese social perception. *Ethos, 14,* 305–320.

Lamb, M.E., & Easterbrooks, M.A. (1981). Individual differences in parental sensitivity: Origins, components, and consequences. In M.E. Lamb & L.R. Sherrod (Eds.), *Infant social cognition: Empirical and theoretical considerations* (pp. 127–154). Hillsdale, NJ: Erlbaum.

Lawton, E.L. (1926). Address of welcome. In *Intelligent parenthood: Proceedings of the Mid-West conference on parent education, March 4, 5, and 6, 1926* (pp. 1–5). Chicago, IL: University of Chicago.

Lebra, T.S. (1976). *Japanese patterns of behavior.* Honolulu, HI: University Press of Hawaii.

Lebra, T.S. (1984). *Japanese women: Constraint and fulfillment.* Honolulu, HI: University Press of Hawaii.

Levine, R.A. (1977). Child rearing as cultural adaptation. In P.H. Leiderman, S.R. Tulkin, & A. Rosenfeld (Eds.). *Culture and infancy: Variations in the human experience* (pp. 15–27). New York: Academic Press.

Lewis, M., & Brooks-Gunn, J. (1979). Toward a theory of social cognition: The development of the self. In I. Uzgiris (Ed.), *New directions in child development: Social interaction and communication during infancy* (pp. 1–20). San Francisco, CA: Jossey-Bass.

Loeb, R.C., Horst, L., & Horton, P.J. (1980). Family interaction patterns associated with self-esteem in preadolescent girls and boys. *Merrill-Palmer Quarterly, 26,* 203–217.

Lytton, H. (1977). Correlates of compliance and the rudiments of conscience in two-year-old boys. *Canadian Journal of Behavioral Sciences, 9,* 242–251.

Lytton, H. (1979). Disciplinary encounters between young boys and their mothers: Is there a contingency system? *Developmental Psychology, 15,* 256–268.

Lytton, H. (1980). *Parent–child interaction: The socialization process observed in twin and singleton families.* New York: Plenum.

Maccoby, E.E., & Martin, J.A. (1983). Socialization in the context of the family: Parent–child interactions. In E.M. Hetherington (Ed.), *Socialization, personality, and social development. Vol. 4. Handbook of child psychology.* New York: Wiley.

Martin, J.A. (1981). A longitudinal study of the consequences of early mother-infant interaction: A microanalytic approach. *Monographs of the Society for Research in Child Development, 46*(3, Serial No. 190).

Minton, C., Kagan, J., & Levine, J.A. (1971). Maternal control and obedience in the two-year-old. *Child Development, 42,* 1873–1894.

Miyake, K., Chen, S., & Campos, J.J. (1985). Infant temperament, mother's mode of interaction, and attachment in Japan: An interim report. In I. Bretherton & E. Waters (Eds.), *Growing points of attachment theory and research. Monographs of the Society for Research in Child Development, 50* (209, 1–2).

Mussen, P.H., Harris, S., Rutherford, E., & Keasey, C.B. (1970). Honesty and altruism among preadolescents. *Developmental Psychology, 3,* 169–194.

Ogbu, J.U. (1981). Origins of human competence: A cultural-ecological perspective. *Child Development, 52,* 413–429.

Parke, R.D. (1974). Rules, roles, and resistance to deviation in children. In A. Pick (Ed.), *Minnesota symposia on child psychology* (Vol. 8, pp. 111–144). Minneapolis, MN: University of Minnesota.

Parke, R.D. (1977). Punishment in children: Effects, side effects and alternative strategies. In H. Hom & P. Robinson (Eds.), *Psychological processes in early education* (pp. 71–97). New York: Academic Press.

Parke, R.D. (1978). Parent-infant interaction: Progress, paradigms, and problems. In G.P. Sackett (Ed.), *Observing behavior: Vol. 1. Theory and applications in mental retardation* (pp. 69–93). Baltimore, MD: University Park.

Patterson, G.R. (1986). Performance models of antisocial boys. *American Psychologist, 41,* 432–444.

Radin, N. (1971). Maternal warmth, achievement motivation and cognitive functioning in lower class pre-school children. *Child Development, 42,* 1560–1565.

Radin, N. (1973). Observed paternal behaviors as antecedents of intellectual functioning in young boys. *Developmental Psychology, 8,* 369–376.

Reese, H.W. (1982). A comment on the meanings of "Dialectics." *Human Development, 25,* 423–429.

Riegel, K.F. (1975). Toward a dialectical theory of development. *Human Development, 18,* 50–64.

Riegel, K.F. (1976). The dialectics of human development. *American Psychologist, 10,* 689–700.

Rogoff, B. & Lave, J. (1984). *Everyday cognition: Its development in social context.* Cambridge: Harvard University.

Salkind, N. (1985). *Theories of human development,* (2nd ed.). New York: Wiley.

Scarr, S. (1984). *Mother care/other care.* New York: Basic Books.

Scarr, S., & McCarthy, K. (1983). How people make their own environments: A theory of genotype-environment effects. *Child Development, 54,* 424–435.

Schaefer, C. (1978). *How to influence children.* New York: Von Nostrand Reinhold.

Schaefer, E.S. (1959). A circumplex model for maternal behavior. *Journal of Abnormal and Social Psychology, 57,* 266–235.

Schaffer, H.R., & Crook, C.K. (1980). Child compliance and maternal control techniques. *Developmental Psychology, 16,* 54–61.

Seegmiller, B.R., & King, W.L. (1975). Relations between behavioral characteristics of infants, their mothers' behavior, and performance on the Bayley mental and motor scales. *Journal of Psychology, 90,* 99–111.

Shaver, D.R. (1985). *Developmental psychology: Theory, research, and applications.* Monterey, CA: Brooks/Cole.

Sigel, I.E. (Ed.). (1985). *Parental belief systems: The psychological consequences for children.* Hillsdale, NJ: Erlbaum.

Sroufe, L.A., & Ward, M.J. (1980). Seductive behavior of mothers: Occurrence, correlates, and family origins. *Child Development, 51,* 1222–1229.

Stayton, D., Hogan, R., & Ainsworth, M.D.S. (1971). Infant obedience and maternal behavior: The origins of socialization reconsidered. *Child Development, 42,* 1057–1069.

Sternberg, R.J. (1984). Towards a triarchic theory of intelligence. *Brain and Behavioral Science, 7,* 269–287.

Sternberg, R.J., & Wagner, R.K. (1986). *Practical intelligence: Origins of competence in the everyday world.* New York: Cambridge University Press.

Stevenson, H., Azuma, H., & Hakuta, K. (1986). *Child development and education in Japan.* New York: Freeman.

Stolz, L.M. (1967). *Influences on parent behavior.* Palo Alto, CA: Stanford University.

Takahashi, K. (1982). Attachment behaviors to a female stranger among Japanese two-year-olds. *Journal of Genetic Psychology, 140,* 299–307.

Takahashi, K. (1986). Examining the strange-situation procedure with Japanese mothers and 12-month-old infants. *Developmental Psychology, 22,* 265–270.

Tudor-Hart, B. (1966). *The intelligent parent's guide to child behavior.* New York: Delacorte Press.

Valsiner, J. (1984, September). *'Intelligence' as person-environment relationship in structured action contexts.* Paper presented at the 23rd International Congress of Psychology, Acapulco, Mexico.

Wachs, T.D. & Gruen, G.E. (1982). *Early experience and human development.* New York: Plenum.

Watson, J.B. (1928). *Psychological care of infant and child.* New York: Norton.

Watson, J.S. (1972). Smiling, cooing, and "the game." *Merrill-Palmer Quarterly, 18,* 323–340.

Weeks, M.H. (1914). What constitutes a good mother. In M.H. Weeks (Ed.), *Parents and their problems: Child welfare in the home, school, church and state, Vol. 1.* Washington, DC: National Congress of Mothers and Parent-Teacher Association.

Weisz, J., Rothbaum, F.M., & Blackburn, T.C. (1984). Standing out and standing in: The psychology of control in America and Japan. *American Psychologist, 39,* 955–969.

Winder, C.L., & Rau, L. (1962). Parental attitudes associated with social deviance in preadolescent boys. *Journal of Abnormal and Social Psychology, 64,* 418–424.

Wulbert, M., Ingles, S., Kriegsmann, F., & Mills, B. (1975). Language delay and associated mother-child interaction. *Developmental Psychology, 11,* 61–70.

Yarrow, L.J., Rubinstein, J., & Pederson, F. (1975). *Infant and environment.* New York: Wiley.

Yarrow, M.R. (1963). Problems of methods in parent-child research. *Child Development, 34,* 215–226.

Zahn-Waxler, C., Radke-Yarrow, M., & King, R.A. (1979). Child-rearing and children's prosocial initiations toward victims of distress. *Child Development, 50*, 319–330.

Zussman, J.V. (1980). Situational determinants of parent behavior: Effects of competing cognitive activity. *Child Development, 51,* 792–800.

CHAPTER 3

Parents' Protection of Children from Dangers*

Tommy Gärling and Anita Gärling

Environmental Psychology Research Group
Department of Psychology
Umeå University
Umeå, Sweden

INTRODUCTION

All mammals care in some way for their offspring in order to ensure its survival (Gubernick & Klopfer, 1981; Sluckin & Herbert, 1986). Such care of the young is accomplished in many different ways, depending on the characteristics of the species and its adjustment to the environment, that is, how members of the species feed, what dangers threaten them, and so forth. It has been questioned, therefore, whether our understanding of the complexities of human parenting is much increased by knowledge about parental behavior in lower animals (Mussen, 1982).

In humans more than in any other species, learning plays a primary role for the ontogeny of parental behavior. Attempts at understanding this role has predominantly focused on the early mother-to-infant bonding (Klaus & Kennell, 1982) which explains parents' attachment to the children and their motivation to take care of them (but see Sluckin, Herbert, & Sluckin, 1983). In this chapter we are interested in why parents pursue their caretaking goals in certain ways. A general

* Our own research reported in this chapter was financially supported by the Bank of Sweden Tercentenary Fund. We would like to express our gratitude to Anders Böök for his valuable comments on an earlier draft.

assumption is that many important parental behaviors are guided by beliefs (Sigel, 1985), and we will try to give some limited answers to questions such as what kinds of beliefs regulate parents' behavior and how beliefs and behavior are interrelated.

Feeding, providing comfort, transfer of knowledge, and protection from dangers are basic functions of parental care. Whereas developmental psychology has mainly concerned itself with the transfer-of-knowledge/socialization function (Maccoby & Martin, 1983), we will focus here on the function of protection from dangers. Our intention is specifically to analyze a problem of great social significance, namely the possible failure of parents (and nonparent caretakers) to protect children from accidental injuries in the home and in the residential neighborhood (Baker, O'Neill, & Karpf, 1984).

An analysis of parental attempts at socialization was recently provided by Dix and Grusec (1985), based on theories of causal attribution (Harvey, Ickes, & Kidd, 1976, 1978, 1981; Jones, Kanouse, Kelley, Nisbett, Valins, & Weiner, 1972). Because this analysis is very similar to ours in relation to accident protection (e.g., Svensson-Gärling, Gärling, & Valsiner, 1985), we will be able to draw on the work of Dix and Grusec (1985). A similar analysis of two basic functions of parental behavior may, furthermore, warrant some more general conclusions about the belief regulation of this behavior. There are also other influential theories of how behavior is regulated by internal cognitive structures (e.g., Feather, 1982; Kuhl & Atkinson, 1986). We will most heavily draw on the theory of reasoned action proposed by Fishbein and Ajzen (1975; see also Ajzen & Fishbein, 1980, and Ajzen, 1985).

In the next section we examine parents' protective behaviors. The factors that regulate these behaviors are then discussed, followed by a presentation of some of our own research on parents' perceptions of accident risks for children. In a concluding section we attempt to sketch an agenda for further research which is compatible with the framework which is developed throughout the preceding sections.

PARENTS' PROTECTIVE BEHAVIORS

Children are subject to a wide range of hazards in their everyday environments, some of which may be poorly understood by laypeople (Kane, 1985). What parents can do is obviously to carefully supervise children in environmental settings, to select and structure such settings so that they become more safe for the children, and to teach the children how to protect themselves. Unfortunately, almost nothing appears to be known about to which extent and in which ways parents are actually engaged in these protective behaviors. Time allocation studies of adults and children (e.g., Björklid, 1982; Bloch & Walsh, 1985; Clarke-Stewart & Hevey, 1981) are not directly relevant.

What we will do here is to try to give as clear definitions as possible of the basic types of protective behaviors mentioned above. We will also offer some hypotheses about how these behaviors are related to each other and to other parental behaviors. In each subsection we will make some comments about what we think will happen at different ages of the child. Age of the child is obviously one of the most important factors which affect parents' protective behaviors although by no means the only one. More will be said about such factors in the next section.

Types of Protective Behaviors

Three basic types of protective behaviors are undertaken by parents. One is to supervise children in environmental settings. A second is to select and structure such settings. A third is to teach the children how to protect themself. Each will in turn be discussed below.

Supervising children in environmental settings. Very few environments are completely safe for children. Therefore, at least at certain ages and in certain environmental settings/situations, children are continuously supervised. That mothers may be sensitive and vigilant in performing such tasks have been demonstrated in laboratory experiments investigating mother–infant interaction (Schaffer & Collis, 1986). Supervision is not confined to observations of the child's behavior. Changes in the environment and other people's behavior should be equally important to monitor.

Supervising children presumably involves primarily a readiness to interfere if something is perceived as threatening. However, it also provides an opportunity to identify situations in which the child can be taught about dangers as well as an opportunity to identify needs of "restructuring" environmental settings. The total frequency of supervising is likely, first, to increase as the child becomes more mobile when growing older, then to decrease as the child has learned how to protect himself or herself. The character may also change. When the children grow older, parents may be more inclined to supervise changes in the environment (and to structure the environment) and others' behavior rather than the children's behavior.

Selecting and structuring environmental settings. Parents are contributing to the children's safety by selecting and structuring their environments. Choosing a residence will, for instance, determine the children's exposure to hazards for many years to come. A home which has been selected is, to varying extents, restructured by parents to render it safer for the children. Groups of parents often try to restructure their neighborhoods to increase, for instance, traffic safety. There are also such protective behaviors at a smaller scale. In the home, small children are often physically restricted, for instance by placing them in playpens. Furthermore, parents do not allow older children to play everywhere in the neighborhood, which, it has been found, determines their home range as well as their cognitive maps of the neighborhood (Torell & Biel, 1985).

As was alluded to above, the frequency of parents' attempts at selecting and structuring environmental settings for the children may not decrease as fast as the frequency of supervision when the children grow older. Furthermore, these attempts should be quite frequent already when the child is an infant. Again, there may be changes in character. Physical factors in the environment which may cause injury are probably primarily focused on when the children are relatively small, whereas parents later may try to make safe environments attractive for their children.

Teaching children how to protect themselves. An important goal for parents should be to teach children to avoid dangers. Such teaching takes on many forms. As soon as children become mobile, they are taught about dangerous spots in the home by means of warnings. Later, parents use various disciplinary techniques to control children's behavior (Grusec & Kucynski, 1980; McLaughlin, 1983; Trickett & Kuczynski, 1986), and, still later, children may be brought to an understanding of dangers akin to the parents' understanding. Children are likely to learn by other routes as well. Some of the learning may, for instance, occur by children's modeling of the parents and by social reciprocation (Hall & Cairns, 1984).

Temporal Organization of Protective Behaviors

Protective behaviors are a certain class of parental behaviors only because their goal is protection. In everyday intercourse a parents' supervision of a child has, of course, several aims such as, for instance, being prepared to react if the child shows signs of distress. The same is certainly true for selecting and structuring environmental settings and teaching the child. Parental behaviors thus simultaneously serve several functions. Different functions may have different priority at particular moments in time, in different settings, and for different parents and children, resulting in different characters of protective behaviors.

Even though the different protective behaviors may be seen as rather distinct, it is likely that, in everyday parental behavior, they are interwoven in different ways. First, to some extent the different behaviors are substitutable. A mother may select/structure an environmental setting which will partly relieve her of the burden of constantly supervising the child. When teaching has had an effect, the need to structure an environment and to supervise a child is reduced. Secondly, the different protective behaviors may be instrumental for each other. For instance, structuring an environmental setting may not lead to protection but may facilitate supervision which leads to protection. Supervising and structuring environmental settings may be instrumental in the process of teaching the child to protect himself or herself. Environmental settings can be structured to provide learning opportunities, and supervision may fulfill the subsidiary function of identifying these learning opportunities.

FACTORS REGULATING PARENTS' PROTECTIVE BEHAVIORS

Analyses of parental behaviors have often been undertaken at a global level (Maccoby & Martin, 1983). In such analyses certain stable properties characterizing parenting over time are related to relevant outcome variables. Another approach to the study of parental behaviors seeks to understand the details of its regulation by means of a microanalysis of the interaction between parent and child. Both these types of analyses of the factors that regulate parents' protective behaviors will be attempted here, but the latter type is emphasized and will be presented first.

Microanalysis

There are many things a person believes (with some certainty) to be true about various aspects of reality. That such beliefs are important for how one acts is furthermore generally agreed upon (e.g., Feather, 1982; Kuhl & Atkinson, 1986). In the domain of parental behavior, Sigel (1985), among others, argues that beliefs are important regulators of many of parents' behavior towards children.

One of the more influential theories about the regulative effects of beliefs on behavior or action is the theory of reasoned action proposed by Fishbein and Ajzen (1975; see also Ajzen & Fishbein, 1980). This theory states that an intention to perform an action is related to how likely and to what degree one believes it leads to positive consequences as well as to one's motivation to comply with what one believes important others think. Recently, Ajzen (1985) has extended the theory to actions which may not with certainty be successfully executed.

Whether or not one attempts to execute an action is therefore, in the extended theory, related also to beliefs about how likely and important the consequences of failing to perform the action are, not only to beliefs about the likelihood of and consequences of succeeding to perform it.

The theory of reasoned action is a general framework for conceptualizing how behavior or actions are related to beliefs. In order to explain how beliefs are formed, other theoretical conceptualizations must be envoked. An example is the analysis by Dix and Grusec (1985) of how parents' socialization attempts are regulated. This analysis draws on theories of causal attribution (Harvey, et al., 1976, 1978, 1981; Jones, et al., 1972). In focus are "misdeeds" which parents attempt to control because they are in conflict with their socialization goals for the children. Why do parents then act as they do when they encounter certain child behaviors, sometimes punishing the child, sometimes doing nothing? Dix and Grusec assume that parents, first, infer whether the behavior is caused by a stable disposition rather than the situation. Secondly, if parents infer it is, they punish the child, because they believe this is likely under these circumstances to promote their goal (although other factors are also important). Another possibility mentioned by Dix and Grusec is that the causal attributions lead to affective responses (Weiner, 1985) on the basis of which parents act. The eventual outcome may be increased effectiveness of control over undesirable behavior, or less such control, depending on how accurate the assessments are.

An account of the regulation of parents' protective behaviors drawing on these conceptual frameworks must both address the question of why such behaviors are at all undertaken as well as the question of which ones are undertaken. These questions will both be discussed in turn.

Why protective behaviors are undertaken. At the heart of protection from dangers is that it entails future-oriented actions which aim at preventing something from happening (or, more generally, to create a beneficial situation), not reactions to something which has happened (Holden, 1985; Valsiner, 1985). Parental regulation of "misdeeds," as analyzed by Dix and Grusec (1985), appears to start with a perceptual classification of the child's behavior when it is observed. A fine-grained analysis may, however, reveal that a parent more often acts in advance in order to prevent such behaviors from occuring. Thus, both the regulation of "misdeeds" and protection from dangers may rely on parents' ability to pick up information on the basis of which they can form beliefs about what is going to happen. It may still be true that the children elicit the parents' actions (Bell & Harper, 1977) by acting in ways that arouse them.

The protection of children from accidental injuries seems to require a readiness on the part of the parents to act on the basis of risks which they assess. An important question which will be illuminated by means of empirical findings in the next section is how such risk assessments are made. Sometimes, direct previous experiences may play a crucial role, if they can be recalled from memory (Tversky & Kahneman, 1973). More often, however, the ability to foresee accidents may in some way rely on knowledge parents have acquired from other, indirect sources. The explanatory function of causal attributions has frequently been in focus (as in the research by Dix & Grusec, 1985). However, as Eiser (1983) notes, causal attributions also have an important predictive function which deserves attention. In this vein, a case has been made for the possibility that assessments of risk (probability) depend on causal factors. For instance, Ajzen (1977) found that subjects considered base-rate information as relevant only if they could see a causal relation between this information and the possible occurrence of an event which they had to predict. Similar findings were reported by Tversky and Kahneman (1980). Gärling, Svensson-Gärling, and Valsiner (1984) reasoned that, if factors are present which one perceives as necessary and/or sufficient causes of an accident to a child, then the perceived likelihood of such an accident should increase. In line with this reasoning, parents' (and nonparents') judgments of the likelihood of traffic accidents to children living in different residential neighborhoods were found to be related to how strongly various prevalent causes attributed to the accidents were rated.

If attributions of causes to accidents play a decisive role in their prediction and control, the question must be raised of what factors account for the causal attributions. In his normative analysis of causal attribution, Kelley (1972a) states that causes are inferred from observations of systematic covariation of cause and effect. However, if only partial direct observations can be made, or if information is obtained from secondary sources (Wells, 1981), causal models or schemata may be used to attribute causes to events (Kelley, 1972b, 1983; Nisbett & Ross, 1980). Others have suggested that causal schemata and observations interact in determining causal attributions. For instance, Ajzen and Fishbein (1975) in effect argued that causal schemata direct attention to more conclusive information which can be observed. More recently, Einhorn and Hogarth (1986) have proposed that the inferred strength of a causal relationship has three necessary conditions: the availability of one (or several) salient cause(s), temporal precedence of the cause(s), and the possibility of inferring mediating causal links. Observed covariation of cause and effect is not a necessary condition, but will if it exists increase the inferred strength of the causal relationship.

Although particular accidents or near-accidents are not ruled out as potential learning experiences, we argue that risk assessments are largely based on models parents have acquired about the functioning (and malfunctioning) of various environmental or behavioral settings (Gump, 1975) of which children form parts. Such a setting is, for instance, the playground, the children playing there, and the adults supervising the children. The home, including the members of the family, guests, etc., is an example of another such setting. Some of the acquired beliefs may transcend particular settings, but, as Gärling (1985) points out, it is still important to take into account both the possibility of learning about the setting (e.g., how predictable events are) and to what degree this knowledge has been acquired. Salient examples are, for instance, traffic in a neighborhood, which may be quite unpredictable (difficult to learn about), whereas a playground may be predictable but less known to a parent. The home is presumably both predictable and known. The consequence is that parents' risk assessments may vary in accuracy depending on how accurate their beliefs are about the particular setting.

Among those beliefs which may transcend particular settings are beliefs about children, their interests, competencies, and skills (Svensson-Gärling, et al., 1985). The argument has been made that assessments of children should be made in relation to particular contexts (Valsiner, 1984) but it may still be the case that context-free descriptions are salient in parents' beliefs (Sameroff & Feil, 1985). Spencer and Blades (1985) argued, on the basis of contradictory evidence, that parents may underestimate children's competence but overestimate their actual performance. This suggests that a distinction between competence and performance may be valid, although if the findings referred to hold up in further research, parents' beliefs about how competence is realized in actual performance may need to be investigated more in depth.

Given that a parent has acquired adequate knowledge of a setting, we assume he or she will be able to "mentally simulate" events in the setting under various imagined conditions (Kahneman & Tversky, 1982). In this way it would be possible for the parent to foresee what will happen. The mental simulation may vary in difficulty. In a predictable and well-known environmental setting, the simulation is similar to the retrieval of scripts (Schank & Abelson, 1977). If the circumstances are novel, the simulation has to rely more on construction and will probably be more demanding and less accurate.

If a situation is assessed as dangerous, a parent may undertake a protective behavior because its consequences are believed to eliminate the danger (to have positive consequences). An additional but probably less important determinant of the behavior is a parent's belief that important others (spouse, society, etc.) have a positive attitude to him or her undertaking the protective behavior. Under certain circumstances, affect (fear) may mediate between risk assessments and parents' protective behaviors, exactly as Dix and Grusec (1985) suggest that affect mediates parents' responses to "misdeeds." This may apply to supervision more than to other protective behaviors (selecting/structuring environmental settings and teaching the children about dangers) because, in general, the risk identified may be close in time to the potential accident. Thus, a parent who identifies causes of potential accidents (e.g., a car coming) when supervising his or her child may react (by, e.g., lifting the child away from the road) on the basis of the fear his or her assessment gives rise to. It may be questioned whether the regulation of the behavior is similar in this case to when one has more time to foresee the consequences of protective actions (Kruglanski & Klar, 1985). However, under other circumstances, for instance when a parent teaches a child, fear may play much less role. Even though a parent simulates accident-prone events when assessing the risk (Kahneman & Tversky, 1982; Svensson-Gärling et al., 1985), there is no reason to believe that this means he or she feels as much fear as when a similar event sequence is actually unfolding.

Which protective behaviors are undertaken. Having discussed why parents undertake protective behaviors at all, we are now left with the question of why parents choose a certain protective behavior rather than another one. For instance, why do parents not teach a child about dangers instead of supervising him or her? And why do they not select/ structure the environment for a child rather than supervising him or her? In actual practice no such choice may exist, because the protective behaviors are dependent on other behaviors as well as on each other. Only to the extent the protective behaviors are independent of other behaviors and substitutable does the question of choice arise.

The main point we would like to make here is that a choice between the protective behaviors is dependent on parents' beliefs about the child's development and its consequences for his or her behavior in particular settings. Supervision may be seen by parents (and by others) as a basic means of protection. A parent may feel he or she has the situation under close control. Therefore, the positive consequences in terms of the protection goal are apparent. Some basic training and structuring of the environment are perhaps judged as necessary complementary means of protection, but it is not until later that they are seen as having positive consequences of their own.

Even though supervision is perceived as an efficient means of protection, supervising a child has negative consequences as well. Such negative consequences may be particularly salient if there are other competing cognitive activities (Zussman, 1980). Furthermore, at some point parents are likely to stop supervising the children in structured settings because they believe this is no longer necessary. Stopping to supervise the children may later extend to other settings, less familiar and less structured by the parents. We assume that such decisions rely on beliefs about children's development of skills in relation to the demands so that they, according to the parents' judgments, can act safely on their own. They may also rely on other inferences about the children within particular settings, such as what attracts their interest, etc.

An equally critical, related decision is when parents should start to teach the children about dangers and when they can trust that such teaching has lasting effects. Here again, beliefs about the child's development should be crucial. In addition, parents' beliefs about how children at different ages are best taught various things (McGillicuddy-De Lisi, 1985) should also affect their decisions. Teaching about dangers should, however, in general be less substitutable than supervision and selecting/structuring settings because of its subsidiary socialization goal which may dominate over the immediate protection goal.

Global Analysis

At a global level of analysis, effective protection is, naturally, a relevant outcome variable. Our preceding analysis suggests that frequency and quality of parents' protective behaviors should be one factor which could possibly predict this outcome variable, but there are certainly other factors too. One may, furthermore, ask what factors predict the frequency and quality of protective behaviors.

Apart from parental protection, we mention here two other factors which should have direct effects on effective protection of a child. One factor is characteristics of the child, such as skill level. Another factor is residential conditions which affect a child's exposure to hazards. As Figure 1 illustrates, parental protection has indirect effects in addition to direct effects, to the extent that the child's skill is partly a result of the parents' teaching efforts. Furthermore, to the extent the residential conditions are the results of parents' choices and structuring, there may also be indirect effects through them.

Basically, according to our microanalysis of the regulation of parental protection, the better a parent is at selecting/structuring environmental settings, at supervising children, and at teaching them, the more effective he or she should be at protection. Experience may be singled out as one important factor, perhaps the most important one, but there is a long history of research on parenting styles which perhaps should not

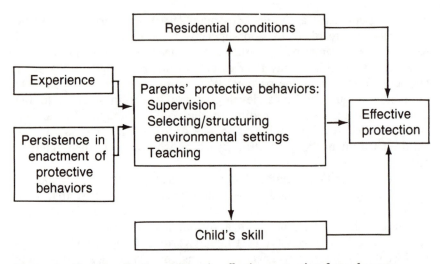

Figure 1.   Factors affecting children's effective protection from dangers.

be ignored. A review by Maccoby and Martin (1983) identifies two dimensions, demandingness and responsiveness, respectively, on the basis of which a fourfold classification can be made of authoritarian-autocratic (high demandingness-low responsiveness), indulgent-permissive (low demandingness-high responsiveness), authoritative-reciprocal (high demandingness-high responsiveness), and indifferent-uninvolved (low demandingness-low responsiveness) types of parenting styles. Although such style differences appear to be highly relevant, no specific hypotheses suggest themselves on empirical or conceptual grounds. One may also speculate whether protection is a parenting function which is less affected by style variation. "Minimal parenting" (Zussman, 1980) may still be satisfactory with respect to the protection goals, although less satisfactory with respect to other goals, such as, for instance, the socialization goal.

Another classification system discussed by Maccoby and Martin (1983) is also based on two dimensions, namely frequency of goal conflicts within a family and the degree to which resolutions of such conflicts are balanced (i.e., satisfy goals that are compromises between parents' and children's goals). This classification system brings into focus a conflict entailed by parental protection which has not yet been mentioned, namely, the conflict that may arise because of the opposition from the child when parents are trying to interfere in the interest of protecting him or her from dangers. Children who, through parents' successful teaching attempts, have attained an understanding of dangers similar to that of the parents may be more ready to accept such interference. Nevertheless, conflicts will arise, and parents may possibly not always be persistent in enforcing the attainment of their protection goals when in conflict with the goals the child may have. It may be particularly difficult to be persistent because dangers are uncertain events which may or may not materialize and about which knowledge is far from perfect. Thus, it would not be too difficult to revise one's perception of the likelihood of such an event if a child resists actions taken on the basis of such assessments. Even though experience may be important here as well, we propose that some measure of persistence in enacting protective behaviors may also predict, partly independently of experience, if parents' protective behaviors lead to effective protection.

Experience may refer to many things, ranging from experience as a child of one's own parents to formal parental education when grown up (Maccoby & Martin, 1983). Distinctions may, furthermore, be made between general and specific experiences, as well as between declarative and procedural knowledge acquired from experience (Sigel, 1985). However, we specifically refer here to experiences of the functioning of the everyday settings in which children grow up. If a parent is the primary caretaker, if the child is not his or her first one, and if there is a previous record of accidents and near-accidents, this might have provided the most important previous experiences, although we do not rule out the role of vicarious experiences through the mass media, parental education, etc.

PARENTS' RISK PERCEPTIONS

The study of subjective risk assessments has attracted interest because it is believed it can contribute to the management and regulation of risks in the society (e.g., Fischhoff, Svenson, & Slovic, in press; Slovic, Fischhoff, & Lichtenstein, 1984). This research has been concerned with questions such as how accurate subjective risk assessments are, how subjective risk assessments are made, and how risks are represented psychologically.

Judging the probability of the occurence of uncertain events such as accidents to children is a difficult task. Often, it cannot be performed unless the required judgments are simplified. Previous research (Kahneman & Tversky, 1973) has identified several heuristics which render such judgments simpler. One is called the *representative* heuristic and is used when a judgment of the probability that an event belong to a specified class or process is called for. A second, the *availability* heuristic, comes into play when one is asked to judge the probability of an event.

The *adjustment-from-an-anchor* heuristic, finally, is used in numerical assessments of probability when a relevant value (anchor or reference value) is available.

The argument was made above that parents acquire beliefs about the functioning of the various environmental settings in which their children reside. On the basis of such acquired beliefs, as well as, to some extent, on the basis of recalled previous experiences of accidents and near-accidents, parents may assess the accident risks to which children are vulnerable. Such assessments are in turn the basis for undertaking protective behaviors.

The availability heuristic (Tversky & Kahneman, 1973) implies that the likelihood of an event is rated on the basis of the ease with which the event is recalled. If one has encountered accident-prone events and they are easy to recall, the likelihood of such events should thus be judged as high. In two studies, we investigated the role of specific previous experiences of accident-prone events for mothers' perceptions of accident risks to children at varying ages. Female university students who were not mothers also participated as subjects. Because these subjects would have had less own experience of accident-prone events involving children, their risk assessments should differ from the mothers' assessments. We also expected that a group of students from the school of education would differ from another group of students from the dentist school, because the former group had had more experience with children.

In a third study we investigated whether and to what extent mothers' and students' based their risk assessments on causal models of accident-prone events rather than on recalled previous experiences of particular such events.

Study 1

Seventy-two women volunteered as subjects in Study 1. All of them were living in a number of residential neighborhoods in Umeå (a Swedish city with 80,000 residents). Twenty-four were mothers sampled from a general population, and an equal number came from each student population. An equal number of the mothers had at least one child in the age ranges 2 to 4, 5 to 6, 7 to 9, and 10 to 12 years, respectively. Most of them had more than one child. The mothers were on average about 10 years older than the students.

By means of a questionnaire, graphical scale ratings were obtained of the risk that a child in the age ranges 2 to 4, 5 to 6, 7 to 9, and 10 to 12 years, respectively, would have an accident with nontrivial consequences where the subjects lived. On the assumption that the subjects would have to recall particular accidents (or near-accidents) when rating the risk, they were, immediately thereafter, asked to list such events in the order they had been recalled.

The results averaged across each subject group (parents, expert and nonexpert nonparents) are plotted in Figure 2. In accordance with the hypothesis that the availability heuristic is used to rate the risk, both rated risk and number of recalled accident scenarios decrease similarly with the child's age. The expected differences between the subject groups were, however, not statistically reliable, and a content analysis of the recalled scenarios furthermore showed that, in almost no cases, the scenarios referred to personal experiences but to generic classes of accidents to which children are vulnerable. The most frequently mentioned classes were (in approximate order of frequency): traffic accidents, falls, burns, cuts, poisonings, drownings, squeezings, and suffocations.

Study 2

Study 2 asked how parents and nonparents assess the risk of particular classes of accidents. Risk was rated for those accident classes or types which were most frequently mentioned in Study 1. In this case the availability heuristic seems even more plausible, since subjects would have to recall more specific accident scenarios which may not be possible in any other way than by referring to one's own previous experiences.

The data collection procedure was exactly the same as in Study 1, except that subjects were asked to rate the risk that a child would have an accident of the specified type. Another 16 subjects participated from each of the populations from which subjects were recruited in Study 1.

Table 1 shows that rated risk and the number of recalled accident scenarios again decrease similarly across the child's age (with the exception for traffic accidents where no decrease was observed in neither case). Parents and expert nonparents furthermore rated risk as higher and recalled more scenarios than nonexpert nonparents, although only the former difference reached statistical significance. However, the statistical relationship between rated risk and the number of recalled accident scenarios was weak at an individual level. A content analysis of the accident scenarios furthermore revealed that, in a majority of cases, the accident scenarios were subclasses of the generic accident classes. For instance, after having judged the risk of a traffic accident, subjects mentioned scenarios like being hit by a car when biking, when crossing the street as a pedestrian, etc. Thus, the scenarios were more specific than in Study 1 but they were not personally experienced to any greater extent.

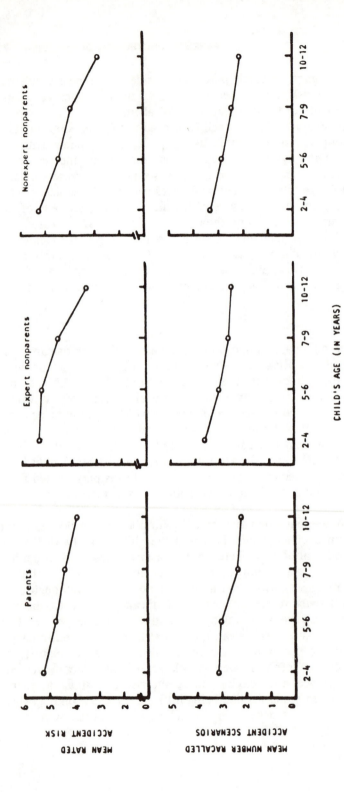

Figure 2. Parents' and nonparents' rated risk and number of recalled accident scenarios.

Table 1. Rated Risk of Accidents (M) and Number of Recalled Accident Scenarios (f) by Parents and Nonparents

| | Child's age in years | | | | | | | |
| | 2–4 | | 5–6 | | 7–9 | | 10–12 | |
Type of accident	M	f	M	f	M	f	M	f
	Parents							
Traffic	4.7	2.1	5.6	2.4	4.8	2.4	3.7	2.1
Falls	4.9	2.6	3.8	2.6	3.1	2.1	2.2	1.9
Burns	3.8	2.6	3.3	2.6	2.9	2.6	2.4	2.3
Cuts	3.1	2.1	3.2	2.4	2.9	2.4	1.8	2.1
Poisonings	3.1	2.3	2.1	2.1	1.4	1.9	0.9	1.6
Drownings	2.6	1.9	2.7	1.9	2.2	1.8	1.4	1.6
Squeezings	4.9	2.4	3.5	2.1	2.3	1.7	1.3	1.3
Suffocations	2.9	1.6	1.7	1.8	1.7	1.4	1.0	1.3
	Expert nonparents							
Traffic	5.5	2.2	5.3	2.3	5.2	2.1	4.2	2.1
Falls	5.7	2.2	4.0	2.0	3.0	1.9	2.1	1.9
Burns	5.1	2.2	3.7	2.1	3.2	2.1	2.8	2.1
Cuts	4.2	2.3	4.2	2.3	3.4	2.1	2.6	2.1
Poisonings	5.6	2.3	4.0	2.1	3.0	1.9	1.9	1.3
Drownings	3.6	1.8	3.3	1.9	2.3	1.8	2.4	1.8
Squeezings	5.5	1.8	4.5	1.6	3.4	1.4	2.1	1.6
Suffocations	4.5	1.6	2.6	1.7	1.8	1.6	1.0	1.3
	Nonexpert nonparents							
Traffic	3.5	1.8	3.5	1.9	3.5	2.0	2.9	2.0
Falls	3.5	1.9	3.3	1.9	2.5	1.8	1.5	1.4
Burns	3.6	2.4	3.0	2.5	2.5	2.1	1.7	1.9
Cuts	2.5	1.5	2.7	1.6	2.5	1.8	1.9	1.6
Poisonings	3.4	1.8	2.0	1.9	1.1	2.0	0.8	2.0
Drownings	1.9	1.8	1.4	1.7	1.6	1.3	1.3	1.3
Squeezings	3.7	1.3	3.5	1.3	2.4	1.3	1.6	1.2
Suffocations	2.4	1.3	1.4	1.3	1.0	1.1	0.6	1.0

Study 3

When faced with the task of assessing the risk a child runs of having an (unspecified) accident, a parent may recall (rather generic) accident-prone events, and the perceived risk may be related to number of such recalled events. However, if a salient, specified such risk is evaluated, the results of Study 2 showed that some other heuristic may be at work. A representative scenario may in this case be recalled or con-structed (Kahneman & Tversky, 1982). Because causal connections are embedded in such a scenario or script (Schank & Abelson, 1977), it is conceivable that the likelihood of the scenario is rated on the basis of the strength of these causal connections. For instance, if the absence of the mother's supervision is perceived as important for the possible occurence of an accident to a small child, then one would rate its likelihood as high if the mother does not supervise the child.

Study 3 investigated the role of causal models for mothers' risk assessments. Twenty-four descriptions of accident scenarios were prepared in accordance with subjects' reports in Studies 1 and 2. All of them had the following basic structure: (a) A mother and her child are interacting in a setting (the home, the backyard, or the immediate surrounding neighborhood). (b) For some reason (a phone call, a neighbor calling, etc.), the mother leaves the child alone or exerts no control (by walking behind, by biking in front of, etc.). (c) The child acts in an unsafe way (by running out in the street, climbing the windowsill, opening the kitchen oven, etc.) with an injury-causing accident as consequence. The type of accident was varied in the scenarios. In one-third of them the child was hit by a car; in one-third he or she fell, from a roof or from a tree, from the second floor, or in a stair case; and in one-third he or she was burned, from contact with a hot kitchen stove, or from contact with some hot objects on the stove. The characteristics of the child were independently varied with respect to age and sex. In an equal number of scenarios the child was 3, 5, 8, and 11 years old, respectively, and at each age the child protagonist was, in a randomly chosen half of the scenarios, a boy, in the other half a girl.

The subjects who participated in Study 3 were still another 16 subjects from each of the populations from which subjects were recruited in Studies 1 and 2. They were presented all the descriptions and asked, first, to imagine that parts (a) and (b) of each description had occurred; secondly, to predict on graphical scales how likely it was that the accident described in part (c) actually would occur; and, finally, as soon as they had rated the likelihood, to state why they rated the accident as likely as they did. The prediction format of the task was chosen because previous research (Fischoff, 1975) has shown that prediction may differ from explanation, and prediction seemed to be more relevant in the present case.

A possibility is that subjects searched their memory in order to match the scenario with similar, previously experienced accident-prone events which in turn would determine the degree of risk they perceived. The hypothesis investigated was, however, that subjects based their ratings of risk on the strength of causal factors present in the scenario. The reasons given by the subjects in each respective group favored this latter possibility: 93%, 98%, and 95% of the reasons given by parents, expert nonparents, and nonexpert nonparents, respectively, were causal, whereas the few remaining reasons referred explicitly to previous experience of similar events. The overwhelming majority of causal reasons referred to the child protagonists' motivations to engage in the behavior leading to the accident and his or her skill in doing that without an accident occurring. Other reasons mentioned were that the mother left the child (for scenarios with the youngest children), that the environment was unsafe, and that other people involved in the accident, like drivers, failed to be cautious.

It was possible to make predictions about the actual ratings of likelihood on the basis of the notion that one believes that children's skill to manage safely increases with age, and that, at least in young ages, girls are more careful and skilled than boys. These predictions are not born out in either of the subject groups, as shown by the results in Table 2. It is possible that the ratings of likelihood were based on more complex interactions between the characteristics of the child (age and sex) and on other factors than the subjects were able to convey when giving reasons for their ratings.

Conclusions

The results of Studies 1 to 3 suggested that parents' assessments of the accident risks children are vulnerable to are not based primarily on their recall of previous experiences of accidents or near-accidents with children. Such previous experiences may still be important in various ways, although not exactly as suggested by Tversky and Kahneman (1973). If previously experienced accidents are recalled, they may be given disproportionate weight (Nisbett & Ross, 1980). They may also, together with other acquired information (through mass media, safety education, etc.), constitute the general knowledge base the subjects drew

Table 2. Parents' and Nonparents' Rated Likelihood of Accident Scenarios

| | Child's age and sex | | | | | | | |
| | 3 years | | 5 years | | 8 years | | 11 years | |
Type of accident	Boy	Girl	Boy	Girl	Boy	Girl	Boy	Girl
			Parents					
Traffic	4.0	6.9	4.8	6.4	7.0	6.2	2.9	5.5
Fall	5.6	5.5	2.2	5.6	5.8	4.4	4.2	2.0
Burn	4.1	5.1	4.6	5.0	4.3	4.6	5.2	4.0
			Expert Nonparents					
Traffic	5.7	7.3	7.0	7.0	5.9	7.4	4.5	7.2
Fall	5.8	5.7	2.9	6.8	6.5	5.8	5.7	4.2
Burn	5.0	6.9	5.4	7.1	5.7	5.6	7.9	5.3
			Nonexpert Nonparents					
Traffic	5.1	8.0	6.0	5.6	6.4	5.7	3.1	6.0
Fall	4.2	4.5	2.9	5.1	5.8	4.6	5.0	4.7
Burn	5.3	6.0	3.6	6.0	4.8	4.0	6.3	5.7

on when they rated the accident risk in Study 1. Number of recalled types of accidents in that study was related to the rated risk, but the recalled scenarios were not very often personally experienced events, and no large and reliable differences between mothers and the student groups were observed.

When the risk of a particular, salient type of accident, for instance a traffic accident, is being evaluated, the results of Study 2 showed that the number of recalled possible such accidents may be less important. Instead, subjects may, as the results of Study 3 suggested, draw on beliefs about how such specified accidents are caused. Previous experiences are of course one source of information from which causal beliefs are acquired, but such previous experiences may be of a general kind, like, for instance, experiences of how different behavioral settings function, how children develop, and so forth.

Both assessments of risks of various kinds of accidents and of such specific accidents under particular conditions seem to be involved when parents try to protect children. When selecting/structuring an environmental setting or teaching a child about dangers, it is essential that a parent is able to assess various risks. When a child is supervised, particular risks should become salient and assessments of such called for. We have demonstrated that different heuristics may be used in these different assessments but that their assessments probably rely on the same systems of beliefs which parents have of children and their environments. These beliefs seemed to be shared by nonparents, although they should partly have been acquired in different ways by parents and nonparents.

AGENDA FOR RESEARCH

In this chapter we have proposed a framework which conceptually linked our studies of parents' assessments of accident risks to how parents protect children from dangers. We first defined different types of protective behaviors parents undertake and discussed how they are temporarily organized and coordinated. Thereafter, we offered some hypotheses about the regulation of protective behaviors. A basic hypothesis was that a determinant of parents' protective behaviors is assessments of risks which parents are engaged in. Along with the presentation of our framework, relevant literature was briefly reviewed. This review indicated that knowledge about the protection function of parenting is scarce. It seems appropriate then, in a final section, to discuss how this state of affairs can be changed. We will do that by listing those problems which we believe are in most need of being researched.

Because so little is known about parents' protective behaviors under natural circumstances, it seems clear that more information about such everyday parental behaviors should be most welcomed. A problem is that different types of protective behaviors are likely to be interwoven with each other and coordinated with other parental behaviors. Furthermore, there may well be large differences, depending both on the characteristics of the families investigated and on the particular conditions under which they live. Methodologically, questionnaire studies relying on parents' reports seem to be the only feasible alternative but have been criticized because they provide little information about the actual interaction between parents and children (Schaffer & Collins, 1986; Maccoby & Martin, 1983). Nevertheless, important questions about how protective behaviors and other parental behaviors are interrelated, as well as questions about the character and frequency of each type of protective behavior and their interrelationships, can possibly be answered. Equally important is to try to gain information about factors that affect the character and frequency of protective behaviors.

More studies are also needed of parents' risk assessments. It is not difficult to see several problems worthy of further research. A basic problem which cannot easily be solved because there is no self-evident definition of objective risk is to assess how accurate parents are. Do parents underestimate dangers to children? Do such underestimations vary with the child's age and with other factors such as various forms of experiences, mood, and the degree to which the parents' protection goals are in conflict with the child's goals? Studies directed to these questions need to be made so that they allow simultaneous assessments of objective risks, for instance by means of longitudinal designs in which both accident records and parents' risk assessments are obtained. In such studies it may also be possible to learn more about the knowledge base parents draw on when assessing risks for their children.

Another set of questions concern the relationship between parents' and children's risk assessments. Techniques have been developed by means of which even rather young children's risk assessments can be studied (Grieve & Williams, 1985). There are also a few studies of how parents' risk assessments, as well as their predictions of children's risk assessments, compare with children's actual risk assessments (Sheehy & Chapman, 1985). Further studies are needed, however, to answer questions such as whether, to what extent, and under what circumstances children underestimate dangers as compared to their parents. Equally important would be to illuminate differences in heuristics used by parents and children (Valsiner, 1985), possibly as related to parents' amount and type of teaching attempts.

Finally, we would like to point out the need for studying more closely the relationship between risk assessments and protective behaviors, preferably by means of realistic laboratory experiments. A prototypical study is that by Zussman (1980), in which a mother or father brought two of his or her children to the laboratory. The experimenter asked the parent to perform a subsidiary problem-solving task while the children were observed playing. Zussman's main concern was whether the character of supervision and teaching changed as a function of subsidiary task performance. Under such "minimal parenting" conditions, avoiding dangers may be a relatively more important determinant of the parents' behavior than other goals. By systematically varying the observation room in the laboratory, parents' ways of restructuring the environment could be studied as well. Correlations could furthermore be sought between risk assessments by parents (and children) and actual protection by parents.

REFERENCES

Ajzen, I. (1977). Intuitive theories of events and the effects of base-rate information on prediction. *Journal of Personality and Social Psychology, 35,* 303–314.

Ajzen, I. (1985). From intentions to actions: A theory of planned behavior. In J. Kuhl & J. Beckman (Eds.), *Action control: From cognition to behavior* (pp. 11–39). Berlin: Springer.

Ajzen, I., & Fishbein, M. (1975). A Bayesian analysis of attribution processes. *Psychological Bulletin, 82,* 261–277.

Ajzen, I., & Fishbein, M. (1980). *Understanding attitudes and predicting social behavior.* Englewood Cliffs, NJ: Prentice-Hall.

Baker, S.P., O'Neill, B., & Karpf, R.S. (1984). *The injury fact book.* Lexington, MA: Lexington Books.

Bell, R.Q., & Harper, L.V. (Eds.). (1977). *Child effects on adults.* Hillsdale, NJ: Erlbaum.

Björklid, P. (1982). *Children's outdoor environment.* Lund: Liber.

Bloch, M.N., & Walsh, D.J. (1985). Young children's activities at home: Age and sex differences in activity, location, and social context. *Children's Environments Quarterly, 2*(2), 34–40.

Clarke-Stewart, K.A., & Hevey, C.M. (1981). Longitudinal relations in repeated observations of mother-child interaction from 1 to 2 ½ years. *Developmental Psychology, 17,* 127–145.

Dix, T.H., & Grusec, J.E. (1985). Parent attribution processes in the socialization of children. In I.E. Sigel (Ed.), *Parental belief systems* (pp. 201–233). Hillsdale, NJ: Erlbaum.

Einhorn, H.I., & Hogarth, R.M. (1986). Judging probable cause. *Psychological Review, 99,* 3–19.

Eiser, J.R. (1983). Attribution theory and social cognition. In J. Jaspars, F.D. Fincham, & M. Hewstone (Eds.), *Attribution theory and research: Conceptual, developmental and social dimensions* (pp. 91–113). London: Academic Press.

Feather, N. (Ed.). (1982). *Expectations and actions: Expectancy-value models in psychology.* Hillsdale, NJ: Erlbaum.

Fishbein, M., & Ajzen, I. (1975). *Belief, attitude, intention and behavior: An introduction to theory and research.* Reading, MA: Addison-Wesley.

Fischhoff, B. (1975). Hindsight ≠ foresight: The effect of outcome knowledge on judgment under uncertainty. *Journal of Experimental Psychology: Human Perception and Performance, 1,* 288–299.

Fischhoff, B., Svenson, O., & Slovic, P. (1986). Active response to environmental hazards. In D. Stokols & I. Altman (Eds.), *Handbook of environmental psychology* (pp. 1089–1133). New York: Wiley.

Gärling, T. (1985). Children's environments, accidents, and accident prevention: A conceptual analysis. *Children's Environments Quarterly, 2*(4), 4–8.

Gärling, T., Svensson-Gärling, A., & Valsiner, J. (1984). Parental concern about children's traffic safety in residential neighborhoods. *Journal of Environmental Psychology, 4,* 235–252.

Grieve, R., & Williams, A. (1985). Young children's perception of danger. *British Journal of Developmental Psychology, 3,* 385–392.

Grusec, J.E., & Kuczynski, L. (1980). Directions of effect in socialization: A comparison of the parent's versus the child's behavior as determinants of disciplinary techniques. *Developmental Psychology, 16,* 1–10.

Gubernick, D.J., & Klopfer, P.H. (Eds.). (1981). *Parental care in mammals.* New York: Plenum.

Gump, P.V. (1975). Ecological psychology and children. *Review of Child Development, 2,* 75–126.

Hall, W.M., & Cairns, R.B. (1984). Aggressive behavior in children: An outcome of modeling or social reciprocity. *Developmental Psychology, 20,* 739–746.

Harvey, J.H., Ickes, W.J., & Kidd, R.F. (Eds.). (1976). *New directions in attribution research* (Vol. 1). Hillsdale, NJ: Erlbaum.

Harvey, J.H., Ickes, W.J., & Kidd, R.F. (Eds.). (1978). *New directions in attribution research* (Vol. 2). Hillsdale, NJ: Erlbaum.

Harvey, J.H., Ickes, W.J., & Kidd, R.F. (Eds.). (1981). *New directions in attribution research* (Vol. 3). Hillsdale, NJ: Erlbaum.

Holden, G.W. (1985). How parents create a social environment via proactive behavior. In T. Gärling & J. Valsiner (Eds.), *Children within environments* (pp. 193–215). New York: Plenum.

Jones, D.E., Kanouse, D., Kelley, H.H., Nisbett, R.E., Valins, S., & Weiner, B. (Eds.). (1972). *Attribution: Perceiving the causes of behavior.* Morristown, NJ: General Learning Press.

Kahneman, D., & Tversky, A. (1973). On the psychology of prediction. *Psychological Review, 80,* 237–251.

Kahneman, D., & Tversky, A. (1982). The simulation heuristic. In D. Kahneman, P. Slovic, & A. Tversky (Eds.), *Judgment under uncertainty: Heuristics and biases* (pp. 201–208). Cambridge, England: Cambridge University Press.

Kane, D.N. (1985). *Environmental hazards to children.* Phoenix, AZ: Oryx Press.

Kelley, H.H. (1972a). Attribution in social interaction. In E.E. Jones, D.E. Kanouse, H.H. Kelley, R.E. Nisbett, S. Valins, & B. Weiner (Eds.), *Attribution: Perceiving the causes of behavior* (pp. 1–26). Morristown, NJ: General Learning Press.

Kelley, H.H. (1972b). Causal schemata and the attribution processes. In E.E. Jones, D.E. Kanouse, H.H. Kelley, R.E. Nisbett, S. Valins, & B. Weiner (Eds.). *Attribution: Perceiving the causes of behavior* (pp. 151–174). Morristown, NJ: General Learning Press.

Kelley, H.H. (1983). Perceived causal structures. In J. Jaspars, F.D. Fincham, & M. Hewstone (Eds.), *Attribution theory and research: Conceptual, developmental and social dimensions* (pp. 343–369). London: Academic Press.

Klaus, M.H., & Kennell, J.H. (1982). *Parent–infant bonding.* St. Louis, LA: Mosby.

Kruglanski, A.W., & Klar, Y. (1985). Knowing what to do: On the epistemology of actions. In J. Kuhl & J. Beckman (Eds.), *Action control: From cognition to behavior* (pp. 41–60). Berlin: Springer.

Kuhl, J., & Atkinson, J.W. (Ed.). (1986). *Motivation, thought, and action.* New York: Praeger.

Maccoby, E.E., & Martin, J.A. (1983). Socialization in the context of the family: Parent-child interaction. In P. Mussen & E.M. Hetherington (Eds.), *Handbook of child psychology* (4th ed., vol. 4, pp. 1–101). New York: Wiley.

McGillicuddy-De Lisi, A.V. (1985). The relationship between parental beliefs and children's cognitive level. In I.E. Sigel (Ed.). *Parental belief systems* (pp. 7–24). Hillsdale, NJ: Erlbaum.

McLaughlin, B. (1983). Child compliance to parental control techniques. *Developmental Psychology, 19,* 667–673.

Mussen, P. (1982). Parenting, prosocial behavior, and political attitudes. In L.W. Hoffman, R. Gandelman, & H.R. Shiffman (Eds.), *Parenting, its causes and consequences* (pp. 111–121). Hillsdale, NJ: Erlbaum.

Nisbett, R.E., & Ross, L. (1980). *Human inference: Strategies and shortcomings of social judgment.* Englewood Cliffs, NJ: Prentice-Hall.

Sameroff, A.J., & Feil, L.A. (1985). Parental concepts of development. In I.E. Sigel (Ed.). *Parental belief systems* (pp. 83–105). Hillsdale, NJ: Erlbaum.

Schaffer, H.R., & Collis, G.M. (1986). Parental responsiveness and child behavior. In W. Sluckin & M. Herbert (Eds.), *Parental behaviour* (pp. 283–315). Oxford, England: Basil Blackwell.

Schank, R., & Abelson, R.P. (1977). *Scripts, plans, goals and understanding: An inquiry into human knowledge structures.* Hillsdale, NJ: Erlbaum.

Sheehy, N.P., & Chapman, A.J. (1985). Adults' and children's perceptions of hazard in familiar environments. In T. Gärling & J. Valsiner (Eds.), *Children within environments* (pp. 51–64). New York: Plenum.

Sigel, I.E. (1985). A conceptual analysis of beliefs. In I.E. Sigel (Ed.). *Parental belief systems* (pp. 345–371). Hillsdale, NJ: Erlbaum.

Slovic, P., Fischhoff, B., & Lichtenstein, S. (1984). Behavioral decision theory perspectives on risk and safety. *Acta Psychologica, 56,* 183–203.

Sluckin, W., & Herbert, M. (Eds). (1986). *Parental behaviour.* Oxford, England: Basil Blackwell.

Sluckin, W., Herbert, M., & Sluckin, A. (1983). *Maternal bonding.* Oxford, England: Basil Blackwell.

Spencer, C., & Blades, M. (1985). Children at risk: Are we underestimating their general competence whilst overestimating their performance. In T. Gärling & J. Valsiner (Eds.), *Children within environments* (pp. 39–49). New York: Plenum.

Svensson-Gärling, A., Gärling, T., & Valsiner, J. (1985). Parents' knowledge of children's competence, perceptions of risk and causes of child accidents, and residential satisfaction. In T. Gärling & J. Valsiner (Eds.), *Children within environments* (pp. 65–88). New York: Plenum.

Trickett, P.K., & Kuczynski, L. (1986). Children's misbehaviors and parental discipline strategies in abusive and nonabusive families. *Developmental Psychology, 22,* 115–123.

Torell, G., & Biel, A. (1985). Parental restrictions and children's acquisition of neighborhood knowledge. In T. Gärling & J. Valsiner (Eds.), *Children within environments* (pp. 107–118). New York: Plenum.

Tversky, A., & Kahneman, D. (1973). Availability: A heuristic for judging the frequency and probability. *Cognitive Psychology, 5,* 207–232.

Tversky, A., & Kahneman, D. (1980). Causal schemas in judgments under uncertainty. In M. Fischbein (Ed.), *Progress in social psychology* (pp. 49–72). Hillsdale, NJ: Erlbaum.

Valsiner, J. (1984). Conceptualizing intelligence: From an internal static attribution to the study of the process structure of organism-environment relationships. *International Journal of Psychology, 19,* 363–389.

Valsiner, J. (1985). Theoretical issues of child development and the problem of accident prevention. In T. Gärling & J. Valsiner (Eds.), *Children within environments* (pp. 13–36). New York: Plenum.

Weiner, B. (1985). An attributional theory of achievement motivation and emotion. *Psychological Review, 92,* 548–573.

Wells, G.L. (1981). Lay analyses of causal forces on behavior. In J.H. Harvey (Ed.), *Cognition, social behavior, and the environment* (pp. 309–324). Hillsdale, NJ: Erlbaum.

Zussman, J.U. (1980). Situational determinants of parental behavior: Effects of competing cognitive activity. *Child Development, 51,* 792–800.

PART TWO

Adult-Child Interaction within Environmental Settings

INTRODUCTION

Following the analyses of the cognitive side of organization of child-environment relationships (Part One), the contributors to Part Two of this volume outline different ways in which adults and children are jointly involved in interaction within particular environmental settings. That such joint involvement is an important aspect of child development is no news for developmental psychology. However, the *context-bound nature* of adult–child joint action is only rarely given serious theoretical attention (Bronfenbrenner, 1979), and its explicit empirical investigation that preserves the context while studying selected phenomena is practically absent from contemporary child psychology. The contributors to Part Two work towards overcoming that gap in contemporary developmental psychology, each from a different empirical basis. However, all three chapters in Part Two share a common theoretical emphasis that is linked with the cultural-historical traditions of thought in psychology.

In contemporary developmental psychology, increasing interest in Lev Vygotsky's theoretical heritage is evident. A Vygotskian perspective on children's social development is most directly represented in this part of the volume by the contribution of the group of Yugoslavian psychologists led by Nada Ignjatović-Savić (Chapter 4). Yugoslavian developmental psychology in general, even if it is not extensive in terms of empirical research conducted at different research institutions, is far advanced in the theoretical field. Similarly to developmental psychologists from other countries in Europe—both East and West—Yugoslavian developmental psychology has synthesized various theoretical tendencies and traditionally separate disciplines in a highly prodctive way (see Ivić, 1978; Ivić & Marjanović, 1986). The chapter by Ignjatović-Savić, Kovăc-Cerović, Plut, and Pešikan is one example of such synthesis. In the theoretical sphere, the authors start from, and advance further, Vygotsky's theoretical notions about the ways in which children's social interaction with others facilitates their own development. Contrary to contemporary efforts in Soviet (and likewise in American) psychology to present Vygotsky's theoretical heritage as a complete and elaborate theoretical system, many of the fundamental notions in Vygotsky's writings were actually left incomplete for various reasons (Van der Veer, 1984). Furthermore, contemporary "followers" of Vygotsky, both in the Soviet Union and in the West, have rarely attempted to develop his theoretical system to its full capacity. Analyses of Vygotsky's ideas in contemporary psychology often remain one-sided (see Valsiner, 1987, chap. 4), and his name is sometimes brought in to provide halo for empirical investigations that have little in common with his theoretical ideas.

A good particular example of an idea put forward by Vygotsky and frequently cited in contemporary child psychology, but very rarely accurately understood (nor developed further), is the concept of the *zone of proximal development*. It is exactly this concept that Ignjatović-Savić et al. set out to elaborate—both theoretically and empirically. In the theoretical vein, they relate the zone of proximal development with other "zones" that are introduced *(zone of future development, zone of actual development,* and *zone of past development)*. The alignment of these "zones" on the basis of the developmental time parameter makes it possible to conceptualize Vygotsky's zone of proximal development *within* the context where developmental goals of the child's (expected) future are linked with actual relapses (otherwise known as *regressions—*see Bever, 1982) in the child's actions in social interaction contexts. On the empirical side, the investigators demonstrate a careful analysis of *dyadic* forms of interaction that include both the adult and the child within the given environmental setting. The Ignjatović-Savić et al. study is perhaps the first existing empirical elaboration in developmental psychology of Vygotsky's methodological strategy of *analysis into units* (see Vygotsky, 1986, chap. 1), applied to the phenomenology of adult–child interaction.

The study by Paula E. Hill and Jaan Valsiner (Chapter 5) is, on the one hand, based on the traditional attachment theory (Bowlby's theoretical model), but, on the other, reverses its homeostatic emphasis. The historically formed "layer" structure of Bowlby's attachment theory is analyzed by the authors. That analysis reveals a paradox in the "youngest" sediment of Bowlby's theory—his integration of features of the control-systems theory into his thinking by the end of the 1960s. Namely, the flexibility of setting goals makes it highly probable for the developing child to transcend the "set goal" of attachment-bond pres- ervation that is posited by Bowlby (on the basis of his psychoanalytic core ideas) to be *the* goal which is homeostatically maintained in the course of the second year of life. The empirical part of the Hill and Valsiner study entails observations of the ways in which toddlers make use of their mothers, as well as of their structured home environments, to engage previously unfamiliar adults in joint action. The focus of the analysis is on the temporally organized active strategies that toddlers use to that end. In line with the methodological imperative that requires the analysis of individual cases longitudinally as the only fully adequate research design for developmental research (see Valsiner, 1986), the authors present elaborate behavioral data on individual cases.

Finally, Dutch psychologists René van der Veer and Marinus H. Van IJzendoorn (Chapter 6) attempt to integrate some aspects of Vygotskian theorizing with the traditions of attachment research that are quite widespread in contemporary child psychology. Attachment research has largely been occupied by empirical efforts to distinguish different attachment "types," as well as aimed at finding out the potential long-term correlates of the attachment types. Rarely has attachment been viewed in process terms. Van der Veer and Van IJzendoorn treat attachment types of toddlers as index variables which signify different structures of child–adult interaction. Thus, for toddlers belonging to A, B, or C types of attachment, expected organization with their social environments may differ in consistently organized ways. For instance, the quality of attachment may provide its flavor to the children's acting within their zones of proximal development, thus feeding into the cognitive development of the children. If that is the case, reflection of these ways could be expected to be found in adult–child joint action later in childhood. The authors report findings from a longitudinal study, where the context of children's attachment qualities at the end of their second year of life is shown to make a difference at the age of 5 years, when the process of mother–child interaction while solving puzzles was studied.

REFERENCES

Bever, T.G. (Ed.). (1982). *Regressions in mental development: Basic phenomena and theories.* Hillsdale, NJ: Erlbaum.
Bronfenbrenner, U. (1979). *The ecology of human development.* Cambridge, MA: Harvard University Press.
Ivić, I. (1978). *Čovek kao animal symbolicum: razvoj simboličkih sposobnosti.* Belgrade: Nolit (in Serbo-croatian).

Ivić, I., & Marjanović, A. (Eds.). (1986). *Traditional games and children of today.* Belgrade: UNESCO & Institute of Psychology.

Valsiner, J. (Ed.). (1986). *The individual subject and scientific psychology.* New York: Plenum.

Valsiner, J. (1987). *Developmental psychology in the Soviet Union.* Brighton, England: Harvester Press.

Van der Veer, R. (1984). *Cultuur en cognitie.* Groningen, The Netherlands: Wolters-Noordhoff (in Dutch).

Vygotsky, L. (1986). *Thought and language.* 2nd ed. Cambridge, MA: MIT Press.

CHAPTER 4

Social Interaction in Early Childhood and Its Developmental Effects

Nada Ignjatović-Savić, Tünde Kovač-Cerović, Dijana Plut, and Ana Pešikan

University of Belgrade
Yugoslavia

It is only through communication, through the mutual acting of man upon man, that the "man within a man" unfolds for oneself as well as for others. To be-that means to communicate in a dialogue. (M. Bakhtin, 1967, p.p. 333–334)

It is difficult not to be an interactionist today. It is one of the most common names in psychological circles. However, it says no more about its owner than do names like Smith or Dupont. It is actually a common name for a collection of various theoretical and methodological approaches. It is necessary that both these elements be specified in order that the interaction between interactionists be developmentally prospective. There are interactionists who incline toward individualistic conceptions about human nature and its development. These deal with the social as if it were something outside the individual, estranged from him or her and forced on him or her as an external pressing force, or as a condition or motivator of development. The individualistic approach is conspicuous even in Piaget's *interactional* theory of mental development, which represent the theoretical framework most generally applied to the study of child's sensori-motor development.

One should keep in mind that "interaction" in this theory, at least when dealing with the subject matter of early development, has a very specific meaning. Namely, Piaget's fundamental theoretical assertion is that sensori-motor intelligence develops in the course of the child's interaction with physical reality, i.e., that it arises from the child's *individual* practical action in the world of physical objects. Piaget's attitude concerning the role of social factors in this period of development is very explicit and clear.

> During the sensori-motor period the infant is, of course, already subject to manifold social influences; people afford him the greatest pleasures known to his limited experience—from food to the warmth of the affection which surrounds him—people gather around him, smile at him, amuse him, calm him; they inculcate habits and regular courses of conduct linked to signals and words; some behavior is already forbidden and he is scolded. . . . *But from the point of view of the subject himself, the social environment is still not essentially distinct from the physical environment* [italics added] at least up to the fifth of the stages of sensori-motor intelligence that we have distinguished (chap. IV). . . . *The infant reacts to them [i.e., persons] in the same way as to objects* [italics added] namely with gestures that happen to cause them to continue interesting actions, and with various cries, but there is still as yet no interchange of thought; since at this level the child does not know thought; *nor, consequently, is there any profound modification of intellectual structures by the social life surrounding him* [italics added]. (Piaget, 1959, p. 158)

We have resorted to this extensive quotation from Piaget because we believe that it comprises all the important controversial points inherent to the individualistic conception of early development. We shall summarize them:

1. The baby is an asocial being yet to be socialized. The adult merely appears as the means of satisfaction of the basic biological needs, and as an instrument of social pressure (they inculcate habits, give orders, scold, and forbid certain kinds of behavior).
2. The preverbal child makes no intellectual distinction between the social and the physical environment.
3. There is no cognitive exchange between the adult and the child during the sensori-motor period.
4. Social factors have no constructive role in early mental development. Sensori-motor intelligence has its origin only in the child's individual action on physical reality.

Although Piaget undoubtedly deserves credit for stressing the active role of the subject as a factor in his own development, it seems to us that he has unjustifiably underestimated the role of social interaction in early development. Actually, the Piagetian framework does not include the development of social interaction in early childhood even as a research problem. The problem simply does not fit into the theory's assimilation schemes.

The essence of our interactionistic standpoint is that it does not view social interaction in early childhood as just another aspect of development worthy of investigation, but attributes to it a definite and significant role in the child's entire psychological development. We view social interaction as a formative factor in the development of a number of psychological functions, specifically those which are uniquely human.

These ideas originate in L.S. Vygotsky's cultural-historical theory of psychological development, an approach which in many important points radically differs from Piaget's view.

As this theory forms the basic conceptual framework of our research, we shall briefly summarize its fundamental assertions, commenting at greater length on the points relevant to the subject matter of our concern.

The Basic Theses of Vygotsky's Theory of Development

1. The infant is a social being. His or her first actions are directed at adults and realized through them.

> The infant's dependence on adults determines the fundamental peculiarities of the child's relationship to reality (and to himself): *these relationships are always mediated through other people* [italics added], always being refracted through the prism of the relationship with another person. . . . The relationship of the child to reality is thus a social relationship from the very beginning. In that sense, we could label the young infant a maximally social being. (Vygotsky, 1984, p. 281)

The most recent empirical results, obtained in ethological and psychological studies of early social responsiveness, social perception, attachement, and preverbal communication, bear witness to the fact that the baby displays at a very early age a particular sensitivity, preference, and ability to respond selectively to stimuli coming from people, i.e., to social stimuli (Trevarthen, Hubley, & Sheeran, 1975; Schaffer, 1971; Ainsworth, Blehar, Waters, & Wall,, 1978; Thoman, 1979; Gouin Decarie & Richard, 1982). Therefore, it seems justifiable to speak of the primary *sociality,* and not the *associality,* of the child.

2. The "cultural-biological paradox of mental ontogenesis" (Vygotsky, 1960) follows from this. There is no temporally and developmentally separate development of the natural, biological, and cultural functions, but the child rather starts on the course of cultural develop-

ment before the natural one has been completed. In other words the child is from the very beginning of his or her life incorporated in the world of cultural objects and interacts with adults who are the bearers of cultural meaning.

3. This further implies that all functions of individual adaptation are socially mediated. The social mediation is twofold:

(a) The child always encounters an *adult-made environment*. Such an environment bears the brand of the surrounding culture: beginning with the choice of the physical objects surrounding the baby, the manner of handling of the baby, etc., to the system of knowledge, beliefs, customs, values, social institutions, etc. which are characteristic for the given culture.

(b) The other form of social mediation is theoretically much more significant, in that it clearly shows the constructive role of social factors in the formation of individual psychological functions:

> it is only *through others* [italics added] that we become what we are, and that rule applies not only to the personality as a whole, but also to the history of each individual function. (Vygotsky, 1960, p. 196).

This thesis deserves special attention because it implies a change in the conceptual and methodological inventory of psychology. Namely, in the history of psychology the complex dialectics of the relationship between the individual and his or her social environment have been viewed either through the prism of separating and confronting these two entities or by reducing the individual to the social (as in classical behaviorism and in sociologistic interpretations of human nature in general). In both of these cases the unit of psychological analysis is the individual, i.e., individual activity. Such a state of events is very well illustrated by the following comment, expressed by Bruner, Olver, and Greenfield (1967):

> We are, alas, wedded to the idea that human reality exists within the limiting boundary of the human skin! (p. 321)

Vygotsky's reply to the aforementioned comment from Bruner et al. would be, therefore, that there exists something which transcends *the boundary of the human skin* and precedes individual mental operations, both temporally and developmentally.

> Every function in the child's cultural development appears twice: first on the social level, and later on the individual level, first between people

(interpsychological) and then inside the child (intrapsychological). (Vygotsky, 1960, p. 48)

In other words, the germ of the child's higher mental functions appear *somewhere between* the adult and child; the individual psychological process is at first *divided between* two individuals, representing a form of mutual acting (inter-action) between child and adult, to become later an intrapsychological category, i.e., an individual characteristic of the child. The connections are not only temporal but also causal. Without this specific form of interaction, there can be no development of the cultural functions which are distinctive characteristics of the human species.

4.   It is also important to stress that, according to Vygotsky, the *relationship* between partners in this developmentally significant interaction has to be *asymmetrical*. Not every form of cooperation is, therefore, a constructive factor in intellectual development, but only the cooperation between a child and a person who possesses more knowledge than the child *about the reality* they are acting upon together, as well as knowledge *about what the child can do.*

5.   The theoretical concept which specifies the mechanism of the influence of interaction with the adult on the child's mental development is the concept of the *zone of proximal development.* Not all participation of the adult in interaction with the child has equal developmental value. A decisive role in development is played precisely by cooperation within the zone of proximal development, i.e., within the developmental area of those functions presently "in an embrionic state."

This joint activity possesses certain specific characteristics. There is role division: one part of the action is performed by the adult, the other by the child, or there appears an alternating succession of the one's and the other's activity—the partners mutually complete and coordinate each other's actions, but what is important is that the organization of the activity in its entirety cannot be attributed to either of the participants alone, but is located somewhere "in between," in the activity of the dyad as a psychological unit.

To clarify this we shall refer to Ivić's elaboration of the influence of interaction on the development of the symbolic function (see also Ivić, 1986a, 1986b):

For, in the asymmetrical dyad that the child-adult dyad is, the child, in beginning, has only the means for affective communication and, while this system of affective communication is just in the process of formation, the adult participant in the dyad attributes meaning to the child's practical actions and brings semiotic means into communication.

In such a dyadic relationship, certain practical actions performed in the course of common activities acquire a signalling, communicative meaning, because the adult interprets a child's practical action as a signal, a message. Here, actually, we have the basic mechanism of the creation of semantic symbols: *the mechanism of social feedback* [italics added]. It consists in that the effects which certain behavior provokes in another person and the reaction of the other person change in turn it's course, function and structure. Social feedback differs from ordinary feedback, among other things, in that the reflected information comes from another person who appears as some sort of outer Self, as the *alter ego* [italics added]. This *alter ego* [italics added] does not provide a simple echo but is an active reaction, and where a child is concerned, the alter ego consisting in the adult constantly interprets performed behavior in the light of his own understanding of this behavior, which is at a higher level than the child's understanding . . . A real psychological unit would not consists in the child's individual system of behavior, for the system has its extensions in the adult. (Ivić, 1978, pp. 179–180)

The adult appears here as a real external amplifier, a constituent of the child's mind. But, this does not mean that the developing person is a mere object of social-cultural influence which shapes his or her mind. Although there are tendencies toward that kind of interpretation, Vygotsky had an entirely opposite vision of the factors of development. For him, as for Piaget, the child is an active (but also an inter-active) agent in his or her own development.

In the first place, the initiative for communication comes from the child as much as from adult:

For a very young child (aged 1–3), the social and the physical (practical) components of a situation are sufficiently differentiated. Therefore, the child comes to exhibit an interesting pattern of behavior: When he fails or when it is impossible to attain his objective, the practical situation is transformed into a social one. (Vygotsky, 1984, p. 307)

In other words, the child asks for cooperation himself or herself, drawing the adult into communication. The child is an active participant in the interaction, not only because he or she initiates the contact, but also because he or she determines the content and dynamics of the interaction.

Besides, the child further elaborates the above mentioned "in-betweens" which occured in his or her interaction with the adult, mainly in free play.

Play is the source of development and creates the zone of proximal development. The child *moves forward* [italics added] essentially through play activity. (Vygotsky, 1976, p. 552)

This Vygotsky's assertion must be interpreted, it seems to us, in the following manner: In play activity the child himself or herself takes on *both roles*—that of the other toward himself or herself, and, vice versa, gradually thus gaining control over that which he or she previously could only perform with the help of the adult. But the play situation gives the child a great degree of freedom—he or she spontaneously recollects something that has actually happened in interaction with the adult, this not being a mere reproduction but a free reconstruction of it according to the child's current strivings. Play is, therefore, a transitional stage in the interiorization of the social relationship (just as egocentric speech is a phase of transition between social and internal speech). Through play the previous joint activity is brought under control of the subject and then internalized, thus becoming a real psychological process.

Therefore, although the interaction with the adult is the ultimate *cause, or source* of development, the product of internalization (i.e., individual mental functioning) is not a direct copy of social exchange but a child's *active* assimilation of its components.

Empirical Elaborations of Vygotsky's Ideas

Some of Vygotsky's ideas presented here have been accepted and empirically elaborated by Russian, European, and American psychologists, so we will briefly comment on their work.

Researchers of the Genevan school of genetic social psychology (W. Doise, G. Mugny, A.N. Perret-Clarmont) have undertaken a critical analysis of Piaget's findings and conception of cognitive development, i.e., his epistemological individualism, from a standpoint which could be conceived of as Vygotskian. Starting from the thesis that cognitive coordination between individuals is based on individual cognitive coordination, they performed a series of empirical investigations into the effects of social interaction (between children or between adult and child) on cognitive development in children. By using variations of classical Piagetian tests, they demonstrated that operational capacities that were absent in the individual during the pretest could be elicited, or even fully mastered, during the posttests following situations of social interaction where the partners had to take into account each other's view point (Perret-Clermont, 1980; Perret-Clermont & Brossard, 1985; Doise & Mugny, 1981). According to them, "socio-cognitive conflict" is the basic mechanism in the construction of individual cognitive structures, i.e., in the genesis of developmental changes in the individual.

The non-conserving subject is led to re-structure his thinking as a result of the emergence of a conflict between his point of view and his partner's differing one, when the situation calls for common agreement or joint action (p. 313).

But, although their basic thesis is that social interaction is a constructive factor in intellectual development, these authors also assert

that the child must have reached a minimum operational level if the sociocognitive conflict is to have any effect on his or her cognitive development. Some cognitive prerequisites are thus essential for the child to benefit from the situations of social interaction! (Perret-Clermont & Brossard, 1985, p. 313)

The problem of the formation of these cognitive prerequisites remains open (or is Piagetian-type of auto-regulation implicated here?). In other words, they don't give an answer to what kind of interaction is responsible for the appearance of *new* cognitive structures, which *could* not have developed *without it,* but to what kind of interaction *speeds up* the transition from one level of cognitive development to the next. By focusing on concrete operational thinking, as well as the sociocognitive conflict and the coordination of the viewpoints of partners, they neglect the developmentally more important type of interaction (especially in early phases of development), namely, that of *joint activity* of the adult and child in which the adults action appears as a completion (complement) to the child's yet undeveloped mental action.

Although these authors do not elaborate the concept of the zone of proximal development, it is implicitly present in their research. Namely, those experimental situations which contained a certain cognitive distance or difference between the cognitive viewpoints of the children in interaction have been found developmentally productive. So it is again the adult (the experimenter here) who appears as the significant (and ignored) variable, as he or she is the one who previously assesses the developmental level of future partners in interaction and arranges the situation in such a manner that a preoperational child is faced with a child who is somewhat more mature, and the interaction is thus in the zone of proximal development of the less developed child. In sum, the authors of the Genevan school give a significant contribution to the understanding of the nature of cognitive development, but their experimental paradigm does not offer the possibility for deductions about the formative role of interaction, only about interaction as a motivator and a stimulating factor in development.

The emphasis on the constructive role of social-cultural factors in a child's development is a key point which is common to all Russian followers of Vygotsky.

Gal'perin (1966), Talyzina (1981), El'konin and Davydov (1962) and their collaborators developed various variations of the thesis about the interiorization of the interpsychological relationship as the fundamental process in development, but the way in which this theoretical concept is operationalized in their research differs significantly from ours. It is generally conceived as the child's acquisition of behavioral forms structured by the social environment, the result being that the child later on independently performs the learned actions on a mental plan (e.g., "the theory of a stage by stage development" of mental actions, as in Gal'perin and Talyzina). It is obvious that the subject's role in this process is passive, that he or she has no initiative in choosing either the content and the manner of the knowledge acquisition, or the persons who mediate this knowledge. Such a notion of man and the developing child is closer to behavioristic than to Vygotsky's conception.

A standpoint very close to ours in the basic theoretical postulates is that of Lisina and her group, which has been working together since the 1960s (Lisina, 1974a, 1974b, 1974c, 1978, 1980; Ruzskaia, 1974; Ruzskaia & Reinstein, 1985; Boguslavskaia, 1974). Lisina's main research problems are concerned with the nature and developmental forms of interaction (obshchenie) in ontogenesis: which needs and motives initiate interaction, what the developmental assignments of interaction are, what the means and operations are which help to actualize interaction. However, although Lisina treats interaction with an adult as a constructive factor in development, the subject matter of her research is interaction itself, and not its developmental effects. She also stresses the importance of the asymmetrical quality of interaction with an adult, but we give particular attention to the operationalization of this idea, especially the concept of the zone of proximal development, i.e., the developmental directedness of interaction. However, the main difference between Lisina and our study of interaction is in the methodology of data collection and analysis. Lisina studies interaction within the framework of an experimental design and records behavior of adults and children separately. Our unit of analysis is the dyad's activity, a record of the behavior of both partners simultaneously, while the interaction takes place both in structured and unstructured situations.

One of the main interpreters of Vygotsky in the USA, Wertsch, also deals with the theoretical and empirical elaboration of the concept of the zone of proximal development and the postulates about interiorization of psychological functions. In our opinion, Wertsch's research procedure is also not suitable for the study of the constructive role of interaction, i.e., the transformation of inter- into intrapsychological functioning.

Using simple tasks which require, for example, a "copy object" to be constructed in accordance with a "model object" from various "pieces," Wertsch observes the child's effort to master the task with the help of the mother. He found that the proportion of the other-regulated steps in problem solving decreases with age and concluded that the older child has mastered this activity on the intrapsychological plane. A considerable shortcoming of this design is that there is no pretest and posttest measure of the child's competence; i.e., there is no indicator of how the child solves the problem alone, without help from the mother, which would be necessary in order to be able to conclude that it is the observed shared activity with the mother that enables the child to solve the problem independently. However, even if we were to disregard this omission, it remains to be noted that Wertsch actually deals with the microgenesis of the process of learning the performance of one given activity and not the genesis of the novum in the child's intellectual functioning as a result of social interaction (see also Wertsch, McNamee, McLane and Budwig, 1980). Wertsch's approach is very similar to that of the Russian authors who speak of the formation of mental operations in stages, as can be seen especially in his explanation of the mechanism of interiorization:

> there are several possible mechanisms involved in the transition from social to individual functioning, but one seems particularly important in the kind of setting under consideration here. This is the procedure *of carrying out a task first and later coming to understand it.* [italics added] (Wertsch & Sammarco, 1985, p. 289)

Actually, he gives no proof that the child has mastered the strategy of solving problems of this type. In Piaget's terminology, there is no proof that there is true developmental progress here and not accommodative change induced by a certain kind of social stimulation. Moreover, the very procedure of giving the *same* task to children of various ages bears witness that there is no consideration of the child's zone of proximal development.

The idea of the zone of proximal development is actually most often used as an alternative model to classical intelligence testing in children (Brown & French, 1979; Guthke & Lehwald, 1984) or as a diagnostic instrument in testing mentally retarded children (Campione, Brown, &

Ferrara, 1982). This undoubtedly signifies considerable progress in the field of mental testing. The interpretation of the scope of the zone of proximal development as a measure of the learning potential offers an elegant solution to certain problems of mental testing, but, in our opinion, it does not encompass the complete meaning of the concept of zone of proximal development. It impoverishes this concept in its most valuable aspect—its power to explain *the dynamics* of the influence of social interaction on individual development. Actually, the situations used by these researches in the testing procedure are irrelevant from the standpoint of the development of psychological functions (they often use classical intelligence test items), and social interaction is reduced to giving strictly prescribed helping instructions.

As far as we can judge, zone of proximal development may have a dual meaning. On the one side, it comprises those activities which the child can perform only with someone's help and not alone. In that sense, the zone of proximal development is operationalized within the assisted test/individual test framework and means a characteristic of the individual (the child) which is similar to readiness or learning potential. It remains, therefore, a concept of individualistic psychology. In this framework, the objective assessment of the zone of proximal development of each individual child encounters serious difficulties (it has a paradoxical status, as described by Valsiner, 1985); it is deduced post hoc (if the child has mastered some new activity with someone's help, it is asserted that this activity was in the child's zone of proximal development). Does that mean that, if a child masters *any* set of activities in cooperation with somebody, we are to conclude that these activities were in the child's zone of proximal development? What, then, is the developmental meaning of the zone of proximal development, and what is its role in developmental theory in general? In this sort of usage, isn't the concept stripped of its explanatory role in the understanding of the constructive influence of the social environment in individual development?

We tend to view the zone of proximal development as a *mechanism* which explains or at least describes the way in which the social environment is included as a constructive factor in the child's development, and to operationalize it differently, placing it in the very tissue (or network) of social interaction. As the activities within the child's zone of proximal development we take a special kind of shared activities of the child and an adult where their roles are complementary. The adult behaves as the child's extension (although he or she is not necessarily aware of it), fitting into the child's autonomously motivated activities, completing and finishing them, and providing him or her with higher-level comprehension of them. It is often the child who initiates and includes the adult into his or her current activity. Such shared activities may be called *joint activities in a true sense,* since the behavior of the child and the adult in them cannot be separated even microanalytically. Their developmental future is to be transformed into the child's intrapsychological activity. This operationalization, of course, as the aforementioned ones, includes the growing out of the current level of achievement with the adults' help.

In sum, it is not just a question of the proper time when a new form of behavior is to be promoted, but the proper way this has to be done. This notion is in accordance with the mainstream of our speculations about the constructive impact of social interaction.

The Laboratory of Comparative Human Cognition sums up the contributions of the studies inspired by Vygotsky's theory, especially the concept of the zone of proximal development, as providing:

1. a theory of the structure of the task, which yields information about the proper distance between teacher and students
2. a theory of the role of the adult
3. a description of the system of interactions between adult and child during which the child comes to take responsibility for doing more and more of the task (Laboratory of Comparative Human Cognition, 1982, p. 702).

Judging by all we have said, it seems that the third type of contribution is the sparest, not having gone much further than a mere descriptive statement that the adult's contribution in shared, interactive problem solving progressively decreases while the child's increases. We suppose that the difficulties inherent in interactional analysis constitute the main reason for this shortage (see Hinde and Herrman 1977, Schaffer 1977, Shugar 1980).

A BRIEF OVER-ALL PRESENTATION OF OUR PROJECT

The main goal of our project, in the most general terms, is to explore the developmental effects of adult–child interaction, i.e., to collect the empirical evidence which would in the long run enable us to verify some implications of the hypothesis about the constructive role of social interaction in the child's development. We believe that, to this end, it is strategically most justified to begin with the study of early stages of development, and that was decisive in our choice of the age of our subjects (6–21 months).

In the first phase of our research, we try to determine the connections between certain characteristics of social interaction and various aspects of the child's development in the sensori-motor period (cognitive, social, affective, symbolic, and language development). The obtained results were to serve later on as the basis for the prediction of some parameters of the child's further development.

Beside these general goals, the project has a number specific ones, depending on the individual interests of the project collaborators, which we shall not describe at this point.

The Subjects and Some Characteristics of Their Cultural Environment[1]

Our *subjects* are 50 children aged 6 to 18 months. The sample is constituted by children from normal, integral families, who do not attend a public nursery. There are an equal number of boys and girls, and of mothers with elementary, secondary, and higher education.

The entire sample is from Belgrade, Yugoslavia's capital city, with a population of about 1.5 million. In Yugoslavia (and in Belgrade as well) different ethnic groups, talking different languages, live together. All families participating in our project were from the Serbian ethnic group. We considered it important for all the children in the sample to come from the same language environment, since one of the aims of our project is the investigation of language development and of the impact of adult–child interaction on it.

We shall give some information about the way of life in Belgrade families. Most families live in two to three-room apartments, occasionally even in one-room ones. There is rarely a nursery room; children sleep in a room with their parents and spend the day in the living room. Families with one or two children are the most common (the number of children in the family wasn't a criterion for inclusion in the sample), and only rarely are there three or more children. However, because of the general deficit in living quarters, nuclear families often do not live alone but with either pair of parents of the couple. The older generation then participates in all family activities, including the raising of children. Besides, living is rather open and sociable, the exchange of informal visits is very frequent, communication is partic-

---

[1] The part of the research project we are presenting here was initiated at the Institute for Psychology in Belgrade in 1982, under the guidance of Ivan Ivić and Nada Ignjatović-Savić, and is entitled "Interaction Between Children and Adults, Its Development and Developmental Effects." It is an extensive and intense follow-up study of children from ages of 6 mos. to 7 yrs. The first phase of data collection was completed in 1985, and the study we are presenting here represents only the beginning of the exploitation of the data gathered.

ularly intense in the neighborhood and with relatives, and children usually actively participate in all this. This hospitality could primarily be thanked for the fact that our team was almost always received in a friendly and cordial manner, although the participation of the families in the project was entirely voluntary and was not reimbursed in any way. The reason for dropping out of the sample was only very rarely refusal to cooperate on the family's part, but was much more commonly the child's illness at the time of the planned investigation. The bringing up of children in our families is considered to be primarily a woman's duty, and most fathers participate in it only sporadically, taking over only activities which they find pleasurable, such as walking or bathing the child. Even that much is not done by all fathers, and not always. Women in Yugoslavia are mostly employed. Real housewives are almost exclusively women who have no vocational qualifications. Other unemployed women are those who have just finished school. It is also not rare for a woman to marry before completing her education, in order to continue studies at a slower pace after having children. (All these categories of mothers can be found in our sample). Working mothers get a paid maternity leave until their child is 1 year old; after that, child care is usually taken over by the grandmother if she lives in the same household or at least the same city, or by public children's institutions (for 40% of the children). Very few families, usually well-to-do ones, engage a paid person to take care of their child while they are away.

METHODS

In order to accomplish our research goals we first had to collect as representative data as possible about adult–child interaction and about the child's development. As we wanted to get, as far as possible, a faithful picture of the baby's family life, we decided upon a naturalistic study.[2]

The relevant behaviors of the children and their mothers were observed and videotaped in natural settings, i.e. at their homes. Our choice of the mother as constant partner to the child was imposed by the fact that she is the one who is predominantly occupied with the child of this age, at least in the urban environment of our present-day

---

[2] A combination of the cross-sectional and longitudinal procedures was employed in the research. A cross-sectional investigation was done on samples of 10 children at each of the following age levels: 6, 9, 12, 15, and 18 months (a total of 50 children), and the same children underwent the same procedure 3 months later.

culture. But if there were any exceptions regarding this usual family situation, we also made additional observations of the child's interaction with some other member of his family (father, grandfather, grandmother, etc.).

Two observers and a cameraman arrived at the home at a time prearranged with the mother to maximize the likelihood that the child would be awake and in a good mood. These were three visits to each family made on 3 successive days, each lasting for about 3 hours. The whole procedure was repeated 3 months later (magic number 3!).

The unavoidable problem in every psychological investigation is how to control the influence of context on the subject's behavior. This is not simply a question of laboratory vs. naturalistic study, because in both alternatives we encounter similar problems. Namely, the kind of situation in which observation takes place, the subject's interpretation of the nature of the investigation, etc., all affect the obtained results. In order to control for such factors and secure a broader and better basis for prediction, we designed a wide scope of situations for observation and checked with the mother the representativeness of the behaviors recorded in each of the situations (after the observation was completed).

Without going into details concerning the organization of this large project, we shall rest here on a description of the categories of situations that we used as a source of data (with indications of their content).

In the first, unstructured or free activity, situation, we wanted to see what the mother and the child usually do at that time; i.e., we asked them to behave as if we were not present. Therefore, the choice of the content of the interaction, and even the very existence of the interaction, was left to them (for example, the mother could just sit and read newspapers, and/or the baby could play alone).

For the second, more structured kind of situations, we specified the content or the context of interaction. Those were:

1. A feeding situation.
2. A situation of mother–child shared activity related to physical objects: we only introduced a new polyfunctional toy and told the mother to present it to her child in whatever way she liked.
3. A situation of mother–child shared activity related to a new, strange person (the same instructions as in the previous situation).
4. A situation of mother–child shared activity related to a picture book (similar instructions).
5. A situation in which the mother helps the child to solve a sensori-motor problem in his or her zone of proximal development.
6. Situations in which the mother teaches the child to perform a

simple sequence of actions (which was determined by the experimenters).

7. All the interactional situations taken from a somewhat modified Ainsworth's procedure for studying attachment.

In our opinion, both kinds of interactional situations are necessary if we are to make deductions about the relationship between interaction and the child's development. For example, we may get a certain picture of the mother–child shared activity with objects, i.e., what they do with a toy when forced into this kind of activity (the second kind of situation), but we also need to know how often and in what way do such opportunities arise in their everyday life (first kind of situation).

The third type of situation consists of individual assessment of the child. In order to get a full picture of the child's development, we performed a number of experimental investigations of its various aspects: social cognition, mirror self-recognition, learning and memory capacities, attachment. We also applied three standard procedures for determining:

1. the level of symbolic and speech behavior in the child, using Ivić's Scale of Symbolic and Language Development;
2. the level of Piagetian-type cognitive development, using the Casati-Lezine Scales of Sensorimotor Intelligence (Casati & Lezine, 1968);
3. the level of psychomotor development, using the Bayley Scales of Infant Development (Bayley, 1969).

The fourth situation is an extensive semistandardized interview with the mother, which is supposed to lend information about the general conditions for the child's development (the family situation, the milieu and subculture in which the child is growing up, the parent's values, what they expect of the child, what they perceive in the child's development, their attitudes on child-rearing and education, the concrete actions in child care and rearing, etc.).

Procedure of Data Collection in the Free-Activity Situation

The observation took place in the child's home, in the room most often occupied by the child and his or her partner in interaction.[3] The observational period lasted 20 minutes and did not commence until

---

[3] The choice of the room in which the video-recording took place depended on where the mother stated that she and her child usually spend their day. It was most often the dining room, with one corner adapted for the child (with toys, playpen, etc.).

the pair was adapted to the presence of the video-operator and the observers, which was usually about 30 minutes after entering the home. This situation of unstructured interaction always preceded other situations observed, in order to keep it unaffected by other structured and problem-focused situations. The time of the observation was chosen by the mother as the natural time of day for the interaction between her and her child. The mothers were told that we were interested in the observation of children in their natural family settings, and they received the minimal instruction to do what they otherwise did and not to pay attention to us. The following demands minimally restricted the mother–infant interaction: they had to spend their time in one room[4] (which could effect an increase in the unresponsiveness of the mother to the child's wish to go out), and the child's attempts to address the observers had to be discouraged (the periods of interaction colored by the child's attention to the observers and his or her reaction to the video equipment are identified as an artifact and excluded in the analysis of data).

The representativeness of the data gathered in this situation was controlled in two ways:

• by the comparison of data obtained through the analysis of interaction with the relevant data obtained from an interview conducted with the mother a few days before the videotaping session;
• by recording mother's own estimate of how representative "what we just saw" was of what the mother and child do when they are together.

If there was any doubt on the basis of these sources that the situation of spontaneous interaction was not representative enough, the subjects were omitted from further analysis.

Methodological Issues in the Analysis of Interaction

Anyone who is preparing to embark on an empirical investigation of social interaction, i.e., the complex mutual influences and interchanges between partners, encounters in the very beginning several problems. There is a continuous stream of mutually dependent behavior going on, and it should be decided how to select units for observing and recording out of that piece of life.

The first problem is, therefore, that of segmentation. It means, first

---

[4] We had to close the door so that the child wouldn't leave the observer's and the video operator's field of vision.

of all, the choice of *what* is to be picked up by the procedures for data collecting. As there is yet no theory about the development of social interaction (see Yarrow & Anderson, 1979), or a taxonomy of interactive behavior in early childhood, the choice of categories is a matter of the researcher's intuition as well as the specific objectives of their studies. Generally, those who are only trying to describe certain characteristics of adult–child interaction—i.e., who are interested in the development of interaction per se—decide on molecular units and record simple behaviors that can be directly observed (eye contact, tactile contact, vocalization, etc.).

If the objective is to predict certain aspects of the child's development on the basis of interaction, molar units are to be chosen, derived from those characteristics of interaction which are considered to be relevant. However, the theoretically deduced thesis that certain characteristics of interaction will give certain effects is rarely the point of departure in these cases, but a greater number of interactional variables serves to derive, later, the most sensitive predictors by using statistical procedures (cf. Clarke-Stewart, 1973).

Another problem related to segmentation is how to find the units of analysis which "possess all the basic traits which are characteristic for the whole" (Vygotsky, 1977), i.e., such systemic units or "minimal Gestalts" that preserve the systemic features of the whole. In other words, interactionist research has uncovered the need for new, thus-far unknown variables in psychological analyses—the "dyadic variables"—and a new unit of analysis—the "shared action of the dyad." In order to truly analyze interaction, the unit must contain information about the behavior of both the partners; i.e., one must record what the dyad as a *whole* does at a certain moment. The difficulty of this task is witnessed by the fact that a good many of those who study interaction still employ individualistic inventories of infant variables and maternal variables. The habitual methodological practice is to record what one partner does *separately* from what the other does, and, later, to look for the relationship between these two independent sets of data. The characteristics of interaction thus deduced are a reconstruction from a broken-down whole. In that manner we have a significant loss of essential information about the whole. For example, if we treat the components of the joint activity as separate events, i.e., as "child's unsuccessful attempt at reaching" and "mother's giving the desired object to the child," and then sum them with other reactions of giving and reaching, we are missing the most important point, namely, that the giving completes the child's reaching in such a way that it accords to the latter the meaning of a communicational gesture. This remark applies to the particularization of any shared activity and not only to joint activities in a narrow sense (i.e., activities in the zone of proximal development).

One way to "grasp" the dynamics of the mutual action is to record each time "when the child does this and mother that in response" as one unit. However, this approach, which has rarely been used, anyway also has its limitations. First of all, it succeeds in including only one side of the interchange and not the mutual relationship (only child —→ mother, instead of child ⇌ mother). Besides, we cannot but agree with the following critique:

> Although categories of contingency and cooccuring-parent and infant behavior have been significant improvement over monadic categories, they are still limited to describing *isolated elements* [italics added] of the total parent infant exchange . . . More detailed information about the process of reciprocal interaction between parent and infant has been obtained when the systems for continuous recording of behavior have been used. (Yarrow & Anderson, 1979, p. 215).

Continuous recording opens another problem—the analyses of the sequential flow of units of behavior. So, beside the general problem of how to determine the beginning and the end of a unit of common activity and to differentiate this from parallel but overlapping behavior of partners, there is another problem: to find a system for the analysis of such a sequential flow of behavior in which those segments of behavior coming later give meaning to previous ones. Attempts to solve this problem are still mere "groping in the dark."

The next problem connected to all developmental studies is that the same adult–child behavior does not have the same meaning at two age levels, and, vice versa, that different behaviors at different age levels may have the same meaning. How do we simultaneously grasp developmental changes and the stability (if there is any) in the interaction of a given mother–child pair?

We shall now present how we tried to cope with these problems.

Our System of Interaction Analysis

The theoretical postulates which form the foundation of our entire project dictated an elaboration of a specific methodology of analysis of interactional data. In the first place, our theoretical credo has led us to search for a such way of coding the interaction in unstructured situations which would satisfy the following demands:

1. The *total* behavior of the two partners has to be recorded. That is

necessary because this situation serves as a source of information about what the mother and child usually do when they are together. Namely, it is supposed to offer a representative sample of their everyday life together and to serve for discovering the various patterns of interaction characteristic of each pair. Supplemented by the data obtained in other, more structured situations, it is to provide a basis for the prediction of the child's further development.

2. The basic, minimal unit of analysis must contain information on *the dyad's* shared activity.

3. Units of analysis must be comparable; i.e., they must have the same meaning regardless of the child's age.

4. The unit of analysis must contain information not only about the cooccurrence but also about the dynamics of the relationship between the mother and child behavior.

5. The coding system must allow for data on the process of interaction, i.e., the sequential ties between units.

How did we deal with all these "must's"?

The Units of Analysis of Interaction

The analysis focuses on the recording of the *content of interaction,* i.e., the domain of mother and child activity, as well as on the *character of interaction.* According to content, we distributed the observed activities of mothers and children into 10 behavioral domains which cover virtually all forms of behavior of children at the age levels under observation. These are, primarily, affective, sensori-motor, social, symbolic, motor, and speech behaviors and/or interactions. Because of our special interest in the child's social development, we added to this list some more specific categories of social behavior: social-sensorimotor behavior, social-communicative behavior, and social rituals. Besides, in order to be able to code the entire course of interaction according to this system, we included the domain of physical child care, which represents a notable part of interaction at the ages under study but cannot be listed under the aforementioned categories.

Our assessment of the character of interaction depended, in the first place, on whether the contents of interaction were the subject of activity of both partners or only of one of them. It often happens that, although the partners are, generally speaking, interacting—i.e., they are taking account of each other—not *all* their contents are common to both: the mother sometimes ignores some aspects of the child's activity, and vice versa.

Therefore, we differentiate:

- Shared activities, where both partners are actively participating and engaged with the same contents ("a" units).
- Nonshared activities ("b" units), where only one of the partners deals with certain contents. Within these, we may recognize:

b_1 units: The child is actively occupied with something, while the mother does not participate in this activity although she is in interaction with the child as far as other contents are concerned, e.g., the child is piling blocks; the mother participates in this in no way but asks the child: "How does Grandma cough?" The child replies with an imitation cough without pausing in the activity with building blocks. Therefore, this segment of interaction contains two units: a shared action unit of symbolic content and a nonshared action—b_1 unit—with sensorimotor content.

b_2 units: The mother is active, trying to introduce some content into the interaction, but the child does not join that particular activity, although they are in interaction with respect to other contents. E.g., the mother and child are piling blocks together; the mother is handing him the blocks one by one and asks besides: "How does Grandma cough?" The child gives no reply, only taking the blocks from the mother. This segment of interaction also contains two units: a shared-action unit with sensori-motor content, and a nonshared action (b_2 unit) whose content is symbolic.

However, not all shared activities are of the same nature, either. In accordance with the theoretical postulates of this study, it is important to differentiate them in terms of their *developmental directedness*. We are primarily referring to the distinguishing of activities within the zone of proximal development as developmentally the most important form of organization of the mother's and child's shared activity. However, the child's future development is not only indicated by the zone of proximal development but also by its relationship to other forms of adult–child interaction. For the prediction of the child's further development, it is not only important to determine the duration and contents of shared activity in the zone of proximal development, but also the proportion of this type of interaction in relation to others. There also exist theoretically relevant differences between these other kinds of activities, which are not explicitly described in Vygotsky's theory but may be deduced from it.

In our opinion, it is possible to distinguish conceptually four kinds of shared activities according to their developmental directedness, these being:

1. shared activity in the zone of proximal development—the already mentioned joint activity (a_1);
2. shared activity in the zone of actual development—the child is entering into interaction with his already developed schemes of behavior; the adult responds to that as an active participant of the exchange but does not include anything developmentally new into it. Interaction here is characterized by total symmetry of roles of both partners (a_2);
3. shared activity in the zone of future development—has certain characteristics of interaction in the zone of proximal development, asymmetry in particular, as the adult tends to offer the child a new set of activities; this set of activities, however, is not yet present in the child even in traces, so that the adult's attempt remains with no effect (a_3);
4. shared activity in the zone of past development—the shared activity is directed at those areas and ways of behavior which the child has already overcome in his development (a_4).

Here we have become aware how our vocabulary is individualistically tinted. Terms for the description of the dyad's activity are hard to find. Perhaps an iconic language will help clarify what we mean (although it is not suitable for the presentation of relationship dynamics). Figure 1 shows the conceived structure of the described shared activities.

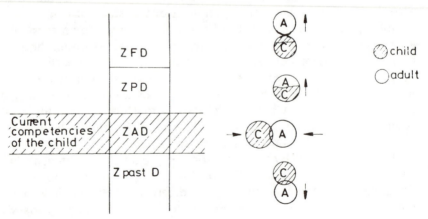

Figure 1. The kinds of shared activities of dyads according to developmental directedness

The basic unit of our analysis is obtained, therefore, by crossing two criteria:

1. What is the content, i.e., domain of activity (of the 10 that were mentioned);
2. What is the character of interaction; i.e., what is its developmental directedness—if we're dealing with a shared activity (there are two kinds of nonshared and four kinds of shared activity).

Thus we get 60 (10 × 6) unit categories for coding interaction!
The list of units of our interaction analysis is given in Figure 2.
Using an example, we shall illustrate the "working" of our coding system and the advantages of these unit categories as compared to contingency categories.

> The child attempts to open a matchbox, does not succeed, and starts showing signs of distress.
>
> Mother A: takes the child up in her arms, cuddles him, and finally calms him.
>
> Mother B: fitting into the child's activity, she succeeds in bringing him about to open the box and thus calms the child.
>
> In Clarke-Stewart's system of analysis, both of these behaviors would be classified in the contingency category under the title "maternal responsiveness." However, although both mothers really are sensitive to the signs of the child's distress and react accordingly, the developmental meaning of these two interactive behaviors is entirely different: Mother A oversees the fact that the child has a sensorimotor cognitive problem and answers only his affective needs with her behavior. In our system of transcription, this would be coded as follows (this is a somewhat simplified record, because a transcript also includes other information which will be mentioned later on):

$$SM_0\ A \longrightarrow \text{ or}$$ – the mother does not participate in the child's sensorimotor activity (b_1)
– there is shared activity in the zone of actual development in the affective domain (a_2)

Mother B answers both the child's cognitive and affective needs. With the mother's help, the child finds the solution to the problem and changes his mood. This is coded as follows:

$$SM \nearrow\ A \longrightarrow \text{ or}$$ a_1–there is shared activity in the zone of proximal development in the sensorimotor domain (a_1)
a_2–there is shared activity in the zone of actual development in the affective domain (a_2)

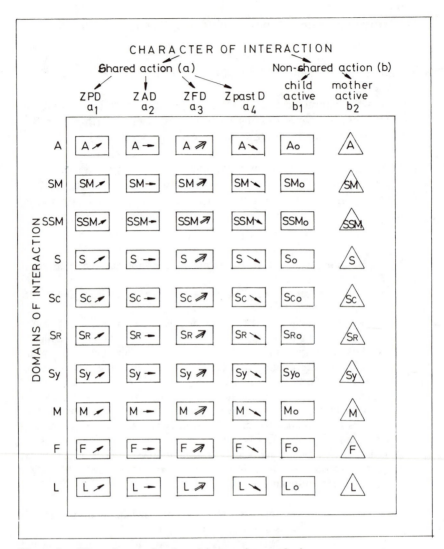

Figure 2.   The scheme of units of interaction analysis

This system of units preserves the original (authentic) configurations of mother and infant behavior, but also allows cross-age comparison. Namely, by classifying behavior into these molar units determined by the content and character of mother-and-child activities, we obtain relevant data which retains the same meaning regardless of age level. Thus we can compare the interactional pattern of a single mother–child pair in various time frames, as well as the patterns of various pairs. This system of units also represents a basis (a starting point) for the more detailed microanalytic coding of the behavioral forms which make up each unit.

Beside the mentioned unit-defining parameters, the transcript also contains the information on whether it is the mother or the child who initiates a given activity; i.e., who is the *initiator* of each single content of interaction. The information about the initiative is therefore recorded at the level of each interactional unit. We believe that the information about which of the partners is "responsible" for the domain of shared activity is important for the discussion of the role of the adult in the child's development and in that of his or her social nature.

The Procedure of Transcription of Data (The Technique of Analysis)

As we also intend to perform the analysis of the process, i.e., the course of interaction, we chose continuous instead of interval or point coding. Our coding procedure consists in recording the original temporal sequence of units and allows the possibility of analyzing the dynamics of their succession, but we still have not found a suitable way of doing this.

The total behavior of mother and child in the situation of free activity is recorded continuously as a sequence of interactional units or units of the child's individual activity:

Although the situation of free activity was relatively brief and both partners were present all the time, not all the pairs spent all the time in interaction. Hence the necessity to include the units of individual activity.

The duration of an individual activity determines a *noninteractive episode.* The duration of at least one interactive unit determines an *interactive episode.* However, an interactive episode may consist of several units taking place simultaneously (if the observed interchange is complex). Therefore, the duration of episodes of interaction may vary, depending on the duration of units constituting them. A change in any of the units making up an episode signifies the transition to a new episode.

A unit of interaction changes when either the *character* or the *content* of the shared activity change. Using an example from our transcript, we shall illustrate how a change in the content, i.e., domain, of the shared activity brings about a change in the unit and hence also the episode.

Subject 407 (age 1;3)

Code signs	Unit description	Behavior description
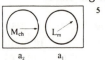	a₂–the child's motor activity encouraged by the mother (zone of actual development) a₁–mother-introduced speech in the zone of proximal development	The child is kicking a ball. Mother returns the ball to the child's foot and verbally encourages his activity at the right time: "Kick it, strongly! Now!"
	a₂–the child's affective need to which the mother responds (zone of actual development) a₁–mother-introduced speech in the zone of proximal development	The child kicks the edge of the bed and begins to cry. Mother takes him up, strokes the hurt place, and affectionately talks: "Leggy hurts, leggy hurts."

The inner structure of an episode may have various degrees of complexity. The more *simple* episodes contain only one or two units, while the *complex* episodes are comprised of three or more units; for example:

A *simple* episode: subject 209 (age 1;0)

Code signs	Unit description	Behavior description
	a₂–the child's sensorimotor activity encouraged by the mother (zone of actual development)	Standing in a play pen, the child throws a rubber bunny outside. Mother picks it up, gives it back

---

[5] ◯ : interactive episode
☐ : interactive unit

A *complex* episode: subject 208 (age 0;9)

Code signs	*Unit description*	*Behavior description*
		to the child, and this activity repeats itself. Both are silent.

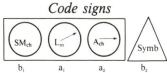

Code signs	*Unit description*	*Behavior description*
	a₁–mother-introduced sensorimotor activity in the zone of proximal development	Mother quickly covers a toy the child has been playing with, with a napkin, and says: "Now you can't find it!" then pulls the napkin so that the child can glimpse the toy. The child removes the napkin, takes the toy, and laughs at mother. She, laughing herself, kisses the child.
	a₃–mother-introduced speech far above the child's understanding (in the zone of future development)	
	a₂–an affective exchange between mother and child (zone of actual development)	

Interactive episodes also differ from each other in their degree of interactivity: they may contain shared activities with various degrees of participation of each of the partners, or different shared-action and non-shared-action units.

In order to clarify this we will cite an example of an episode with non-shared-action units:

Subject 214 (age 1;0)

Code signs	*Unit description*	*Behavior description*
	b₁–child-introduced non-shared sensorimotor action	The child is sitting in his mother's lap and trying to put a larger block into a smaller one simultaneously resting his back against mother,
	a₁–mother-introduced speech in the zone of proximal development	

a_2–affective exchange (zone of actual development)
b_2–mother-introduced nonshared symbolic action

making cuddly motions. Mother strokes his head with one hand and holds a teddy bear in the other, trying to introduce a symbolic activity: "Let's give the little Teddy to eat. Give the Teddy to eat!" The child does not accept this, but only glances at the bear and continues his activity.

We also recorded the affective tone of a dyad's interaction in every interactive episode, which may be a good indicator of the success of their interaction. The affective tone was assessed on a three-point scale as positive, neutral, or negative.

The above-presented system of interaction analysis may seem over-bulky because of the large number of categories and variables, but, in our experience, its application in the transcription of video taped materials is neither complicated nor unreliable. Our recordings were reviewed by two pairs of observers and the agreement between them, calculated for unit-specific categories of interaction on the basis of 25% of the recorded episodes for each dyad was 0.84.

RESULTS AND DISCUSSION

We used for this chapter just a sample from the rich material that we collected. First of all, we restricted ourselves only to a subsample of videotaped dyads. These are six pairs each from two age groups, which were observed as follows:

	1st observation	2nd observation
younger group	at 9 months	at 12 months
older group	at 15 months	at 18 months

As was said earlier, we analyzed only the situation of free interaction.

From the interaction transcripts, we used only data in which the place of certain behavior in the whole time series was not taken into account, because we wished above all to gain insight into how much time was devoted at each pair to each type of unit, each domain, each category of the character of interaction, and the initiative of each one of the partners in the dyads. The data on this were obtained by accumulating the time of duration of the same units of interaction of each pair in the situation of free activity. However, since the situation of spontaneous interaction did not last for exactly the same time in each dyad, each measure of duration was calculated proportionally with the duration of the situation of spontaneous interaction with each particular pair. This calculation is justified by the fact that we view the situation of spontaneous interaction as a representative segment of the usual spontaneous interaction between the mother and child, and assume that the relationships of certain interaction categories registered with the same pair would remain the same if the duration of the spontaneous interaction changed. With the aim of better understanding the phrase "duration of an activity" or "type of interaction" in subsequent text, will always imply, not the actual, but the pondered duration.

In the interaction transcripts, however, simultaneous units (i.e., complex episodes) appear frequently, so that the sum of the duration (in the above sense) of all the units of interaction exceeds 100 in a different measure with different pairs. This has led us to not use the above measure in cases when comparing different categories of interaction with different pairs, but to transform it to the proportion of duration of a certain unit in the sum of duration of all units (minus those where the language and social domain is present. See explanation in Appendix 3). This measure will be referred to as *percentage of interaction* from now on.

We have tried, on the basis of this data, to describe what the mother and child do when they are free to be with one another in unrestricted circumstances: what the content of their interaction is, how they approach and organize it, what the developmental directedness of their actions is, is it the same for every content or is it content-specific, in what ways and how far do they take one another into account, and how harmonious they are as a pair.

We will present the acquired data in the following sections:

The degree of harmony in the pair's interaction
Who initiates the content of interaction
Complexity of interaction: homogenous vs. heterogenous interaction
The contents of interaction

Analysis of interdyad differences of interaction
Patterns of sensorimotor interaction and the child's achievement
on sensori-motor intelligence scale.

THE DEGREE OF HARMONY IN THE PAIR'S INTERACTION

Our system of analysis of interaction provides for different estimates
of the harmony of a pair.

The harmony of a dyad can, first of all, be decided on the basis of
the degree of the partners' involvement in interaction. Our data basis
allows us to judge this in a more elaborated way than just by simply
intersecting the participation–nonparticipation of both partners and thus
gaining four distinct "dyadic states" named by Bakeman and Brown
(1977) as the quiescent state, the infant-alone state, the mother-alone
state and the coacting state.

We can in fact speak about the degree of the partner's harmony,
i.e., whether the pair is interacting at all, and if their interaction includes
shared activity overall, partially or not at all. Combining such relevant
information about the episode—if it is interactive or not and which
units it contains—we derived the following scale of the partner's harmony, according to which we have categorized the episodes during the
free activity situation:

1. Interactive episodes containing shared-action units.
2. Interactive episodes also containing, besides the shared-action units,
   type b_2 nonshared action units (the dyad is involved in the same
   activity, but not all the domains are shared; the mother tries to
   introduce some domains into the interaction; but the child does
   not accept them). Mere individual activity of the mother, activity
   which was not oriented toward the child, we did not record at all.
3. Interactive episodes which comprise the type b_1 units of nonshared
   action; i.e., the child addresses a domain without the mother's
   active participation. The mother merely watches what the child is
   doing, and there is a minimum of interaction.
4. Interaction episodes where both partners are separately dealing with
   some of the domains. Such episodes therefore comprise two nonshared action units, the first being type b_1 and the second type b_2.
   Such an episode can best be described as an episode of parallel
   but interactive activity, because both partners take the other into
   account.
5. Noninteractive episodes; there is not even a minimum of reference

of the partners to one another; we can no longer speak of a dyad, but of two independent forms of behavior (in these cases, only the child's behavior was recorded).

The pairs were compared according to the percentage of episodes in their interaction which were categorized in the described groups.

The percentage of different categories of episodes in the interaction of each pair is given in Table 1.

The following conclusions can be derived from out sample according to the mode of the partner's organization of activity in the observed situation of spontaneous interaction:

1. Interactive episiodes which contain shared action units are the most frequent mode of organization of activity of the observed pairs. This tendency remains outstanding at all age levels, although with 12- and 15-month-olds great individual differences were found with respect to the frequency of this category of episodes.

The least frequent category of episodes in the observed situation of spontaneous interaction is that of the noninteractive episodes, and neither individual nor age-related differences were noticed with respect to their frequency.

Mother and infant spend almost all of their time in the free activity situation interacting with each other at least in the sense that they take into account some of the activities of the other partner.

2. Interactive episodes with parallel activities of the partners are also rarely found, and their appearance changes from pair to pair and tentatively ascends with age.

3. Another distinguishing mode of organizing interaction, though less frequent than the episodes containing shared action units, are the episodes in which one of the partners is engaged in an activity without the active involvement of the other in the same activity. This mode of interacting appears in approximately one third of all registered episodes, but the pairs differ according to the relative number of these episodes in the total behavior of the pairs.

Minor differences according to the relative frequency of the two types of this mode of organizing interaction (episodes with nonshared action units b_1 and b_2, respectively) have been noticed at different age levels of our sample. However, the mutual relationship between the two types of these episodes differs greatly from pair to pair: with some pairs, the mother does not participate in a number of the child's activities, while with others there are more such activities which the mother wishes to introduce into interaction, but the child does not accept them. Those have content that is much more complex than the current capabilities of the child, which the child does not even try to

Table 1. The Extent of Congruence of the Partner's Activity in Percentage of Episodes Categorized on the 5-point Scale of Harmony Presented in the Text (from 9 to 12 Months and from 15 to 18 Months)

age	code of subjects	INTERACTIVE EPISODES				NONINTERACTIVE EPISODES
		only shared action units	besides shared action units (a) also nonshared action units (b) of the following type:			individual activity of the child
		(a)	(b_2)	(b_1)	$(b_1)+(b_2)$	
		1.cat.	2.cat.	3.cat.	4.cat.	5.cat.
9 months	206	68.4	9.2	15.8	6.6	0
	208	64.3	23.5	8.1	3.1	1
	209	63.1	13.2	15.8	7.9	0
	211	54.9	22	17	6.1	0
	212	67.7	8.6	15	8.6	0
	214	60.2	15.7	12.1	4.8	7.2
the whole subsample		63.2	15.5	13.8	6.1	1.4
12 months	206	50.6	10.6	32.9	5.9	0
	208	42.9	45.2	4.8	7.1	0
	209	66.7	7.8	18.6	6.9	0
	211	59.7	26.9	6	7.4	0
	212	52.1	26.8	12.7	7	1.4
	214	75	19.7	4	1.3	0
The whole subsample		59.4	20	14.7	5.9	0
15 months	402	65.4	19.8	3.7	11.1	0
	403	54.2	13.6	22	10.2	0
	405	71.8	19.2	2.6	6.4	0
	407	81.9	12.5	1.4	4.2	0
	409	44.4	18.1	22.2	15.3	0
	411	55.6	32.3	2	10.1	0
the whole subsample		62.3	20.2	8	9.5	0
18 months	402	56.3	5	18.7	17.5	2.5
	403	43.8	38.4	9.6	8.2	0
	405	67.3	12	11.3	9.3	0
	407	64.8	2.8	21.1	9.9	1.4
	409	67	6.8	20.4	4.8	1
	411	65.4	20.2	2.8	10.6	1
the whole subsample		62	13.8	13.4	9.8	1

accept. (This most frequently occurs with mothers of younger children from our sample and generally consists of the complex S_c and S_y activities.). Besides, b_2 units also include activities whose timing or manner of introduction is wrong, so that the child does not accept them for these reasons. (This occurs more often with older age groups, where the contents of the b_2 unit are mostly S_c, SM, and S_y activities of adequate complexity for the child.) It also happens, especially in the older group, that the relationship between the b_1 and b_2 units dramatically changed from one observation to the next (e.g., at pairs 402,407). These changes, just like the individual differences themselves, were interpreted in the framework of the other interactions' characteristics and will be discussed for some of the pairs in the case studies below.

WHO INITIATES THE CONTENT OF INTERACTION

The relationship between the mother and the child in the introduction of the content of interaction can be analyzed (a) independently or (b) dependently of the actual content of the interaction.

1.   The data presented in Figures 3a and 3b, and the bottom line of Table 2, show that, in our entire sample, it is the children who predominantly determine the content of interaction. With all rankings minimal differences in duration or percentage (up to 1.0) were neglected and treated as equal measures. This tendency is more pronounced at younger age levels (18 months is the age at which there is an equal number of mothers and children showing greater initiative). At older age levels, the discrepancy in the relative amount of initiative by mother and child is smaller, as well.

2.   The mother's and the child's initiative were analyzed in terms of the content they introduced into the interaction.

We noted that the mother and the child initiated different domains of behavior to different degrees. Children at all the observed age levels initiated sensori-motor activities most often, and their initiative in this domain was greater than their mothers'. The mothers most often initiated the social communicative domain of behavior, and their initiative in this domain was predominant in relation to the children's. However, it is worthwhile mentioning that the mothers are not the sole initiators of social communication even at the 9-month age level; two children (out of six) are more active than their mothers in this respect, and only one child failed to show initiative in that domain.

In both the older and the younger children, the order of initiated

Table 2. Ranking of Domains According to the Duration of Initiative of Mother and Child and the Percentage of Interaction which is Accounted for by the Initiative of Mother and Child

	206 I obs. Ch	206 I obs. M	206 II obs. Ch	206 II obs. M	208 I obs. Ch	208 I obs. M	208 II obs. Ch	208 II obs. M	209 I obs. Ch	209 I obs. M	209 II obs. Ch	209 II obs. M	211 I obs. Ch	211 I obs. M	211 II obs. Ch	211 II obs. M	212 I obs. Ch	212 I obs. M	212 II obs. Ch	212 II obs. M	214 I obs. Ch	214 I obs. M	214 II obs. Ch	214 II obs. M
A	1.5	3	2	5	7	3	2	3	2	1	2	2	3	4	4	4	2	2	3	3.5	5	1	2	4
SM	1.5	1	1	1	2	6	1	2	1			3	1		1	3	7		6.5		1	4.5	1	1
S$_{SM}$	4.5	4	6.5	7	6	7.5	3.5	6	6	7.5	7	6	4	6.5	7	6	7	6.5	1	7	5	7	5	5
Sc	4.5	2	4	2.5	3	2	5	1	4.5	3.5	3	1	2	2	2	1	3	4	6.5	2	5	3	4	2
Sr	7	5.5	6.5	7	6	4	5	7.5	4.5	6	7	6	6.5	6.5	5	7	7	6.5	6.5	7	5	7	7	6.5
Sy	7	8	6.5	7	6	7.5	3.5	7.5	7.5	7.5	7	6	6.5	6.5	3	2	7	6.5	6.5	7	5	7	7	6.5
M	3	7	3	2.5	6	1		5	3	3.5	4	6	6.5	3	7	5	5	3	4	3.5	5	2	3	3
F	7	5.5	6.5	4	6	5	7	4	7.5	5	5	6	6.5	6.5	7	7	4	6.5	6.5	5	5	4.5	7	8
% of IA	78%	22%	75%	25%	22%	78%	46%	54%	62%	38%	65%	35%	63%	37%	64%	36%	65%	35%	68%	32%	32%	68%	55%	45%

	402 I obs. Ch	402 I obs. M	402 II obs. Ch	402 II obs. M	403 I obs. Ch	403 I obs. M	403 II obs. Ch	403 II obs. M	405 I obs. Ch	405 I obs. M	405 II obs. Ch	405 II obs. M	407 I obs. Ch	407 I obs. M	407 II obs. Ch	407 II obs. M	409 I obs. Ch	409 I obs. M	409 II obs. Ch	409 II obs. M	411 I obs. Ch	411 I obs. M	411 II obs. Ch	411 II obs. M
A	2	4.5	3	3	4	6.5	4	7	1	3	2.5	1	2	3	1.5	3	6.5	3	2	5.5	1	3	1	2
SM	1	4.5	1	4	2	2.5	3	4	2	2	1	5	1		3	2	1	1	3	4	2	5.5	2	3.5
S$_{SM}$	5.5	6	7	6	6.5	6.5	7	7	5	7	7	7.5	7	6.5	7	6	6.5	6	6.5	7.5	6	7.5	6.5	7.5
Sc	4	1	2	1	3	2.5	2	1	3	1	2.5	2	3.5	1	1.5	1	2	2	1	2	4.5	1	3	1
Sr	7.5	8	7	8	6.5	4	7	5	7	4.5	5	4	7	6.5	7	6	6.5	6	6.5	7.5	7.5	5.5	6.5	5
Sy	5.5	2.5	5	2	1	1	1	2	7	4.5	7	3	3.5	4	4.5	6	6.5	6	6.5	3	4.5	2	4	3.5
M	3	2.5	4	6	6.5	6.5	7	7	4	7	4	7.5	5	6.5	4.5	6	4	6	4	5.5	3	7.5	6.5	7.5
F	7.5	7	7	6	6.5	6.5	5	3	7	7	7	6	7	6.5	7	6	3	6	6.5		7.5	4	6.5	6
% of IA	50%	50%	33%	67%	58%	42%	60%	40%	62%	38%	52%	48%	28%	78%	54%	46%	58%	42%	40%	60%	52%	48%	46%	54%

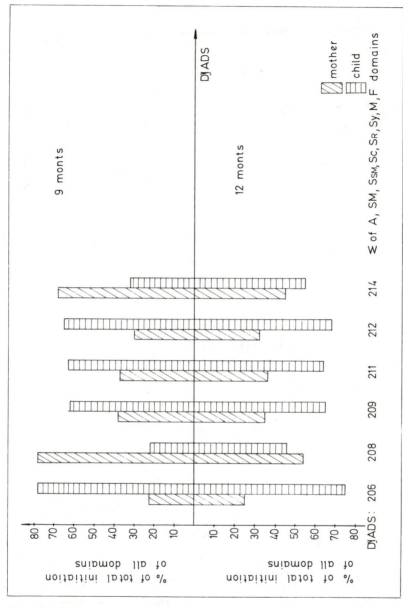

Figure 3(a). Iniciator of the content of interaction (all domains together)

domains in terms of predominance remains virtually the same at the first and the second observation.

Such consistency in the choice of domains was only found in the older children's mothers, while the mothers of the younger group displayed shifts to a greater or lesser degree in this respect. This finding

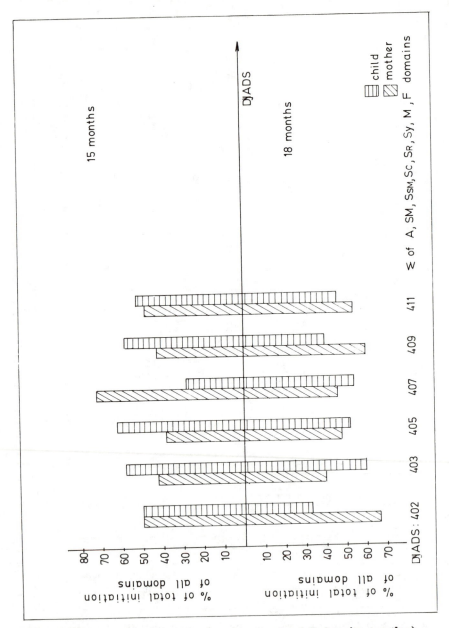

Figure 3(b). Iniciator of the content of interaction (all domains together)

is in accordance with other data which indicate great changes in interaction between the two observation periods in the younger sample.

Table 3.   Rank Correlations of Domains Initiated in the First and the Second
Observation Period for Mothers and Children

code of subjects	YOUNGER 9–12 month		code of subjects	OLDER 15–18	
	child	mother		child	mother
206	0.94**	0.54	402	0.90**	0.81*
208	0.86**	0.47	403	0.92**	0.77*
209	0.73*	0.77*	405	0.84**	0.79*
211	0.66*	0.53	407	0.89**	0.95**
212	0.77*	0.89**	409	0.56	0.46
214	0.70*	0.52	411	0.80	0.87**

* = $p < 0.05$
** = $p < 0.01$

COMPLEXITY OF INTERACTION; HOMOGENEOUS VS. HETEROGENEOUS INTERACTION

As indicated earlier, if, in the interaction of a pair, more than one
domain is registered simultaneously in each episode, i.e., if their episodes
are more complex and of a heterogeneous content, than the sum of
duration of all units will give a surplus over 100% for that particular
pair. In this sense, the sum of duration of all units can be used as the
measure of the content homogeneity of the episodes during the interaction of the pair.

The data shown in Figure 4 indicate, at each of the observed age
levels, great individual differences according to the homogeneity of
episodes during interaction, but we also could distinguish two types of
interaction according to the content of interactional episodes.

• homogeneous type: simultaneously treating mostly one domain of
  behavior. This type of interaction predominates in 9-month-olds.
• heterogeneous type: treating simultaneously more domains of behavior. This type predominates in the interaction at older age levels
  and gradually grows with age.

If each episode comprised only one domain of activity, the sum of
duration would be equal to 100, i.e., total 600 at each age group. We
found that at the 18-month age, each episode is 1.3 times more complex
than the one at 9 months of age, which indicates that the pairs at older
age levels are more prone to carry out several activities at the same
time and that these activities have more facets.

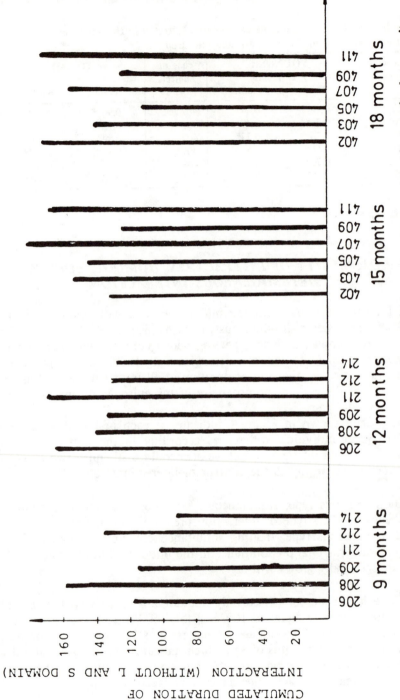

Figure 4. Content homogenity of interaction–individual and group differences according to content homogenity–heterogenity

THE CONTENT OF INTERACTION

The content analysis of interaction is of profound importance and linked to the theoretical postualtes mentioned above. The objective of this analysis is to gain insight into the status of different characters and domains of interaction of pairs in our unstructured situation.

The content analysis of interaction was conducted in three steps:

1. The contribution of the different domains as the contents of interaction was analyzed while the characters of interaction were summed up together.
2. The differences in the contribution of developmentally prospective and conservative treatments of the domains in the interaction were analyzed.
3. The presence of the theoretically most prospective type of treatment (a_1—common action in the zone of the proximal development) was analyzed.

1. Analysis of the Relative Presence of All Domains of Interaction

When an analysis is made of what the contents of interaction are at each of the observed ages, we get the following picture:

The SM, S_c, and A domains are the dominant domains of mother–child interaction at all observed ages, while S_{SM}, S_r, and F are the least frequent to occur. The following developmental tendencies are noted: diminishing presence of SM activities and an increase of symbolic ones at older age levels (15 and 18 months). This fits in perfectly with the well-known concept of the child's development at the sensori-motor

Table 4. Percentage of Interaction Accounted for by Each Domain of Interaction on Each Age Level

		9 months	12 months	15 months	18 months
DOMAINS	A	22.84	18.85	17.00	20.00
	SM	38.91	38.96	28.56	21.06
	S_{SM}	2.10	0.67	0.99	0.47
	S_c	15.55	25.94	30.48	35.65
	S_r	2.42	0.55	0.65	3.79
	Sy	0.33	2.97	14.66	11.93
	M	14.55	9.49	6.46	4.18
	F	3.30	2.58	1.20	2.93
Σ		100.00	100.01	100.00	100.01

stage, which is best presented in Piaget's theory of cognitive development. Exceptionally interesting, however, and essentially different from Piaget's model, is the fact that, already at 9 months, about 16% of interaction consists of communicative exchanges between the child and the mother. It should be noted that our S_c domain comprises the exchange of messages about the physical and social environment, i.e., *cognitive* but not affective exchanges. The latter ones (i.e., the expressions of emotional states) are classified under domain A. Thus, even before the appearance of speech and symbolic functions, the child is a collocutor of the adult. The data on initiatives confirms that frequently it is the child that initiates this content of interaction. According to Ivić, this nonverbal, practical-situational communication (which uses the schemes of actions and situational props, and is developed in the course of shared practical activity between the child and the adult) actually constitutes a direct developmental predecessor of verbal, symbolic communication. The participation of the social communication domain in interaction steeply increases at 12 months and continues to grow with age.

Motor activity as the content of interaction is not as present as the other domains. Its presence is mostly located with 9-month-olds, and it was even absent in the interaction of some pairs.

The data on this domain of interaction should nevertheless be taken with reserve, because conditions in which observations were carried out (staying in a room) limited the gross motor activity which is the first developmental task for older children. Although a child can practice walking, jumping, climbing, and rolling in a room, more adequate environments exist for this (a park, for example).

2. Analysis of Interaction Character for the Most Frequent Domains of the Activity of Pairs

Only five domains are included in the present survey (A, SM, S_c, S_y, and M) because, on the basis of our data, they were singled out as the most frequent content domains of interaction.

We see (Table 5) that interaction, the content of which is affective in all observed ages is almost equally present and most frequently in the zone of actual development (ZAD) of the child (a_2), i.e., that it is reduced to symmetrical affective exchanges between partners. Shared activity in the zone of proximal affective development of the child (a_1) is very rarely present in all surveyed ages.

The SM domain has a paradoxical status: at younger ages (9 and 12 months) when it is the most frequent content of interaction, it is very often inadequately treated. This finding, particularly in conjunction

Table 5. Percentage of Interaction Accounted for by Each Character of Interaction for the 5 Most Frequent Domains

age 9 A

	b_1	a_4	a_2	a_1	a_3	Σ D%
A	2.82	2.82	15.06	2.14	0	22.84
SM	17.91	8.69	9.41	2.20	0.70	38.91
Sc	1.35	1.09	3.63	8.53	0.95	15.55
Sy	0	0	0	0.33	0	0.33
M	1.16	2.78	6.62	3.70	0.29	14.55
Σ_{CH}	23.24	15.38	34.72	16.90	1.94	92.18*

* The rest totaling up to 100% is accounted for by the other 3 domains.

age 9 B

	b_1	a_4	a_2	a_1	a_3	Σ D%
A	4.46	4.35	7.82	1.45	0.77	18.85
SM	13.00	10.77	10.29	4.90	0	38.96
Sc	2.11	4.66	12.03	6.62	0.52	25.94
Sy	0.26	0.21	0.54	1.96	0	2.97
M	3.45	1.64	1.19	3.13	0.08	9.49
Σ_{CH}	23.28	21.63	31.87	18.06	1.37	96.21*

* The rest totaling up to 100% is accounted for by the other 3 domains.

age 15 A

	b_1	a_4	a_2	a_1	a_3	Σ D%
A	0.83	1.06	12.99	2.12	/	17
SM	7.56	5.61	13.08	2.31	/	28.56
Sc	0.79	1.44	18.33	9.74	0.18	30.48
Sy	4.72	0.65	6.79	2.50	/	14.66
M	1.61	1.13	2.12	1.60	/	6.46
Σ_{CH}	15.51	9.89	53.31	18.27	0.18	97.16*

* The rest totaling up to 100% is accounted for by the other 3 domains.

age 15 B

	b_1	a_4	a_2	a_1	a_3	Σ D%
A	2.37	1.51	13.87	2.25	0	20.00
SM	6.95	4.31	7.55	1.82	0.43	21.06
Sc	2.71	4.26	22.92	5.49	0.27	35.65
Sy	4.64	0.40	4.48	2.41	/	11.93
M	1.70	0.17	1.57	0.74	/	4.18
Σ_{CH}	18.37	10.65	50.39	12.71	0.70	92.82*

* The rest totaling up to 100% is accounted for by the other 3 domains.

with the fact that this domain is predominatly initiated by the infant, indicates that SM activity is the most significant domain of the activity for the infant, but not always for the mother. In other words, mothers neglect (b_1) or even inhibit and introduce more babyish SM activities (which the child has already outgrown—a_4). These two characters of SM interaction occur on average three times more often than joint activity in the child's zone of proximal SM development does. The treatment of the child's sensorimotor activity somewhat improves at older age levels (15 and 18 months), but there rarely is joint activity in the zone of proximal SM development (ZP_xD) of the child. However, these group means mask great individual differences, which will be discussed later.

The situation is just the opposite in the case of the social communicative domain of interaction. Not only are there few b_1 and a_4 interaction categories, but this content domain, in comparison with all others, is also most often in the zone of proximal development (ZP_xD) (a_1) in all ages. This points to the hypothesis that our culture is probably more socially oriented, that it values competence in the domain of social reality more than that in the domain of physical reality.

Naturally, such a conclusion is premature and only tentative, because decisions on specific cultural qualities cannot be reached on the basis of a sample of 12 pairs. In any case, the children from our sample initiated S_c and the mothers supported (either by actively responding or promoting) all such activities of child, while they frequently did not react at all or reacted inadequately to activities relating to objects (and toys). The domain of symbolic activities generally does not appear before the age of 15 months. However, the real measure of total symbolic activity could only be obtained by taking into account the data about language behavior. In general for all domains summed up, we can conclude that:

1. At all ages, the interaction classified as zone of actual development (ZAD) is the most frequent to occur—i.e., for the most part, interaction between the mother and the child consists of carrying out activities which the child has already mastered, with the mother's participation and support.
2. At all ages, the interaction classified as zone of future development (ZFD) is the least frequent to occur; i.e., mothers rarely mistake as much in judging the child's capabilities and seldom introduce the tasks which by far exceed child's capability.
3. Zone of proximal development (ZP_xD) and b_1 are almost equally present; they account for about 20% of interaction each, while zone of past development (ZP_tD) accounts for slightly less. Globally, the

data in Table 5 indicates that interaction in older age groups is organized more around the activities in the child's zone of actual development (ZAD) than is the case in younger age groups, hypothetically as a result of the pair's interactional experience with each other.

3. The Prospective vs. Conservative Interaction in Each Domain

Going by the assumed developmental effects, we can bring different categories of the developmental directedness and the character of interaction in general into two global categories: prospective interaction, whose main characteristics is in that it enhances further development, and comprises of interaction in zone of actual development (ZAD), zone of proximal development (ZP_xD) and zone of future development (ZFD); and conservative interaction, which is assumed to have negative effects and comprises of b_1 and zone of past development (ZP_tD). The global presentation of interaction under this dichotomy gives an even clearer picture about the different character of interaction in the five most frequent domains of joint activity, as shown in table 6.

Directly comparing the percentages of the prospective and the conservative interaction for each of the five domains, the above conclusion can be confirmed again.

The SM domain is most prevalent among the conservatively treated domains at all age levels. Interaction in the SM domain is predominatly conservative at the younger age level, while the S_c interaction is predominatly prospective both at the younger and the older age levels.

Affective interaction is predominatly prospective at all age levels, except in 12-month-olds, when it frequently becomes conservative, hypothetically as a consequence of the mother's attempt to introduce control of the negative affects of the infant by ignoring or directly suppressing his or her affective reactions.

The interactions in the domain of motoric activity of the infant at the 9-month age level is generally prospective, but later on the reverse is true (see earlier note).

In general, the comparison of the relative share of prospective vs. conservative interaction shows the predominance of the first over the second. This tendency is more pronounced in older age levels. It looks as if mothers become more conscious of their role in the child's development at the 15- and 18-month age levels.

But the same point applies to everything that has been said so far on the basis of age-group comparisons: there are pronounced individual differences both in the presence of certain domains and in the character of interaction. As a matter of fact, it is these inter-dyad differences

Table 6. Percentage of Interaction Accounted for by Conservative* vs. Prospective* Interaction for the Five Most Frequent Domains

age 9 months

	conserv.	prospect.	difference
A	5.64	17.20	+ 11.56**
SM	26.60	12.31	− 14.29
Sc	2.44	13.11	+ 10.67
Sy	0	0.33	+ 0.33
M	3.94	10.61	+ 6.67
	38.62	53.56	+ 14.94

age 12 months

	conserv.	prospect.	difference
A	8.81	10.04	+ 1.23
SM	23.77	15.19	− 8.58
Sc	6.77	19.17	+ 12.4
Sy	0.47	2.50	+ 2.03
M	5.09	4.40	+ 0.69
	44.91	51.3	+ 6.39

age 15 months

	conserv.	prospect.	difference
A	1.89	15.11	+ 13.22
SM	13.17	15.39	− 2.22
Sc	2.23	28.25	+ 26.02
Sy	5.37	9.29	+ 3.92
M	2.74	3.72	+ 0.98
	25.4	71.76	+ 46.36

age 18 months

	conserv.	prospect.	difference
A	3.88	16.12	+ 12.34
SM	11.26	9.80	− 1.46
Sc	6.97	28.67	+ 21.70
Sy	5.04	6.89	+ 1.85
M	1.87	2.31	+ 0.44
	29.02	63.8	+ 34.78

* conservative: b_1+a_4
prospective: $a_1+a_2+a_3$

** +: more prospective
−: more conservative

which are particularly important for our purpose of predicting children's further development.

ANALYSIS OF INTERDYAD DIFFERENCES OF INTERACTION

Differences According to the Character of Interaction

Table 7 shows the percentages of each character of interaction (for all domains together) for each pair.

As can be seen, there are major individual differences (expressed in percentages) of all the types of shared activity, as well as the b_1 category. Comparing pairs according to the dichotomy of the prospective vs. conservative interaction (Table 8) we notice that, at the 9-month age level, pair 208 has the most prospective interaction by far.

Conservative interaction is the least present here, while at the same time the activity in the zone of proximal development (ZP_xD) of the child is most frequent (45.7%), while the interaction of pairs 209 and 211 is the worst, according to our assessment (their interaction is more conservatively than prospectively oriented). These individual differences, however, highly fluctuate, which is understandable since, in order to be adequate, the mothers must adapt to developmental changes of their child: what was an activity in the zone of proximal development (ZP_xD) becomes an activity in the zone of actual development (ZAD), and after a certain time also in the zone of past developmental (ZP_tD). This also implies the question of whether we can speak about a kind of "developmental sensitivity" for all age levels on the part of the mother, or if such sensitivity is possibly specific for certain age groups, but this problem is out of the scope of our present study.

From the age of 9 months to that of 12 months changes occurred in the developmental directedness: with two pairs the change was in a positive direction, and with two pairs in a negative one, with the correlation for the group amounting to $\rho = -0.41$. Hence, at the 12-month age level, pair 214 has the best interaction, and pair 206 the worst.

Pairs 208 and 214 are the very illustrations for a possible age-level specialization of the mothers: 208 is a "puller" at 9 months and "gives up" at 12 months, while 214 is a "puller" at 12 months but not until that age. However, we cannot say on the basis of just two observations whether this is due to their particular sensitivity or insensitivity for a particular age level.

The comparison of pairs from our older sample, i.e., at 15 months, shows similar interdyad differences as regards the developmental di-

Table 7. Percentage of Each Character of Interaction with Each Pair

9 months

developmental directedness	code of subjects	206	208	209	211	212	214
	a_8	0.0	5.7	0.4	4.8	0.0	0.0
	a_1	6.8	45.7	12.4	7.6	9.4	20.0
	a_2	61.8	28.1	32.3	29.3	45.9	38.9
	a_4	1.5	12.5	27.9	22.1	15.3	21.2
	b_1	29.9	8.0	27.0	36.2	29.4	19.9

12 months

developmental directedness	code of subjects	206	208	209	211	212	214
	a_8	0.0	0.0	0.0	1.0	7.8	0.0
	a_1	6.1	7.1	7.6	32.7	7.5	52.7
	a_2	17.1	43.0	42.6	40.9	35.7	24.7
	a_4	14.8	34.6	25.2	16.5	36.4	12.4
	b_1	62.0	15.3	24.6	8.9	12.6	10.2

15 months

developmental directedness	code of subjects	402	403	405	407	409	411
	a_8	0.0	1.0	0.0	0.0	0.0	0.0
	a_1	26.0	21.9	17.7	18.8	27.2	7.0
	a_2	48.2	35.2	62.4	74.1	39.0	50.3
	a_4	16.8	5.0	9.1	3.5	4.2	30.7
	b_1	9.0	36.9	10.8	3.5	29.6	12.0

18 months

developmental directedness	code of subjects	402	403	405	407	409	411
	a_8	0.8	0.0	0.5	0.0	2.7	0.7
	a_1	15.3	16.3	16.9	3.8	18.4	18.6
	a_2	65.3	36.3	55.8	70.3	52.8	55.5
	a_4	7.3	4.5	6.7	9.6	0.0	14.1
	b_1	11.3	42.9	20.1	16.3	26.1	11.1

Table 8. Percentage of Conservative Interaction

code of subjects	206	208	209	211	212	214
9 months	31.4	20.5	54.9	58.3	44.7	41.1
12 months	76.8	49.9	49.9	25.4	49.0	22.7

code of subjects	402	403	405	407	409	411
15 months	25.8	41.9	19.9	7	33.8	42.7
18 months	18.6	47.4	26.8	25.9	26.1	25.2

rectedness of interaction, but the percentage of conservative interaction is lower for this subsample.

Pair 407 has the best interaction by far—the least amount of developmentally negatively oriented interaction and a large amount of joint activity in the zone of proximal development (ZP_xD), while pairs 403 and 411 have the greatest proportion of conservative interaction in this subsample.

Changes in the character of interaction noted in the observation of these pairs for a 3-month period are not so drastic as in the younger sample, and the sample at 18 months is almost equaled up by the percentage of conservative interaction (thus a correlation which is virtually zero, $\rho=-0.04$).

Patterns of Interaction

If, to this data, the ones on the presence of domains (Figure 5) and on the initiation of certain domains (Table 2) are added, we get a basis for searching for key patterns of mother–child interaction. Without going into an analysis of all the individual differences (in any case, in a sample of this size it can easily happen that each pair becomes the sole representative of a different type), we will further illustrate below, on a number of chosen examples, what we mean by individual differences in interaction patterns. We will show two pairs on the positive, and two pairs on the negative, extremes according to their interaction-indices.

The first two illustrations are dyad of mother and child at 12 months (Table 9a,b,c, and d).

We see that, in the interaction of both pairs, all domains are present

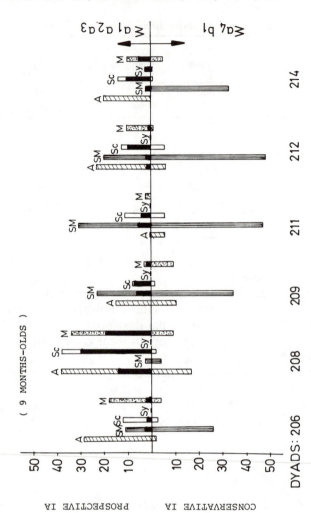

Figure 5a. Potentially Developmentally Prospective versus Conservative Interaction in each Domain (9 Months-Olds)

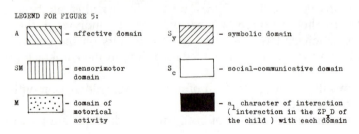

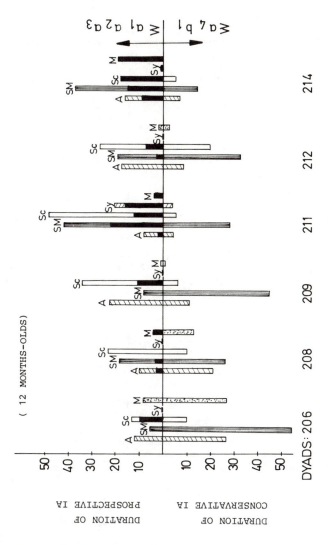

Figure 5b. Potentially Developmentally Prospective versus Conservative Interaction in each Domain (12 Months-Olds)

almost equally (especially the three most frequent and most important ones at this age: A, SM, S_c. However, they differ dramatically in the character of interaction: 50% of interaction with pair 209 is conservative, i.e., the least developmentally prospective interaction. Interaction in the zone of proximal development (ZP_xD) with pair 214 occurs virtually in every domain, while its occurrence is restricted to the S_c domain with pair 209. The reason for this difference can be discovered more

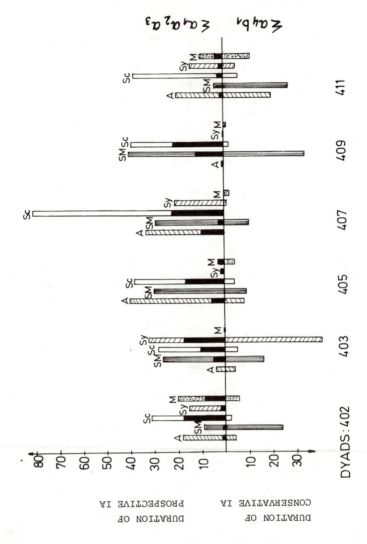

Figure 5c. **Potentially Developmentally Prospective versus Conservative Inter-action in each Domain (15 Months-Olds)**

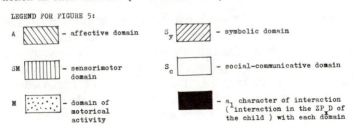

LEGEND FOR FIGURE 5:

A $\boxed{\text{(hatched)}}$ - affective domain

S_y $\boxed{\text{(hatched)}}$ - symbolic domain

SM $\boxed{\text{(lined)}}$ - sensorimotor domain

S_c $\boxed{}$ - social-communicative domain

M $\boxed{\text{(dotted)}}$ - domain of motorical activity

$\boxed{\text{(solid)}}$ - a_1 character of interaction (^{1}interaction in the ZP_D of the child) with each domain

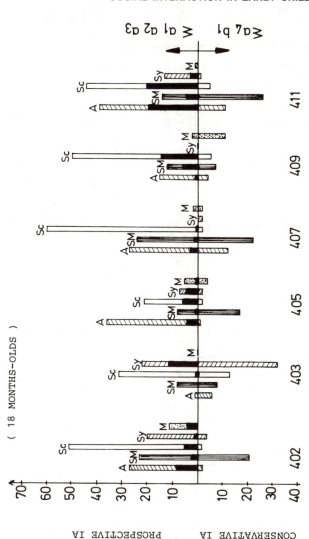

Figure 5d. Potentially Developmentally Prospective versus Conservative Interaction in each Domain (18 Months-Olds)

easily if we take into account the data about initiative. With both pairs, the child takes more initiative than the mother (with pair 209 this is more pronounced—Table 2), and they are similar in their accord in preference of certain domains. What makes them different, however, is the character of interaction in domains which are initiated by the mother or the child. With pair 209, the interaction is the worst in the

Table 9. Percentage of Each Unit of Interaction (Domains × Character) with for Chosen Pairs

Table 9a:

| | child 12 months (pair 209) | | | | | |
	b_1	a_4	a_2	a_1	a_3	Σ
A	0.61	7.96	17.03	0	0	25.6
SM	18.49	16.48	5.93	0	0	40.9
S_{SM}	0	0	0	0	0	0
S_c	4.05	0.74	18.30	7.61	0	30.7
S_r	0	0	0	0	0	0
S_y	0	0	0	0	0	0
M	0.75	0	0.65	0	0	1.4
F	0.65	0	0.75	0	0	1.4
Σ	24.55	25.18	42.66	7.61	0	100%

Table 9b:

| | child 12 months (pair 214) | | | | | |
	b_1	a_4	a_2	a_1	a_3	Σ
A	3.42	2.28	5.96	6.76	0	18.4
SM	5.68	6.31	18.42	11.41	0	41.8
S_{SM}	0	0	0.0	2.98	0	3.0
S_c	0.78	3.76	0.35	14.21	0	19.1
S_r	0.35	0	0	1.14	0	1.5
S_y	0	0	0	0.8	0	0.8
M	0	0	0	15.4	0	15.4
F	0	0	0	0	0	0
Σ	10.23	12.35	24.73	52.7	0	100%

Table 9c:

| | child 15 months (pair 407) | | | | | |
	b_1	a_4	a_2	a_1	a_3	Σ
A	0	0	13.40	5.50	0	18.9
SM	1.94	3.49	15.17	1.20	0	21.8
S_{SM}	0	0	0	0	0	0
S_c	0	0	33.66	12.14	0	45.8
S_r	0	0	0	0	0	0
S_y	0.3	0	11.9	0	0	12.2
M	1.3	0	0	0	0	1.3
F	0	0	0	0	0	0
Σ	3.54	3.49	74.13	18.84	0	100%

Table 9d:

| | child 15 months (pair 411) | | | | | |
	b_1	a_4	a_2	a_1	a_3	Σ
A	1.70	11.09	11.14	0.77	0	24.7
SM	2.87	13.17	2.46	0	0	18.5
S_{SM}	0	0.8	0	0	0	0.8
S_c	1.35	2.19	21.46	1.40	0	26.4
S_r	0	0	1.8	0	0	1.8
S_y	2.75	0.14	7.47	1.05	0	11.4
M	3.39	3.39	4.22	1.90	0	12.9
F	0	0	1.68	1.82	0	3.5
Σ	12.06	30.78	50.23	6.94	0	100%

domain most often initiated by the child (SM), while more interaction in the zone of actual development (ZAD) and zone of proximal development (ZP_xD) appears only in the domain where the mother's initiative is predominant. Nothing of the above-described division was noted with pair 214: interaction is generally prospective equally in all domains, regardless of whether it was initiated by the mother or the child.

This congruence of pair 214 was achieved only at this age level, most probably because the SM activity which was just the child's individual behavior at a younger age now became a content of interaction, because it has started to be promoted and initiated by the mother as well. Pairs 407 and 411 can be contrasted in a similar way at the 15-month age level: both pairs have similar domains present in their interaction (except the developmentally very important $S_{c,}$ which was noted to be about twice as much present with pair 407 than with pair 411), but the character of interaction is different: almost the entire interaction with 407 is prospective in all domains, with a lot of interaction also in the zone of proximal development (ZP_xD—the picture would be even more effective if their data of zone of proximal language development, was registered), while pair 411 has much more conservative interaction, and a negligible amount of interaction in the zone of proximal development (ZP_xD). The mother in pair 407 takes much more initiative than the child, but they agree very well as regards the preferred domains (Table 2). The reverse is true with pair 411: interaction is initiated equally by the mother and the child (50%–50%), but there is almost no accord regarding the preferred domains (Table 2), so that we again have a picture of discord in interaction between the mother and the child—the domains introduced by the mother (S_c and S_y) are proportionally treated the best, while those introduced by the child (SM for example) are treated the worst.

E and R Type

Although our categories of analysis were not designed to capture the very essence of Nelson's (1973) R and E type, we tried to check, on the basis of our data about initiation of different domains, her finding on the existence of these two types of children.

In our system of interaction analysis, the referential type would apply to children who predominantly initiate SM activities, (R type is obviously oriented to objects and actions with objects), while the expressive type would apply to children who initiate the affective and the S_c domain (E type is oriented to persons, feelings, needs, and social relations). In our sample, these three domains appear most frequently, and they are in fact the very domains most often initiated by the children.

The data presented in Table 10 show that the A and SM domains are almost equally initiated by a large number of children, but there are also those who are more or less clearly SM or affective-communication oriented. As far as the above is concerned, there seems to be a sound basis for further discussion and research on the R and E types of children in our culture as well. But, concerning the findings of A. Clarke-Stewart (1973) that girls are more socially oriented and boys more object oriented, we must say that the tendency towards such stereotypes of the male and female role appears only at the age of 18 months, but not earlier.

PATTERNS OF SENSORI-MOTOR INTERACTION AND THE ACHIEVEMENT ON SENSORI-MOTOR INTELLIGENCE SCALE

So far we have dealt merely with the description of interaction. Now we will go a step closer to our main objective.

Going into the constructive role of social interaction is a lengthy and troublesome endeavor, and so exceeds the scope of our present aims. However, on the basis of data collected so far, we can try to consider the point of undertaking such an endeavor. In other words, if we expect that different characteristics of social interaction would have repercussions on the child's further development exactly in the way sketched out by Vygotsky, the failure to find meaningful links between the characteristics of interaction and the current indices of the child's development would to a large extent reduce the plausibility of the hypothesis on the constructive role of interaction in development. With this aim, we carried out a brief check of the links between the characteristics of interaction and the achievements on the scale of SM intelligence.

We applied the Casati & Lezine (1968) SMI scale on all children from the sample at both observation periods. The scale has four subscales and seven types of task sets. We used the average percentage of solved tasks (the sum of the percentage of success for each type of set divided by the number of the types of task sets (7) as the measure of children's achievement on the SMI scale (see Table 11.).

If we keep to Piaget's thesis on the origin of SM intelligence, the amount of the SM domain in interaction or the amount of SM activity initiated by the child should be expected to be in correlation with the child's achievement on the SM intelligence scale, or, at least, if we

Table 10. Percentage* of the Most Frequently Initiated Domains by the Child

9 months

domains / code of subjects	206	208	209	211	212	214
A	28.6	85.6	14.7	6.2	21.5	0
SM	30.0	12.6	61.4	79.5	47.7	100
S_c	9.7	1.8	6.7	9.5	14.6	0
Sex:	F	M	M	F	F	M
Type:		E	R	R		R

12 months

domains / code of subjects	206	208	209	211	212	214
A	30.4	28.5	28.1	5.6	27.0	27.4
SM	38.5	36.1	53.1	60.5	29.4	39.0
S_c	10.5	16.3	14.6	22.2	41.8	11.0
Sex:	F	M	M	F	F	M
Type:				R		

15 months

domains / code of subjects	402	403	405	407	409	411
A	23.3	8.4	48.1	33.4	0	37.7
SM	39.4	25.5	27.9	37.3	67.6	31.2
S_c	13.8	16.4	12.1	13.0	24.6	3.3
Sex:	M	M	M	F	F	F
Type:			E		R	

18 months

domains / code of subjects	402	403	405	407	409	411
A	13.6	8.7	19.6	33.2	30.4	47.3
SM	53.6	12.3	37.6	28.7	18.7	36.1
S_c	17.4	27.7	19.6	32.7	47.0	12.2
Sex:	M	M	M	F	F	F
Type:	R			E	E	E

*Calculated out of the duration of the child's total initiative.

Table 11. Achievements of the Tested Sample on the SMI Scale Expressed Through Percentage of Solved (Successfully Performed) Tasks

code of subjects	A age*	B age*	difference B–A	code of subjects	A age	B age	difference B–A
206	22	34	12	402	46	53	7
208	24	30	6	403	49	64	15
209	30	32	2	405	46	65	19
211	21	38	17	407	59	67	8
212	19	40	21	409	55	57	2
214	16	38	22	411	40	41	1

* The younger children from our sample (9-month- and 12-month-olds) did not solve the 5, 6, and 7 types of tasks at all, and in type 4 achieved only 4 points.

accept a somewhat less confining variation of the thesis, that the amount of the SM domain in interaction reduced by the amount of the a_4 type of shared activity in the SM domain—which depicts the mother's hindering the child's SM activity—is in correlation with the achievements of the child.

Checks of all three above hypotheses have given negative results (see Tables 12 and 13). Correlations of all three indicators with the SMI scale at all age levels are very low and statistically not significant.

On the other hand, even the most global measure which takes into account the character of interaction in the SM domain (e.g., prospective minus conservative sensorimotor interaction) is linked with achievements on the SMI scale at all age levels, except at 18 months, when the symbolic and sociocommunicative activities take the place of the SM domain. The character of interaction in the SM domain is, therefore, not unimportant: Children with whom prospective SM interaction is predominant have better achievements on the SMI scale than those with whom there is more conservative interaction. Besides this global measure of the quality of interaction of SM content, a number of more specific indicators of interaction are also in correlation with the SMI scale, e.g., the duration of zone of proximal development (ZP_xD) at the 15-month age level ($\rho=0.79$), zone of proximal development (ZP_xD) minus zone of past development (ZP_tD) also at the 15-month age level (0.73), but a detailed study and interpretation exceeds the range and requirements of this work. However, we consider that the data presented in the last three lines of Table 13 are especially valuable in the further articulation of the discussion on whether social interaction between the child and the adult has a constructive role in the child's development. The pattern of correlations at the younger age level indicates that major

Table 12. Duration of each Character of Interaction SM Domain

character of interaction	code of subjects		9 months						12 months					
			206	208	209	211	212	214	206	208	209	211	212	214
	(ZFD)	a_3	0	0	0	5.1	0	0	0	0	0	0	0	0
	(ZP$_x$D)	a_1	2.6	0	5.9	4.8	1.1	1.5	0	3.1	0	21.8	2.6	14.1
	(ZAD)	a_2	8.5	2.2	16.9	20.9	18.9	0.6	5.1	15.2	7.8	20.4	16.1	22.8
	(ZP$_t$D)	a_4	0	2.5	17.8	15.2	13.6	14.0	3.6	21.7	21.6	16.7	20.2	7.8
		b_1	26.1	2.2	16.7	32.7	33.5	18.4	50.5	4.9	24.3	11.6	12.2	7.0
	Σ SM		37.2	6.9	57.3	78.7	67.1	34.5	59.2	44.9	53.7	70.5	51.1	51.7

character of interaction	code of subjects		15 months						18 months					
			402	403	405	407	409	411	402	403	405	407	409	411
	(ZFD)	a_3	0	0	0	0	0	0	1.4	0	0.4	0	2.0	0
	(ZP$_x$D)	a_1	1.5	5.3	0	2.1	11.9	0	2.8	0	1.0	1.8	6.0	4.7
	(ZAD)	a_2	7.9	20.7	30.0	27.1	28.4	4.1	18.8	7.5	6.1	22.0	4.3	9.2
	(ZP$_t$D)	a_4	14.5	0.3	4.4	6.2	3.3	22.0	6.4	1.8	5.7	11.0	0	13.6
		b_1	9.2	15.3	4.9	3.4	30.7	4.8	14.9	6.5	11.7	10.7	6.6	11.9
	Σ SM		33.1	41.6	39.3	38.8	74.3	30.9	44.3	15.8	24.9	45.5	18.9	39.4

Table 13. Correlations Between Various Indices of Interaction Concerning SM Activity and the Achievement on Casati-Lezine Scale of Sensorimotor Intelligence

	younger gr.		older gr.	
CORRELATED VARIABLES:	9 months	12 months	15 months	18 months
Total* SM activity —with SMI scale	-0.14	0.24	0.61	0.01
Child's initiative of SM domain—with SMI scale	-0.08	0.24	-0.33	-0.37
SM activity minus ZP,D in SM—with SMI scale	-0.14	0.24	0.61	-0.14
Prospective minus conservative SM IA with SMI scale	0.94[3]	0.30	0.61	0.11
SMI scale (I–II assessment)	-0.81[2]		0.70	
Prospective minus conservative SM IA (I–II observation)	-0.48		0.04	
IA with SMI (I–II observation)	**0.77[1]		***0.99[3]	

[3] $p < 0.01$
[2] $p < 0.005$
[1] $p < 0.10$
* All correlations are rank correlations calculated on the basis of the duration of the relevant categories of interaction and percentage of achievement on Casati-Lezine SMI scale.
** Here the change measures are correlated, namely: (duration of prospective–conservative)II obs.—(duration of prospective–conservative)I obs. with gain—percentage for SMI scale.
*** Here IA indice (prospective–conservative) at 15 months is correlated with SMI achievement at 18 months.

changes in the character of interaction from the 9-month to the 12-month age levels coincides with changes in the achievement on the SMI scale (i.e., children whose interaction with their mothers had changed from 9 to 12 months in a positive direction have much greater gain on the scale of SMI than do children whose interaction has changed in a negative direction). It would be hard to find a more convincing explanation for the $\rho = -0.81$ correlation between the SMI scores at the first and the second observation than the one which sees this as a consequence of the changes in the character of interaction.

At older age levels, the link between the character of previous interaction in the SM sphere (I obs.) and the child's further SM development (II obs.) is quite explicit and unambiguous. This pattern of relationships is exactly the one which fits best into the way we conceptualize the impact of interactional variables on the formation of mental functions. At 18 months, the sensorimotor domain is, in our sample, replaced by other, developmentally more significant, domains (S_c and S_y) in interaction; hence, no relationship can any longer be found between interaction and sensorimotor intelligence at that age, but the SMI achievement reflects what had happened in interaction between the child and the mother earlier on.

The chosen examples of various types of dyads which we have given in a previous section of this work also illustrate this relationship between the character of interaction and the child's achievement on the SMI scale: the child in pair 209 (with a high incidence of conservative interaction in the SM domain) has the smallest gain between the first and the second assessment, whereas the child in pair 214 (where the interaction dramatically changed in the prospective direction, especially in the SM domain) has the greatest gain. The child in pair 407 (with predominantly prospective interaction) has the best achievement on the SMI scale at 15 months and 18 months, while the child in pair 411 (an example of discord in interaction and conservative directedness) is the worst achiever at both ages.

GENERAL DISCUSSION

The problem which motivated our research project concerns the dynamics of the influence of early social interaction on the child's psychological development.

The results which we have presented here originate from an incomplete sample, both of subjects and situations; they rely, therefore, on a very restricted data base within our project and are the product of that phase of research in which the main objective was to elaborate a system for transcribing interaction which would suit our theoretical conceptions.

Still, even on the basis of this first-step analysis, we can already say that various patterns of adult–child interaction are related to various developmental effects. Even very rough indices of the child's intellectual functioning, i.e., achievement on the SMI scale, are related to the character of interaction in the SM domain and change according to developmental directedness of interaction. These findings testify that even those functions generally thought to be natural, such as sensori-motor intelligence, are socially mediated and eventually shaped by culture. We cannot yet definitely say whether this influence is only motivational, or formative as well.

In this paper we stressed the important role of one microcultural variable, that being the character of mother–child interaction in the sensori-motor (SM) domain. The other relevant variables that will be included in our analysis should clarify the obtained picture of the culture-dependent nature of early intellectual development; these variables encompass the way in which parents structure their child's physical surroundings, the parents' attitudes about what a little child's intelligence consists in, whether its development can be stimulated and how, etc.; and also the necessary molecular data on a child's repertoire and organization of SM schemes, on the concrete content and the temporal and structural organization of the adult and child's joint SM activity, and the kinds of strategies which the adult offers the child in approaching and solving SM problems (these data will be obtained in this unstructured, as well as in two other structured, situations). A similar series of research steps is planned in the testing of the relationships between socio-cultural factors and other aspects of the child's development.

The problem of the stability of such relationships, as well as the problem of the long-term effects of early social interaction, evoke some of the fundamental problems in developmental psychology: that of the importance of early experience in further development and that of the nature of developmental changes.

According to Vygotsky's theory, psychological development consists, besides changes within each psychic function, in the change of mutual relationships between these functions, in the change of place and role of particular psychic functions in the mental organization. To go one step further, there can be different patterning of psychic functions going on in children from different cultures or even from the various interactional patterns found within the same culture.

When describing the mother–child interaction, we have noted great differences between the pairs in respect to each of the variables. However, we do not treat these differences as measurement errors, the way individual differences are, as a rule, treated in those psychological fields where the main task is to determine general regularities, such as in normative developmental psychology. On the contrary, the appearance of these differences represents to us a theoretically significant phenomenon that should be accorded special attention. Our basic hypothesis related to this is that interdyad differences, although also interesting from the standpoint of the description of interaction in a cross-section of time, may be considered to be the germ of later individual differences and may be perhaps conceptualized as the starting-point for different developmental courses in different persons. The idea of divergence in the course of development is only a global and so-far insufficiently elaborated idea in developmental psychology. Bruner has made this alternative to Piagetian universalism explicit by speaking of various "developmental styles" (Bruner et al., 1967), while it seems to us that Vygotsky's theory offers a sound theoretical foundation for the idea of divergent courses of development. Namely, if social interaction has a constructive role in development, then it can be expected that variations in social interaction (and not only individual differences in what is "inside the boundaries of the human skin") are not ephemeral differences, but give rise to more lasting different tendencies in further interactions and, indirectly, in total future development of the child.

Interdyad differences which we have noted in our research can most probably be interpreted in this manner. However, we are not yet able to judge whether such an interpretation would be plausible or not.

In the first place, in our analyses we have not drawn on all the sources of interdyad variations. Our analyses concentrated on the assessment of the developmental directedness of interaction in particular domains, with only a global evaluation of the interactional variables in the strict sense. Therefore, it is possible that the discovered patterns of interaction are orthogonal to other sources of variation, such as microanalytic variables, techniques and means of interaction, etc. It is also possible that these other variables have greater differential impact on further development than the variables which we have described here.

Another group of problems center around the consistency in these variations. It is clear that we can hardly attribute the decisive role in determining the direction of further development to interdyad differences which are highly changeable from moment to moment, even if they actually do have such a role. The question is, therefore, what is the "critical dosage" of the same kind of interaction which can be expected to have developmental consequences, and what is a momentary and chance variation. In other words, it is necessary first to find out the interdyad differences which are invariant at least some of the time, and only then to speak of the constructive role of this interaction in further development and, tentatively, about the various courses of further development of different children. The system of analysis of interaction which is presented in this work was conceived with the very intent of obtaining data which are comparable across ages, i.e., which are not related to concrete content and specific developmental stage of the subject. Hence, it enables us to determine the existence of stable patterns of interaction which characterize a given dyad throughout a range of various ages of the child. The data obtained by using such a system indicate dramatic changes in interaction between ages of 9 and 12 months, and much more stable patterns in the older age groups. Can we expect greater and greater stability at successive ages, or are these results accidental?

Another special theoretical problem concerns the way of assessing development, i.e. the choice of criterion measures. The question is, namely, which aspects of individual differences can be considered to be the consequence of interdyad differences in interaction, and which procedures can be used to identify these differences. Vygotsky is, to be true, explicit in the sense that every personal function of the individual has once appeared in interaction. But it is much less clear *what* features of interaction become internalized and *how*. There may be grounds for expecting a rather direct relationship between the consistent prospective interaction in a certain domain, i.e., concerning a certain psychic function of the child, and the later advances in development of this function in the child (adult). However, in our opinion, much more complex chains of causation are more probable. Namely, it is possible to expect that different strategies in problem solving in the broadest sense, or even differences in the mental organization, in the mutual relationships of different psychical functions will appear in the child as a result of the course of his or her interaction with adults in some earlier period.

In any case, it is hardly probable that these individual differences will show up on any kind of achievement tests, so that, in order to verify any of the above problems, we also have to develop new, different procedures for the diagnosis of individual differences.

REFERENCES

Ainsworth, M.D.S., Blehar, M.C., Waters, E., & Wall, S. (1978). *Patterns of attachment.* Hillsdale, NJ: Erlbaum.
Bakeman, R., & Brown, J.V. (1977). Behavioral dialogues: An approach to the assessment of mother–infant interaction. *Child Development, 48,* 195–203.
Bakhtin, M. (1967). *Problemi poetike Dostojevskog* [Problems of Dostoevsky's poetics]. Beograd: Nolit.
Bayley, N. (1969). *Bayley scales of infant development.* New York: Psychological Corp.
Boguslavskaia, Z.M. (1974). Motivy obshcheniia s vzroslymi u detei doshkolñogo vozrasta [Motives for interaction with adults in the preschool child]. In A.V. Zaporozhec, & M.I. Lisina (Eds.), *Razvitie obshcheniia u doshkolñikov* [Development of interaction in preschoolers] (pp. 203–256). Moskow: Pedagogika.

Brown, A.L., & French, L.A. (1979). The zone of potential development: Implications for intelligence testing in the year 2000. *Intelligence, 3,* 253–271.

Bruner, J., Olver, R., & Greenfield, P. (1967). *Studies in cognitive growth.* New York: Wiley.

Campione, J.C., Brown, A.L., & Ferrara, R.A. (1982). Mental retardation and intelligence. In R. Sternberg (Ed.), *Handbook of human intelligence* (pp. 392–490). Cambridge, England: Cambridge University Press.

Casati, I., & Lezine, I. (1968). *Les ètapes de l'intelligence sensori-motrice de l'enfant de la naissance à deux ans.* Paris: Centre de psychologie appliquèe.

Clarke-Stewart, K.A. (1973). Interactions between mothers and their young children: Characteristics and consequences. *Monographs of the Society for Research in Child Development, 38* (6–7, Serial No. 153).

Doise, W., & Mugny, G. (1981). *Le dèveloppement social de l'intelligence.* Paris: Inter Editions.

El'konin, D.B., & Davidov, V.V. (Eds.). (1962). *Vozrastnye vozmozhnosti usvoeniia znanii* [Age related learning capacities]. Moskow: Prosveshchenye.

Gal'perin, P.I. (1966). K ucheniiu ob interiorizacii [Towards one conception of interiorization]. *Voprosy psikhologii, 6,* 25–32.

Gouin Decarie, T., & Richard, M. (1982). La socialization du nourisson. *La Recherche, 13* (139), 1388–1396.

Guthke, J., & Lehwald, G. (1984). On component analysis of the intellectual learning ability in learning tests. *Zeitschrift für Psychologie, 192,1,* 3–17.

Hinde, R.A., & Herrmann, J. (1977). Frequencies, durations derived measures and their correlations in studying dyadic and triadic relationship. In H.R. Schaffer (Ed.), *Studies in mother infant interaction* (pp. 19–45). London: Academic Press.

Ivić, I. (1978). *Čovek kao animal symbolicum* [Man as animal symbolicum]. Beograd: Nolit.

Ivić, I. (1986a). Deux types de la communication prèverbale et le developpement de langage chez l'enfant. *Zbornik Filozofskog fakulteta,* Serija B, *XIV,* 69–73.

Ivić, I. (1986b, May). *Le role formateur des interactions sociales.* Paper presented at the colloque: Interactions sociales et constructions des savoirs. Institut National de Recherche Pedagogique-CRESAS, Paris.

Laboratory of Comparative Human Cognition. (1982). Culture and intelligence. In R. Sternberg (Ed.), *Handbook of human intelligence* (pp. 642–719). Cambridge, England: Cambridge University Press.

Lisina, M.I. (1974a). Vozniknovenie i razvitie neposredstvenno-emotsionalnogo obshcheniia so vzroslymi u detei pervogo polugodiia zhizni [The appearance and development of immediate emotional interaction with adults in the first half year of life]. In A.V. Zaporozhec, & M.I. Lisina (Eds.), *Razvitie obshcheniia u doshkolñikov* [Development of interaction in preschoolers] (pp. 18–64). Moskow: Pedagogika.

Lisina, M.I. (1974b). Vliianie obshcheniia so vzroslymi na razvitie rebenka pervogo polugodiia zhizni [The influence of interaction with adults on development of the child in the first half year of life]. In A.V. Zaporozhec, & M.I. Lisina (Eds.), *Razvitie obshcheniia u doshkolagnikov* [Development of interaction in preschoolers] (pp. 65–112). Moskow: Pedagogika.

Lisina, M.I. (1974c). *Vozrastnye i individualnye osobennosti obshcheniia so vzroslymi u detei ot rozhdeniia do semi let* [Age related and individual peculiarities of interaction with adults in children from birth to age seven]. Doctoral dissertation. Moskow: Avtoref.

Lisina, M.I. (1978). Genezis form obshcheniia u detei [The genesis of the form of interaction in the child]. In L.I. Antsiferova (Ed.), *Printsip razvitiia v psikhologii* [Principles of development in psychology] (pp. 268–294). Moskow: Nauka.

Lisina, M.I. (1980). Obschenie detei so vzroslymi i sverstnikami: obshchee i razlichnoe [Interaction of children with adults and with peers: the general and the specific]. In M.I. Lisina (Ed.), *Issledovaniia po problemam vozrastnoi i pedagogicheskoi psikhologii* [Studies in developmental and educational psychology] (pp. 3–32). Moskow: APN SSSR.

Nelson, K. (1973). Structure and strategy in learning to talk. *Monographs of the Society for Research in Child Development, 38* (1–2, Serial No 149).

Perret-Clermont, A.N. (1980). *Social interaction and cognitive development in children.* New York: Academic Press.

Perret-Clermont, A.N., & Brossard, A. (1985). On the interdigitation of social and cognitive process. In R.A. Hinde, A.N. Perret-Clermont, & J. Stevenson-Hinde (Eds.), *Social relationships and cognitive development* (pp. 309–327). Oxford, England: Clarendon Press.

Piaget, J. (1959). *The psychology of intelligence.* London: Routledge & Kegan Paul.

Ruzskaia, A.G. (1974). Otnoshenie detei doshkolnogo vozrasta k raznym variantam obshcheniia so vzroslymi [The attitude of preschool children toward variations in interaction with adults]. In A.V. Zaporozhec, & M.I. Lisina (Eds.), *Razvitie obshcheniia u doshkolnikov* [Development of interaction in preschoolers] (pp. 179–203). Moskow: Pedagogika.

Ruzshaia, A.G., & Reinstein, A.E. (1985). Rechdetei dvukh-semi let v obshchenii so vzroslym i so sverstnikom [The speech of two-to seven year olds in their interaction with adults and pears]. In L. Kolominskii, & M.I. Lisina (Eds.), *Geneticheski problemy sotsialnoi psikhologii* [Development problems of social psychology] (pp. 88–100). Minsk: Universitetskoe.

Schaffer, H.R. (1971). *The growth of sociability.* Harmondsworth, England: Penguin Booksj.

Schaffer, H.R. (1977). Early interactive development. In H.R. Schaffer (Ed.), *Studies in mother–infant interaction* (pp. 1–16). London: Academic Press.

Shugar, G.W. (1980, July). *Early child discourse analysed in the dyadic interaction unit.* Paper presented at 22nd International Congress of Psychology, Leipzig.

Talyzina, N. (1981). *The psychology of learning.* Moscow: Progress Publishers.

Thoman, E.G. (Ed.). (1979). *Origins of the infant's social responsiveness* Hillsdale, NJ: Erlbaum.

Trevarthen, C., Hubley, P., & Sheeran, L. (1975). Les activitès inèes du nourisson. *La recherche, 6,* (56), 447–458.
Valsiner, J. (1985). Theoretical issues of child development and the problem
of accident prevention. In T. Gärling, & J. Valsiner (Ed.), *Children within
environments: Toward a psychology of accident prevention* (pp. 1–28).
New York: Plenum.
Vygotsky, L.S. (1960). *Razvitie vysshikh psikhicheskikh funktsii* [The develop-
ment of higher psychological functions]. Moskow: APN RSFSR.
Vygotsky, L.S. (1976). Play and its role in the mental development of the child.
In J.S. Bruner, A. Jolla, & K. Sylva (Eds.), *Play, its role in development
and evolution* (pp. 537–555). Harmondsworthe, England: Penguin Books.
Vygotsky, L.S. (1977). Mišljenje i govor [Thinking and speech]. Beograd: Nolit.
Vygotsky, L.S. (1984). Voprosy detskoi psikhologii, In A.V. Zaporozhec (Ed.),
L.S. Vygotsky: Sobranie sochinenii (Vol. 4, pp. 244–385). Moskow: Pe-
dagogika. (Written in 1934).
Wertsch, J.V., McNamee, G.D., McLane, J.B., & Budwig, N.A. (1980). The
adult child dyad as a problem-solving system. *Child Development, 51,*
1215–1221.
Wertsch, J.V., & Sammarco, J.G. (1985). Social precursors to individual cognitive functioning. The problem of units of analysis. In R.A. Hinde, A.N.
Perret-Clermont, & J. Stevenson-Hinde (Eds.), *Social relationships and
cognitive development* (pp. 276–293). Oxford, England: Clarendon Press.
Yarrow, L.J., & Anderson, B.J. (1979). Procedures for studying parent infant
interaction: A critique. In E.B. Thoman (Ed.), *Origins of the infant's
social responsiveness* (pp. 209–225). Hillsdale, NJ: Erlbaum.

1) A – *the affective domain*
   Definition: The expression, cognition, control and exchange of emotions
   code A⟋ (a_1): – the mother names the child's emotion
   – the mother directs the child as to the emotional attitude he or she should have towards something
   – the mother enables the child to control his or her emotions

   code A⟶ (a_2): – the affective exchange of the same emotion
   – complementary affective exchange
   e.g., comforting the child when he or she is sad, calming him or her, etc.

   code A⟱ (a_3): – the mother asks for the child to control his or her emotions, which he or she cannot do
   e.g., the child is afraid of the dark and the mother tells him or her how misconceived this is
   – the mother attempts to name complex emotional states which the child does not yet have (confusion, envy, etc.)

   code A⟍ (a_4): – the mother answers the child's negative emotion with a negative or inarticulate emotion (she reacts like the child itself)
   – the mother does not have a consistent attitude toward the child's emotional expression; she does not articulate her attitude clearly
   – the mother tolerates or even initiates a primitive expression of affect

   code A. (b_1): – the mother does not notice the child's emotion

2) SM – *the sensori-motor domain*
   Definition: Sensori-motor activities and schemes of sensori-motor intelligence
   code SM⟋ (a_1): – introducing schemes which the child does not perform yet independently, but is able to master with the help of the adult
   – combining simpler schemes into more complex ones

   code SM⟶ (a_2): – initiating and supporting the sensori-motor schemes recently mastered by the child

   code SM⟱ (a_3): – introducing a scheme which the child is unable to perform even with the help of the adult
   – posing a sensori-motor problem (sensori-motor intelligence) which cannot even be understood as a problem by the child

code SM↘ (a_4) – interrupting well developed sensori-motor activities of the child
– initiating sensori-motor activities which are more primitive than those which the child has already mastered

code SM. (b_1) – not noticing the sensori-motor activities of the child

3) S_{SM} – *the social-sensorimotor domain*
Definition: The exploration of the physical characteristics of persons (touching the face, hair, playing with hands, etc.)

code S_{SM}↗ (a_1) – the mother introduces a more complex scheme of exploration
e.g., makes faces while the child explores her face

code S_{SM}→ (a_2) – the mother supports the exploratory activities in the child
e.g., she offers her face for exploration-nibbles the finger he or she puts into her mouth

code S_{SM}↗ (a_3) – the mother asks the child to perform too complex social sensorimotor activities
e.g., the mother asks the child to show parts of her face in the mirror

code S_{SM}↘ (a_4) – the mother interrupts the child's exploration
e.g., while the child is exploring the mother's face with his or her hand, the mother turns her head or constrains his or her hand

code S_{SM}• (b_1) – the mother doesn't notice the social sensori-motor activities of the child

4) S – *the social domain*
Definition: Interest for the obervers or the cameraman (paying attention to the observers, trying to establish a contact with them, flirting with observers). Always is interpreted as an artifact of the situation and is omitted from further analysis

5) S_C – *the social communicative domain*
Definition: The skill to send and receive messages, the ability to exchange information. Includes the following components:
1. an understanding and acceptance of the complementary roles of the sender and receiver;
2. the development of a number of means which mediate communication.

code S_c↗ (a_1) – the mother interprets behavior which does not have the meaning of a message as a message, and formulates this message
– the mother elaborates the child's simpler message and answers it only after that

- the mother will not accept a primitively formulated message but demands of the child a reformulation
- the mother adapts the message to the child, but also introduces means which he or she has not as yet mastered

code S_c → (a_2)
- the mother understands the message as the child gives it, but does not try to articulate it any further
- the mother sends the child a message using those means which have already been mastered by the child, i.e., in the same way in which the child would do it himself or herself

code S_c ↗ (a_3)
- the mother expresses the message without using the context
- the mother bombards the child with messages
- the mother demands a too complex articulation of the message of the child

code S_c ↘ $a_4)$
- the mother does not support and even hinders the child's attempts to express a clear message
e.g., the child says "Wah" (Want), and mother replies "Wah, wah, my baby barks!"
- the mother expresses one thing verbally and another thing nonverbally

code S_c • (b_1)
- the mother does not notice the message sent

6) S_R – *the domain of social-ritual behavior*
Definition: All immediate imitations and those behaviors which cannot certainly be identified as symbolical. This category comprises behavior performed in an almost ritual way and triggered both by verbal and nonverbal signals. It is very possible that these social rituals are culture-specific
e.g., the child is asked "Where does the bunny drink water?", and he or she should show the palm of his or her hand with his or her other index finger.

code S_R ↗ (a_1)
- the learning of new social rituals or the perfection of already learned ones

code S_R → (a_2)
- the initiation and support of already adopted rituals

code S_R ↗ (a_3)
- insisting that the child should perform a ritual perfectly or that he or she immediately perform something which he or she has only begun learning

code S_R ↘ (a_4)
- the mother interrupts the child's ritualized activity

code S_R • (b_1)
- the mother does not react to the ritualized behavior started by the child on his or her own

7) Sy – *the domain of symbolical activity*
Definition: Behaviors which suppose the existence of any kind of mental representation
e.g., symbolical games, delayed imitation, memory, etc.

code Sy⟋ (a₁)   – the initiation of symbolical activities which can be performed by the child only with the adult's help, or the elaboration of the existing ones

– the attribution of symbolical meaning to nonsymbolical activity

code Sy⟶ (a₂)   – the initiation and support of the symbolical activities already mastered by the child (but which are not below the child's actual level of development)

code Sy⬈ (a₃)   – the mother introduces symbolical behavior which is far above the child's actual developmental capabilities

code Sy⬂ (a₄)   – the mother interrupts or hinders some symbolical activity of the child's

– the mother pushes the child into more primitive forms of play than he or she already engages in

code Sy . (b₁)   – the mother interprets and comments on symbolical activity as if it were nonsymbolical

– the mother does not participate in the child's symbolical activities

8) M – *the domain of motor behavior*

Definition: Gross motor behavior, not yet totally automatized.

          e.g., independent standing, crawling, walking, jumping, etc.

code M⟋ (a₁)   – the initiation of more complex physical activities than those already mastered by the child

– the voluntary control of the motor behavior which is spontaneously easy to perform

e.g., at 1.0 demand to raise hands and feet upon command (verbally guided gymnastics)

code M⟶ (a₂)   – the creation of conditions for and the support of all those activities for which the child is developmentally mature

code M⬈ (a₃)   – a demand concerning motor behavior which is far surpassing the child's actual level of development

code M⬂ (a₄)   – treating the child as an object

e.g., the mother carries the child, moves the child's hand for him or her

– hindering and interrupting a motor action

code M • (b₁)   – ignoring the motor component of some behavior when it is of importance for the child

9) F – *the domain of physical care*

Definition: Activities of taking care of the child physically when they are at the center of attention.

          e.g., diapering, feeding, nose-wiping, toilet training, etc.

code F⟋ (a₁)   – the mother insists on the child's independent performance of some care-taking activities or on his or her active cooperation

           – care-taking activities, followed by adjusted explana-
             tions of why something is being done

code F⟶ (a_2) – the mother's behavior is adjusted to the child's ability
             to understand what is going on
              e.g., the child participates in the diapering (raises his
                or her feet, turns on his or her side, etc.)

code F↗ (a_3) – mother's exaggerated expectations in terms of the
             child's independence and cooperation in care-taking
             activities

code F↘ (a_4) – treating the child as the object of care, even when
             he or she is able to cooperate
            – keeping the child from satisfying some physical need

code F. (b_1) – the mother does not notice or does not react to the
             child's physical needs

10) L – *the language domain*
    Definition: Verbal communication between mother and child (L), the
             child's vocalization (V), and mother's affective speech (AS).
             The last category includes that kind of mother's speech which
             does not aim at transmitting a message but serves solely the
             purpose of an emotional exchange.
               e.g., "Honey, sweetheart, pet . . ."
             Note: Affective speech (AS) and vocalization (V) are recorded
             without the annotation signifying the character of interaction
             of the pair, and serve as data for a further detailed analysis
             of language development. The remaining language behavior
             was recorded with the annotation of its developmental di-
             rectedness, but was also left out of the analysis because
             language accompanies the behavior of almost all pairs (an
             almost universal domain) and because in almost all the pairs
             it is in the zone of proximal development. Therefore, the
             differences between the pairs ought to be analyzed differently
             in the language domain than in other domains.

CHAPTER 5

Getting to Know Strangers: Toddlers' Construction of Relationships*

Paula E. Hill and Jaan Valsiner

Department of Psychology
University of North Carolina

Human beings establish, maintain, and end relationships with others all through their lives. This activity is made possible by the support from their culturally organized environments. The ways in which interpersonal relations are established and maintained, as well as the environmental settings in which that establishment and maintenance takes place, are structured by the culture.

From the developmental perspective, the establishment and maintenance of interpersonal relationships constitutes a social skill the basic structure of which is provided by the culture through the mediation of the people who surround the developing child. These people—parents, grandparents, older siblings, caregivers, peers, teachers, etc.—play a twofold role in the development of children's interpersonal skills. On the one hand, their presence creates necessities for the child to establish new relationships and maintain existing ones. The caregivers arrange the child's meeting of previously unfamiliar other children and adults and regulate the ways in which the children establish new relationships with them. Thus, the *goals* and *opportunities* for relationship formation

* The research reported here was supported by a Sigma Xi grant-of-aid to the first author, and by the University of North Carolina Junior Faculty Development Award to the second author. A preliminary version of this paper was presented at the International Conference on Infant Studies, New York, on April, 6, 1984. The authors want to express their gratitude to Pamela D. Fleming, Nina E. Tracy, Rebecca Peterson, Claudia Mackie, and Sammy Hill for their help in different phases of the research project.

are provided to the children originally by their caregivers. On the other hand, it is also the *means* of relationship formation that caregivers introduce to the children. They provide assistance to the developing child in his or her learning the complicated system of regulation of interpersonal relations, by canalizing the developing social skills of relationship formation towards culturally acceptable forms.

By the time children become competent members of their culture, they are ready to use culture-provided environmental and normative "resources" of the regulation of interpersonal relationships in flexible ways, taking into account both the characteristics of the partners and those of the settings in which the relationship exists. In the present chapter, we address the issue of the ontogenetic beginnings of children's development of interpersonal action strategies. This issue brings us down on the age scale to the second year of life (toddlerhood). We will first analyze the major theoretical issues of the development of interpersonal skills of relationship formation, and then illustrate those by empirical evidence from a naturalistic experimental study.

THE CONTEXT: CULTURAL EXPECTATIONS FOR CHILDREN'S SOCIABILITY

The ontogenetic timetable for children's establishment of new social relationships is determined by the cultural knowledge about when, how, and whom the developing child is expected to meet. The relevance of the cultural meaning systems in this respect becomes explicit in contexts where parents from different cultures meet. The following example provides an illustration:

> In a small Italian town, a visiting American mother is preparing to take her toddler to the city park, with the intention of "giving her child the opportunity to play with other children." When she announces her intention to take the child to the park, her Italian landlords are puzzled, and suggest that the child can play in their yard instead. The mother's explanation that she wants her child to meet "new" children is met by amused irony—who on earth, in one's sound mind, wants one's toddler to meet unfamiliar children!

Differences between cultures in caregivers' structuring of their children's relationships with others that closely resemble our example have been documented elsewhere in greater detail (see Wolfenstein, 1955). Parents in any culture operate on the basis of folk models that provide them with guidance for what to expect from children at a given age, and how to treat these children. Research on folk models of parenting has revealed intricate cultural timetables of ages at which children are perceived to be capable of different tasks (Harkness & Super, 1983; Super & Harkness, 1986). The age-graded perception of children's capacities is functional for integration of children's activities into the web of the life of the family and community by delegating to them some tasks that they can carry out, and that are relevant for the common good. Children in any culture are involved in everyday chores of the family (see Goodnow, in press), and childhood labor has been used widely in our cultural history.

The integration of developing children into the culture by providing them with communally relevant tasks to perform creates the conditions under which the children have to interact with different people, many of whom are at first unfamiliar. The nature of particular tasks allotted to children determines the nature of their new relationships. Thus, a toddler who participates (together with an adult) in begging activity in a public place will have to submerge his or her new relationships with potential "donors" to the goals of that activity. Likewise, a child who is given the task of selling products at a market has to let the goals of this activity dominate his or her relationships with the unfamiliar (and familiar) people who are expected to become buyers. In a similar vein, children who take part in peripatetic entertainment routines (see Berland, 1982) are expected to develop social skills that allow them to monitor the sentiment in the audience. It is in the context of children's inclusion in the relevant life activities of their families that their interaction skills develop—along the lines charted out by cultural norms.

Cultural Organization of the Development of Children's Interpersonal Skills

The ways in which children's interpersonal skills develop are structured by the cultural expectations of what children are capable (and expected) of doing at different ages, and by the norms of organizing interpersonal relations (between adults, children and adults, and between children) in the culture. These expectations and norms provide for the culturally structured social environments that children are exposed to during their childhoods. They can observe how adults interact with other adults; they learn to interact with adults in culturally appropriate ways. Even their interaction with their peers is culturally organized. In different cultures, these three facets of social interaction can be organized in highly variable ways.

Developing children are necessarily participant observers of the ways in which adults interact with other adults—spouses, relatives, friends, acquaintances of different sex and social status, etc. The opportunity for observational learning about adults' interaction rules is all-pervasive in the lives of children, since every important aspect of organization of their life events is connected with coordinated actions of their caregivers. In other terms—children's development within any culture is *collectively organized,* and the majority of adult–adult interactive episodes that perform the task of such organization can be observed by the children.

The interaction between adults and children is likewise culturally regulated—by social norms pertaining to the form of interaction, and by cultural understanding of its content. As far as the form of interaction is concerned, many cultures limit children's freedom of initiating contact with adults in general, and with unfamiliar, and high-status adults in particular (Wills, 1977). On the side of the content of child–adult discourse, culture structures the adults' *meaning* that they attach to children's actions at large (Leis, 1982) and interaction efforts in particular (see Robinson, in this volume). If children's communication attempts are not considered to be meaningful, those can be ignored by adults. In contrast, if adults consider the vocalizations of very young children to be intentionally meaningful, they may become involved in seemingly "egalitarian" dialogues between adults and babies.

To summarize—the culturally structured life environments of developing children provide the framework within which children's individually specific skills of interacting with others become established. The children are seen by the adults as being capable of different actions at different ages. Given the usefulness of that perceived capacity from the perspective of the adults, children may become participants in the adult life tasks when they are given responsibilities to fulfill those. Their experiences, however, are at first embedded in the context of social relationships within the family and its kinship group, and only later branch beyond the sphere of familiar environmental settings. Thus, the first unfamiliar persons whom the infant and toddler meets are likely to be relatives and family friends, whose benevolent attitude towards the child is beyond doubt. It is the context of family relationships that serves as the basis for the child's establishment of novel ties with previously unknown people.

CHILDREN'S SOCIAL RELATIONSHIPS AND ATTACHMENT RESEARCH

Most of the knowledge available in contemporary child psychology about children's social relationships has been a by-product of psychologists' interest in attachment. In the framework of attachment research, different aspects of children's social relationships have received uneven coverage. For example, the *quality* of *children's* relationships with their attachment figures has been the major theme of empirical investigations, whereas the topic addressed in this chapter—the process of establishment of toddlers' social relationships—happens to be studied quite rarely within that research tradition. Even within the line of research that has purposefully emphasized the role of caregivers as facilitators of infants' exploration of their environment (Anderson, 1972; Hay, 1977; Rheingold, 1969, 1985; Rheingold & Eckerman, 1969, 1970; Ross, Rheingold, & Eckerman, 1972), it is the exploration of physical rather than social environment that has overwhelmingly been in the focus of investigators' attention. Only rarely has infants' and toddlers' approach to novel persons been subjected to systematic investigation (see Ross & Goldman, 1977a,b). What can be the reasons for such unequal coverage of equally interesting research topics? An analysis of the attachment theory and of the ways in which attachment has been studied empirically will provide some tentative answers to that question.

The Status of "Attachment" in Developmental Psychology

Historically, attachment theory is a direct outcome of developments within the psychoanalytic school of thought. Bowlby was an experienced child psychiatrist with a psychoanalytic background long before he invented the "attachment theory." He had done substantial work in the area of disrupted family relationships and their adverse effects on children's personality development (see Bowlby, 1944, 1951). As a result of the psychoanalytic background of Bowlby's thinking, the structure of attachment theory resembles the ideas of Karen Horney to a great extent (Feiring, 1983). More directly, Bowlby himself recognized his indebtedness to Therese Benedek of the "Hungarian School" of psychoanalysis (Bowlby, 1958, p. 358). The clinical background of the other leading figure of contemporary attachment research—Mary Ainsworth—is likewise obvious in her classic work on attachment in Uganda (Ainsworth, 1967).

The psychoanalytic core of Bowlby's attachment theory serves as the foundation for the two "layers" of thought that were later superimposed on it. First, the ethological emphasis was added to the psychoanalytic basis to form the attachment theory (Bowlby, 1958). As Bowlby himself recollects, a friend recommended Konrad Lorenz's animal research to him in the Summer of 1951 (Bowlby, 1980b, p. 649). He was particularly fascinated by the emphasis of ethology on behavioral observations of animals in their real-life environments. Ethology also provided Bowlby with theoretical possibilities to argue for the biological significance of attachment relationships, and their basis— observable attachment behaviors.

The link of Bowlby's attachment theory with cognitive psychology— more particularly with control systems theory—was a later addition to the theory (see Bowlby, 1969). It followed the increasing popularity of psychological explanations that emphasized goal-orientation and self-correction on the way towards goals sought by a person (Miller, Galanter, & Pribram, 1960). The control-systems terminology that Bowlby has been using has not become widely popular among attachment researchers. However, it is particularly that perspective which is of theoretical relevance for the present investigation of toddlers' contact establishment with strangers.

The "attachment bond" and its maintenance. Influence of the work of Benedek relates Bowlby's thinking with the continental-European traditions of developmental psychology of the 1920s–1930s, particularly with the work of Charlotte Bühler and Hildegard Hetzer (see Benedek, 1938). Benedek introduced the idea that emotional relationships with significant others serve as the basis for exploration of the world. She emphasized the relevance of the mother–child "symbiotic bond" and the relevance of clinging or following in the establishment of that bond.

Once the attachment bond has been formed, it provides affective flavor to all other aspects of the child's development, while remaining itself in a homeostatically regulated form, at least for a while. In this respect, an ontogenetic timetable for the formation and maintenance of child–mother relationships that Bowlby provided prior to his invention of attachment theory in the mid-1950s is revealing:

(a) The phase during which the infant is in course of establishing a relation with a clearly identified person—his mother; this is normally achieved by five or six months of age.
(b) The phase during which he needs her as an ever-present companion; this usually continues until about his third birthday.
(c) The phase during which he is becoming able to maintain a relationship with her in absentia. During the fourth and fifth years such a relationship can only be maintained in favourable circumstances and for a few days or weeks at a time; after seven or eight the relationship can be maintained, though not without strain, for a period of a year or more. (Bowlby, 1952, p. 53)

This developmental schedule, which remains present in contemporary attachment research, demonstrates why there has been rather little interest in toddlers' and young children's ways of establishment of new social relationships. First, since the primary attachment relationship is said to form in infancy, when the child's role in it is limited to the set of maturing behavioral means (crying, smiling, following—by gaze and locomotion, etc.), it is the caregiver's caring of the child that leads in the relationship formation. The relevance of the opportunities provided by the caregivers fits well with Bowlby's world-renowned analyses of the effects of parental deprivation on child development (Bowlby, 1951, 1952). When the child's behavioral opportunities develop so that he *can* establish new relationships with other people (e.g., in toddlerhood), it is expected (in the normal case) that the child's already-formed attachment to the mother dominates his or her actions ("he needs her as an ever-present companion"). Consequently—toddlers' active efforts to establish new relationships with others are viewed as secondary in importance to the task of maintaining the attachment bond. Once these new relationships are developing, they are expected to be based on the previous attachment bonds, which are assumed to determine the nature of the new relationships.

Empirical directions in contemporary attachment research. Contemporary empirical attachment research has proceeded in directions rather different from the psychodynamic emphasis on the process of emotional ties that Benedek and Bowlby advocated. Largely bridging the gap between the phenomena-orientation of clinicians and the traditions of psychological measurement, attachment research in the last decade has addressed a number of relatively traditional issues, mostly with little hope of finding new solutions to those. For example, the problem of stability of attachment patterns in populations over age (Bates, Maslin, & Frankel, 1985; Lamb, Thompson, Gardner, & Charnov, 1985; Thompson, Lamb, & Estes, 1982), and also their influence across tasks (Erickson, Sroufe, & Egeland, 1985; Suess, Escher-Graeub, & Grossmann, 1985; Van der Veer & Van IJzendoorn, this volume), cross-cultural differences in the distributions of attachment types (Grossmann, Grossmann, Huber, & Wartner, 1981; Sagi & Koren, 1985; Van IJzendoorn, Tavecchio, Goossens, Vergeer, & Swaan, 1983), and interobserver consistency in diagnosis of attachment categories (Sagi & Lamb, 1985) have been among favorite topics of empirical study.

Most of the studies of attachment have assumed that the attachment between the child and the attachment figure is already established in some qualitative form by the age in which most of the attachment research is done (8–24 months). Therefore, the attachment "type" of a child is expected to be stable (in psychologists' jargon—"reliable"). When a fixed status of attachment is assumed to be the case, it becomes reasonable to study the ways in which these stable attachment conditions relate to other aspects of child development and parenting. The earlier process of attachment formation (in infancy) may include reference to behavior patterns that serve as species-specific "building blocks" with the help of which attachments are constructed and maintained in interaction between the infant and the adult(s). That interaction is not that between equals, though. The adults are expected to arrange appropriate opportunities for the child to become involved in attachment formation. Hence the relevance of the *caregivers'* provision of contact with the babies for the establishment of attachment bonds that has been strongly emphasized in the pertinent research literature (Kennell & Klaus, 1984; Kennell, Voos, & Klaus, 1979; Klaus & Kennell, 1976; Myers, 1984a, b). The dangers of infants' deprivation from contact with parents, real or imaginary, seem to remain a metatheoretical motivating force for much of the contemporary thinking about attachment.

Attachment: static essence or process? Different attachment researchers proceed in somewhat different directions in their thinking about attachment in the second year of life, depending on whether they emphasize the *process* or *state* of attachment between the child and the attachment figure. The first line of thought—concentrating on the process of maintenance and transformation of attachment relationships—is rooted in Bowlby's (1969) introduction of concepts from control systems theory into his theory. Ainsworth's earlier studies were likewise rich in process descriptions of attachment (Ainsworth, 1967). Along similar lines, other investigators have proposed formal schemes that are to explain the process of attachment maintenance (Bischof, 1975; Bretherton, 1985; Bretherton & Ainsworth, 1974) and change in ontogeny (Sroufe, 1979; Sroufe & Fleeson, 1986). The second line of thinking treats attachment relationships as entities that vary within population, and can therefore be studied using the interindividual reference frame (see Valsiner, 1987). Different children are viewed to have established, and currently maintain, attachment relationships of different kinds, that can be classified into different types (A, B, C, and their subtypes). This perspective on attachment deals with it as a stable *state* that varies across children. Not surprisingly, many attachment researchers who have taken this perspective have often attributed the status of *trait* to the attachment types (see analyses of this transition in Blurton Jones, Ferreira, Brown, & Moore, 1980; Waters & Deane, 1982, 1985). The focus on attachment as a state (or trait) leads investigators to questions that emphasize the stability and deterministic functions of the existing attachments rather than the child's construction of new relationships. The deterministic role of the past relationships renders developmental continuity a sought-after empirical phenomenon for attachment researchers who view attachment as a homeostatic state.

For them, developmental discontinuity in the attachment type distribution over age in a population can be seen as an unwelcome indication of the irrelevance of past experiences for the children's future. In this, the state-perspective on attachment is not different from other predeterministic views on development as unfolding of maturational or imprinted developmental "schedules." Such (nondevelopmental) transformation of attachment theory has little in common with Bowlby's version of the control-systems view on attachment process (see below), and largely falls into line with the working models of earlier psychoanalysis.

The nondevelopmental approach to attachment in the second year of life is concerned with "reliable" and valid "measurement" of different children's attachment states (traits). The developmental consequences of these states are discussed and sometimes studied in longitudinal research projects. Theoretically, attachment types distinguished in the second year of life are expected to direct the further development of children into different trajectories in years to come—hence the interest of contemporary attachment researchers in epigenetic views on development (see Bretherton & Waters, 1985). However, the process of maintenance of these attachments as relationships during the second year, as well as efforts to transcend them, have been rarely of interest. Nevertheless, the standard measurement setting of attachment researchers—the "Strange Situation"—provides ample opportunities for the study of the process of attachment maintenance.

Attachment measurement and the process of relationship formation. The standard situation in which attachment states of children are habitually diagnosed was introduced by Ainsworth and Wittig (1969) and given careful elaboration over the 1970s. It consists of eight short episodes, most of which are 3 minutes long, during which the presence of mother and a stranger in the experimental room with toys is varied by design. The procedure is aimed at triggering in the child behavior patterns usual for the child at separation and reunion with the mother (see Ainsworth, Blehar, Waters, & Wall, 1978, p. 37). On the one hand, the Strange Situation is a laboratory version of children's everyday life events, in which they are at times separated from their caregivers. Sometimes such separation involves the caregiver leaving the child with another adult of lesser familiarity to the child. However, it needs to be pointed out that the occurrence of leaving a child with an unfamiliar person not known to the caregiver is an unlikely event in the child's life. The Strange Situation, however, necessarily involves the participation of a stranger who is previously unfamiliar to both the child and the mother. This fits the role of the stranger in this setting as an experimental means the role of which is to accentuate the existing attachment of the child towards the caregiver by triggering explicit attachment behaviors in the former.

Thus, the Strange Situation is a setting modelled after children's everyday lives, but purposefully modified to fit the goals of attachment measurement—the establishment of a given child's attachment type. A paradox common to all psychological measurement procedures is inherent in the Strange Situation. On the one hand, it is expected to be sufficiently valid ecologically to trigger phenomena of attachment in the child. Therefore, the setting has to be quite complex, involving the possibility that "noise" (in the form of unexpected events in the behavior of the child, and the mother) might occur. On the other hand, it has to be maximally standardized so as to satisfy criteria of traditional measurement in the rest of psychology.

As can be seen from this analysis of the Strange Situation, the misfit between the traditional ideal of psychological measurement—that of closed systems—and the open-systemic reality of the situation itself is central to child psychologists' utilization of that measurement situation. The open-systems nature of the Strange Situation is dutifully reflected in its standard description, where Episodes 4–7 can be of different length, given the state of the child when left alone, or the length of time it takes for the child to become re-involved in play with the mother at reunion (Ainsworth et al., 1978, p. 37).

One of the aspects that is often documented in the Strange Situation context, and which reflects the open-systems nature of that situation, is child's wariness towards the "stranger." Despite the designed use of the stranger in the situation to trigger the child's attachment behavior towards the caregiver by way of stranger-wariness, that wariness can be described (from the perspective of the adults) as situation-specific (Sroufe, Waters, & Matas, 1974). This practically means that no standard aspect of the Strange Situation elicits it from all children in a systematic manner. Despite the circumstances used in many laboratory procedures that are explicitly set up to elicit wariness in infants (e.g., Clarke-Stewart, 1978; Maccoby & Jacklin, 1973; Stern & Bender, 1974), that phenomenon occurs only in some of the children at some unpredictable times. The role of the "stranger" in eliciting wariness in the Strange Situation cannot be taken for granted. In fact, Eckerman and Rheingold (1974) reported smiling and visual regard to be common among 10-month-old infants who were left in a room together with an unfamiliar person and toys. No distress in such a challenging *exploration* situation was documented to be present among infants. In a similar vein, working with older (24- to 26-month-old) children, Takahashi (1982) found that half of the children in her sample showed the "stranger" toys, and one third of the subjects approached the "stranger"—without any signs of wariness.

It is the open systems nature of the Strange Situation that makes it in principle inapplicable as a "measurement setting" for attachment in the sense of traditional ideals of closed-systems research methodology. Although for the attachment researchers of the modern days it is claimed to serve sufficiently for classifying children into attachment types, the challenges that this situation furnishes from the children's viewpoint are very different. First and foremost, from the perspective of the child, the Strange Situation is a setting where new demands for adaptation to the environment—integrating objects and persons in the setting— are faced by the child. That adaptation can take different forms that vary across children, and across occasions of the same child. Some children some of the time display attachment behaviors towards the caregiver at his or her departure and return. Others try to engage the "stranger" in interaction, sometimes depending on the "stranger"— caregiver interaction that the child could observe, and at other times irrespective of that interaction. Still some other children may ignore the comings and goings of the caregiver and the "stranger," and con- centrate on the exploration of the toys and acting with those, as a means to adapt to the Strange Situation. All these three basic ways of children's adaptation to that situation are equally realistic, and have been documented in various studies reported in the attachment liter- ature. For the particular purposes of the present chapter, however, only one of the three adaptation mechanisms—that of child's strategies to engage the "stranger" in interaction—is relevant. Much of the little that we know about toddlers' establishment of relationships with others emerges as a side-story from existing reports in studies where the Strange Situation has been used.

Existing knowledge about development of children's social skills. Strictly speaking, the development of toddlers' exploration of novel adults is preceded by orientation behavior towards unfamiliar persons in early infancy (Heymer, 1980). Of course, after the formation of the attachment bond with the caregiver(s) by the third quarter of the first year of life, the infant begins to use the caregiver as a base from the confidence of which he or she explores his or her surroundings. In this respect, the attachment figure ceases to be the object of infant's social interaction, and becomes part of the *context* within which the child explores the surroundings and establishes novel social relationships (Cairns, 1972). Many of these novel relationships are necessary as a part of the young organism's adaptation to changing circumstances (see Cairns, 1977), but some may transcend the immediate adaptational needs and constitute part of the child's own active construction of self through interaction with others.

Research on attachment has provided an occasional access to phenomenology of child–"stranger" interaction. Interesting observations of the process aspect of child–adult attachment and contact-making with strangers have emerged as a by-product of the Strange Situation research. Thus, in Episode 3 (which usually involves a 3-minute-long presence of the stranger in the room with the mother and baby for the first time), children's exploration of, and efforts to establish contact with, the stranger have been well documented:

> Most infants could be described as being in a state of conflict between wary/fearful behavior and sociable behavior, both of which were activated by the stranger. Some behavior could be interpreted as expressing both of the conflicting systems simultaneously—for example, coy behavior, intention movements, and tentative responses to the stranger's offer of a toy. In other behavior, the competing tendencies alternated, as for example when approach to the stranger was followed immediately by rapid movement away from her usually toward the mother. In the latter case, attachment behavior was clearly involved in the conflict, as it was also in instances in which the infant, wary/fearful of the stranger, retreated to the mother as a secure haven from which vantage point he turned to examine the stranger, still wary of her. Attachment behavior was eventually overridden by sociable behavior (or possibly by a combination of sociable and exploratory behavior) in most infants, who were attracted away from the mother by the stranger's inviting him to play with the toy she offered. Wary behavior continued to conflict with the exploratory and/or sociable behavior, however, for few infants in Episode 3 did more than tentatively reach toward the stranger's toy. (Ainsworth et al., 1978, p. 281)

The full context of children's stranger-contacting phenomenology in Episode 3 of the standard Strange Situation should be kept in mind. That episode is divided into three stages, each lasting 1 minute. The first two stages involve no effort by the stranger to initiate interaction with the baby. Thus, Ainsworth et al.'s (1978) observation about the fact that attachment behaviour in this episode was (in most cases) overridden by children's sociable behavior is a remarkable testimony to the young children's contact-making with a stranger in a strongly limited time frame (2 minutes of the 3-minute Episode 3). Similar results have been obtained in other studies where investigators have been alert to children's behaviors directed towards the stranger. Bretherton (1978), for example, found that, in her sample of 48 twelve-month olds, the overwhelming majority (46) of the children smiled at the stranger at least once in the first 2 minutes of the Episode 3 (which in that study lasted 8 minutes) of the Strange Situation. Thirty-two of the infants were observed to show or offer the stranger a toy during the 8-minute episode, whereas only 19 of the children accepted the stranger's first offer of a toy towards the beginning of the episode. Similar findings have been obtained by Ignjatovic-Savic (1986)—12 of 21 9-month-olds, 17 (of 19) 12-month-olds, and 15 (out of 19) 18-month-olds in her sample displayed active efforts to contact the "stranger" at least in one of the five conditions of action pre-set for the "stranger" in the situation. However, only 4 of the 17 15-month-olds demonstrated active interest in the unfamiliar persons. The establishment of the child's contact with the stranger has been shown to be regulated by the contingency of the stranger's actions given those of the child (Levitt, 1980). In case of an unresponsive "stranger," 12-month-olds may only briefly try to establish proximity with him or her (Ross, 1975). When the "stranger" played a more active role in relation to the 11- to 13-month-olds, 25 (of 32) infants would at some time touch the stranger during 4-minute experimental sessions (in contrast, only 2 of 32 infants touched a "passive" stranger under otherwise comparable conditions—Ross & Goldman, 1977a).

The development of exploration by infants and toddlers is closely linked with the presence of the caregiver. While leaving the caregiver will later be important for the preservation of the individual and even the species (Rheingold & Eckerman, 1970), near the end of the first year the infant prefers to have the caregiver present while he wanders. When in the Strange Situation, year-old infants show an increase in exploratory behavior when the mother is present. Her absence depresses exploration and increases the incidence of attachment behaviors (Ainsworth & Bell, 1970). Not only is the mere presence of the mother important for exploration, but her presence also provides emotional flavor to the exploratory activities. In a laboratory situation, Sorce and Emde (1981) found that 15-month-old toddlers displayed less pleasure and exploration when their mothers were reading than when they paid attention to the children. The infants of the mothers who were reading remained closer to the caregiver, showed less active interest in their environment, and made fewer bids for attention.

Furthermore, the Strange Situation is not a setting where the child is involved with two separate dyadic encounters with adults, one known and the other new. Rather, it is a triadic situation in which the child has immediate access to information of how the two adults relate to each other. For example, Lewis and Feiring (1981) have described the ways in which both direct and indirect means of interaction between adults have an effect on the child's relationships. Direct means of interaction on the side of the adult would involve the child immediately, whereas the indirect means have no immediate input in the interaction. Not surprisingly, direct means are known to be stronger and more influential than the indirect ones, but the extent of the influence of the latter can still be present. Feiring, Lewis, and Starr (1984) examined this facet in 15-month-olds, using mothers and two unfamiliar women (Stranger 1 and Stranger 2) in a laboratory "Strange Situation." In one condition, the mother and Stranger 2 conversed as if they were close friends, while Stranger 1 remained aloof. In the second condition, the two strangers interacted in the same friendly manner with each other as had the mother and Stranger 2 in the first condition. In the last condition, all three remained aloof from each other and the child (pretended to read magazines). After that condition, Stranger 2 attempted to make friends with the child. It appeared that the first two conditions had indirectly affected the infants, who demonstrated less worry and greater willingness to interact with Stranger 2, than those infants who had been exposed to the third condition only. The reasons for such selectivity can be variable. When having to make a choice, an infant may prefer to interact with an unfamiliar woman who is relatively unoccupied, rather than try to interact with the other woman who is engaged in talking to the mother, when all the four are in the room together (Bretherton, Stolberg, & Kreye, 1981). This finding is also supported by the study of Fein (1975), in which 18-month-olds vocalized least and remained most distant when their mothers were conversing with an unfamiliar person, as compared to the condition in which the adults were playing a mock game or remaining silent. The toddlers were least distant in the game condition, suggesting the possibility that the nature of the mother–stranger interaction determines the child's conduct in the Strange Situation. Alternatively, as Beckwith (1972) has demonstrated, infants' responsiveness to one interaction partner (e.g., the mother) reduces responsiveness to the other ("stranger"). However, the children may be highly tuned to the nature of the relationships between the parent and the stranger. Clarke-Stewart (1978) attempted to address the issue of how the interaction between the "stranger" and the attachment figure in the Strange Situation affects the child in a more experimental way, varying the nature of interaction between the two adults. Children (within the age range 1–2.5 years) were subjected to conditions in which the two adults interacted in a hostile, neutral, or friendly way. Although these conditions were found not to demonstrate differences in the child's responsiveness to the "stranger," the children were seen more often close to the mother if she was interacting with a friendly "stranger."

All these studies have been phrased within the theoretical context of the attachment theory, and have therefore concentrated on caregiver *versus* "stranger" effects on the child's attachment behaviors. When viewed from the child's perspective, the "Strange Situation" may turn out a setting in which various phenomena that go beyond attachment may be embedded. For instance, the child in a "Strange Situation" can utilize the "stranger" in ways that go beyond the primary attachment bond. Klinnert, Emde, and Butterfield (1983) found that 1-year-olds can use unfamiliar persons as referent-agents when placed into a potentially frightening situation. In their study, the infants were confronted by a toy that was approaching them. Infants who had previously been involved in a short period of interaction with a "friendly" (smiling) "stranger" were observed to display signs of positive affect towards the approaching toy. In contrast, infants who had previously interacted with an "unfriendly stranger" (who had displayed to them signs of fear) were observed to display signs of negative affect at the approach of the toy.

As the preceding review reveals, information about toddlers' establishing contact with unfamiliar persons has been obtained by the use of the Strange Situation. That information, however, is mostly purely empirical and lacks rigorous theoretical analysis, which would be obligatory for any advance in developmental psychology. The presently available empirical information has been loosely connected even with the theory that is closest to the researchers of attachment—Bowlby's control-systems approach to the process of attachment.

Attachment Theory and Relationship Formation

Despite its basically homeostatic core, Bowlby's final version of his attachment theory is certainly not at all insensitive to the dynamic process that underlies attachment maintenance and transformation. His addition of basic ideas of control-systems theory to his previous synthesis of psychoanalysis and ethology made it possible to conceptualize the process of attachment in terms of child–adult interaction (Bowlby, 1969).

Goal-directedness and attachment behavior. The introduction of goal-directedness of behavior of both the child and the caregiver into attachment theory makes Bowlby's approach usable for the study of child's relationships with new persons. Although Bowlby—in line with his ontogenetic timetable of attachment that we outlined above—considers the set-goal of the attachment system in toddlerhood to be maintenance of proximity with the mother *in general* (Bowlby, 1969, p. 180), he understands the moment-to-moment flexibility of the child–adult relationships in particular cases. In the second year of life, the child is said to develop a "will of his own" which makes the attachment/exploration behavioral systems highly dynamic. The child is described as *changing* his goals:

> At one moment he is determined to sit on his mother's knee and nothing else will do; at another he is content to watch her through the doorway. In ordinary circumstances, it seems clear, whatever conditions are at any one time necessary to terminate his attachment behaviour become the set-goal of whatever attachment plan he adopts. Goal-directed attachment plans can vary in structure from being simple and swiftly executed to being something far more elaborate. The particular degree of complexity of a plan turns partly on the set-goal selected, partly on the subject's estimate of the situation obtaining between himself and his attachment figure, and partly on his skill in devising a plan to meet that situation. (Bowlby, 1969, p. 351)

As is evident from this conceptualization of the toddler's goal-oriented maintenance of the attachment by Bowlby, the particular behavioral form of attachment is highly situation- and goal-specific. Bowlby's theory relies heavily on the child's (and, of course, caregiver's) goal setting and goal changing as the guiding force that organizes the particular form that the attachment relationship takes within a given environment. However, it is exactly that emphasis on goal setting that makes it possible for Bowlby's theory to transcend its own limits. For example—instead of axiomatically accepting the idea that in toddler-hood the most general set-goal is the maintenance of proximity to the mother, the open-systemic nature of goal setting by the child and the mother allows for the development of other major set-goals. Consider a case in which the mother promotes the toddler's "making friends" with others—adults, older children, or peers. Under these conditions, the toddler may establish a set-goal of *establishment* of new relationships with any of these interaction partners. In this case, we may happen to observe a toddler actively engaging a peer or older child in interaction and maintaining proximity—with the mother's social facilitation pro-moting it on the background. Or, in the contrary case of adults' discouragement of the child's initiative of engaging unfamiliar adults in interaction with them, the child may internalize the expectancy of being wary of strangers. In either case, it is the culturally structured social environment of the child that canalizes the latter towards one or the other form of dealing with strangers.

Proximity maintenance versus flexibility in goal setting. The particular forms in which stranger-contacting occurs depend on the conditions of the given setting (e.g., presence of alarming events, rebuffs from others), of the child (fatigue, hunger, ill health, pain, cold), and of the role of the primary attachment figure in the setting (mother absent, departing, or discouraging of proximity—see Bowlby, 1969, p. 259). Bowlby's control-systems description of attachment relationships is thus open to the idea that dominance of attachment over exploration can be an episodic, context-dependent occurrence in our observations of toddlers. However, since maintenance of the proximity to the attachment figure is assumed to be the set goal for toddlers, the variability of behavioral observations does not indicate that the relationship may develop into new forms as the child explores the environment on the basis of confidence given by the mother. In essence, Bowlby's theory is axiomatically determined at its abstract level, whereas its treatment of actual phenomena retains and recognizes the dynamic and indeterministic nature of the interaction process. The implications of Bowlby's thinking about attachment come close to those by Piaget on cognition–affect relations (see Lightfoot, in this volume). In both cases, some aspects of the theoretical systems are set up as homeostasis-retaining machines, whereas both theorists are well versed in the immense richness of phenomena that go beyond the principle of balance restoration.

Structure of the Process of Relationship Formation

As we outlined above, research on attachment has largely been concentrated on the maintenance side of the toddler–caregiver attachment, paying only occasional attention to the other side of toddlers' social contacts—establishment of relationships with previously unfamiliar persons. We also showed that Bowlby's most recent theoretical system, based on control systems viewpoint, could in principle be used to explain how new social contacts emerge. However, the function of proximity maintenance as the set-goal in the second year of life—as Bowlby has set it up—does not allow for a productive use of his attachment theory for the study of toddlers' formation of relations.

How, then, could one conceptualize the establishment of a new social relationship by a toddler? Indeed, the previous relationship (attachment) to the caregiver(s) is a legitimate basis for any new relationship. We are here interested in the process by which a toddler's novel relationship develops over time of exposure to a person (adult) whom the child has not encountered before, while the parent is present. The child–parent attachment can be taken for granted as the basis of confidence for the child's overtures towards the stranger. How, then, is the new relationship constructed by the child, with the assistance of the adults?

Joint-action mediation in relationship formation. The core idea of our theoretical conceptualization of toddlers' contact-establishment with unfamiliar adults is the joint action mediation of the interaction process. The role of child–adult(s) joint action becomes evident as a necessary part of the system that regulates child–environment relationships. Toddlers are constantly in the process of actively exploring their environments. The latter oftentimes include human objects, who become targets for exploration. The toddlers, after exploration of people from a distance, may try to involve these adults in joint action with them as a means of establishing new relationships. The particular occurrence of toddlers' effort to engage new persons in joint action is canalized by the caregivers who—in accordance with cultural expectations—either facilitate or suppress the child's initiative in making contact with a new adult. In this respect, toddlers' new relationships are the result of joint action of the children, their caregivers, and the novel persons.

The toddlers' actions in exploration of their environments constitute a temporal chain—the child moves from actions with one object to that with another, to a third object, and so on and so forth. A new adult can be turned an object of investigation by the exploring toddler—in this case, the child approaches the adult and tries to engage him or her in interaction for a while, after which a return to some other object in the environment can occur in the toddler's action. Alternatively, the adult may try to gain the attention of the child, by initiating joint action with the object the child is currently acting with, or proposing an alternative object as the target for joint action. In this latter case, it depends on whether the toddler is ready to accept the adult's initiative or not. In the case of acceptance, the two may proceed with their joint action with the given object, or move (together) to joint action with a different object. If the child rejects the adult's initiative, then the child continues to act with the previous object *not* letting the adult intervene, or "escapes" to another object that the adult is currently not involved with.

Coordination of goal-oriented actions in the triad. The present theoretical description of the process of toddlers' contact-establishing with novel persons within their structured environments involves the notion that the toddler, the unfamiliar adult, and the caregiver are constantly setting goals for themselves that may involve inclusion of any of the other persons in the situation. Thus, the child may suddenly move away from solitary play with an object, go over to the mother and sit on her lap, and start "flirting" with the other adult. In this case we can imply that the child utilizes the "secure base" of mother as a part of his or her goal-directed effort to gain the attention of the other adult that could lead to the establishment of a new interaction routine. This change in the toddler's action may fit with the mother's goals (in case she is trying to facilitate the child's friendly interaction with the other adult), and she may introduce suggestions or demands on the child to move ahead in contacting the stranger. Alternatively, if she is interested in suppressing the child's interest in the other adult for some reason (e.g., the mother and the other adult are in the middle of a serious discussion, and the mother does not want to diverge from that into child-oriented discourse), she can attempt to redirect the toddler's object of activity by trying to draw the child's attention to another object in the environment. The actions of the other adult are then crucial for the success of the mother's goal-directed effort. That adult may himself or herself facilitate the toddler's initiative by responding favorably to it—thus possibly becoming engaged in an interaction episode. Or, alternatively, the other adult may be unwilling to be disturbed by the child's initiative and chooses to ignore it. The coordination of the goals of the three participants is therefore the main mechanism through which the toddler's novel relationship with a previously unfamiliar adult is negotiated over time.

Furthermore, all three participants in the situation can at any time *reset* their goals. Thus, the mother may decide to abandon her effort to suppress the persistent initiative of the toddler to contact the other adult, and move to facilitate the child–stranger contact-making. The other adult may also, at any time, abandon his or her previous goal (e.g., of "becoming friends" with the child) and set a new one (e.g., getting some important business done with the mother of the child). In a similar vein, the child can at any time alter his or her goals. In the case of toddler–parent–stranger triads in any setting where goal setting and resetting is little constrained, the establishment of the toddler's new social relationships with a previously unfamiliar adult is a dynamic process in which the coordination of the contemporaneous states of goals of the three participants regulates interaction.

However, there is an inherent theoretical difficulty in the reliance on goal setting and resetting in the description of relationship formation. Goals are implied entities that need to be inferred from the knowledge of the structure of the situation, in conjunction with the participants' actions within it. Singular goals are rarely present—most often, we have to infer the existence of a *goal structure,* where different goals are organized in a hierarchical system (see Kindermann & Valsiner, in press). The complexity of the goal structure is even greater than mere simultaneous presence of multiple goals. Some of the goals may occur in that structure in some indeterminate or fuzzy form, the presence of which is difficult to document in any given instance. This is all the more difficult, since the goal structure may undergo constant change.

In the empirical part of this chapter, we will elaborate on the process by which toddlers establish contact with previously unfamiliar adults. The analysis provided in this chapter includes the results of previously reported findings (Hill & Valsiner, 1984), and extends those in the direction of greater specificity of the process of relationship formation.

"MAKING FRIENDS" WITH A STRANGER: THE EMPIRICAL STUDY

The present study was undertaken to study how the ways in which toddlers act when exposed to an unfamiliar person within a familiar environmental setting, and how the parent(s) of the given toddler, organize the establishment of social contact between the child and the new person. In line with these aims, the traditional Strange Situation was substantially transformed in two directions. First, the "stranger" had to be exposed to the child in a setting thoroughly familiar for the child (and unfamiliar to the stranger). Such a setting is the child's home environment. Thus, the whole experiment had to take place in the child's home. Secondly, the frequent "comings and goings" of adult participants in the standard Strange Situation—which are of stimulus value for the diagnosis of children's "attachment type"—are antithetical to the process-oriented research goals of this study. Therefore, the present study involved a relatively lengthy period during which a "stranger" and the child's parent(s) were jointly present in the setting, conducting themselves in ways that would facilitate the child's efforts to engage the "stranger" in social interaction. The experimental setting of the present study was made up so as to resemble an ordinary visit by an unfamiliar adult to the home—from the (presumed) perspective of the toddler. The only "strange" feature of the setting was the presence of another adult, whose role was to videorecord the whole sequence of the actions of the child.

The Subjects and Procedure

The list of potential subjects was first obtained by examining the birth records of a middle-sized (100,000 inhabitants) town in North Carolina. Criteria for being selected as a potential participant in the study included a lack of medical complications at the time when the child was born, no older siblings, and a minimum of 12 years of education (equals secondary education) of both parents. Parents of the subjects were initially contacted by telephone, at which time the study was briefly described, and a preliminary home interview was scheduled. Sixteen families participated in the study, 5 with male and 11 with female children. All children were first-borns and had no younger siblings.

For the interview, the main experimenter (the first author) visited the child's home and met the parent(s). The procedure was explained to them, and they were instructed to do anything they considered feasible to facilitate their child's friendly meeting of the "stranger" during the planned home session, while keeping the child's attention away from the person who would be involved videorecording the session. This explicit instruction to the parents distinguishes the present study from the few other investigations in the literature where the parents' role in similar settings has been limited to their passive presence devoid of efforts to direct the child's behavior (e.g., Ross & Goldman, 1977a, p. 639). Parent(s) were also given a questionnaire to fill out. The questionnaire included open-ended questions that pertained to the parents' perception of the child's conduct in different settings (e.g., contacts with strangers in and outside home), information about the network of child's social contacts (regularity and amount of contact with different babysitters, nonparent kin, acquaintances), and about the child's development history (approximate ages at which the child had started to creep/crawl, stand, walk independently). The purpose of the questionnaire was to use the parents' knowledge as a complementary information source to be added to the videotaped observations.

Participating families were visited repeatedly in the course of the second year of life of the child (see Table 1 for ages of children at particular visits). The procedure at each visit was the same:

1. *Base observation.* Experimenter 1 (henceforth S1—"stranger 1"), in most of the cases the first author—entered the home of the child, carrying video equipment, was greeted briefly by the mother, and started to videorecord continuously all the conduct of the child. (It should be kept in mind that the parent had been previously instructed to redirect the child's attention from S1 to some other object). The base observation period lasted at least 5 minutes.

2. *The presence of the "stranger."* This episode started with the "stranger" (experimenter 2—S2—previously unknown to both the child and the parent) indicated his or her arrival. The parent (often with the child) would go to open the door for S2, while S1 continues to videotape the child's conduct. After a brief introduction of himself or herself by S2, the parent invites S2 in and asks him or her to take a seat. S2 proceeds to converse with the parent for some minutes, while making himself or herself available for the child's possible contact-making overtures. If the child did make efforts to engage the "stranger" in joint action, S2 would let himself or herself

be drawn into it. If the child made no effort to that end during S2's initial interaction with the parent, S2 would try to engage the child in joint action. Either way, length of episode 2 ranged from 6 to 20 minutes in full.

3. *The departure episode.* At a certain appropriate moment, S2 declared his or her intention to leave, thus setting the stage for the departure "ritual" which involved saying "good-bye" to both the child and the parent, moving towards the exit escorted by the parent and the child, and actually taking the leave. S1 continued to videotape the child's conduct for another 5–10 minutes after S2's departure.

Different persons (males and females—all but one were college students) served in the role of S2 in the study. The same child encountered different persons in the role of S2.

The children from all 16 participating families were first studied when they were within the age range 12.5 to 15.75 months. For six children, the experiment was repeated three times (at different ages of the individual children) within the age range of 13.5 to 21.75 months. In the case of five children among the six, the sex of the S2s whom they encountered in the course of the experimental session was counterbalanced. The remaining child in that subgroup encountered only female strangers on all four occasions. Counterbalancing of male/female S2s was also done for three additional children, who for various organizational reasons could be studied only three times (age range of repetition of the procedure: 19.75–21.75 months). The rest of the subjects (N= 7) were exposed to the repeated experimental situation only once (in the age range 14–22 months), and, in 13 out of the 14 cases, the role of S2 was played by females.

Since the emphasis of analysis of empirical materials in this study is put on individual cases and changes in those over time, the exact distribution of study ages for individual children in the sample is important. This information is presented in Table 1.

It is evident from Table 1 that the individual cases studied cover toddlerhood in a relatively systematic manner. About half of experimental episodes were conducted within the age range 12–16 months (23 out of all 47 episodes conducted). Ten episodes were conducted in the 17- to 18-month age range, and the remaining 14 episodes took place in the 19- to 22-month age range.

Data Analysis

Data analysis in psychological research usually involves two stages. First, the data are derived (constructed) on the basis of the observed

Table 1. Description of the Schedule of Observations for the Individual Cases in the Sample

No.	Sex	Name	Age at observation (months) / sex of S2 (M/F)										
			12	13	14	15	16	17	18	19	20	21	22
1.	M	Jonathan D.		13/F	14/F								
2.	F	Jennifer W.					15.5/F						22/F
3.	M	David B.	12.5/F								20.75/F		
4.	M	Scott S.			14/F							21/F	
5.	F	Taylor S.	12.75/F							19.25/F			
6.	M	Matthew P.	12.5/F								20.5/F		
7.	F	Lyndsay H.					15.75/M						22/F
8.	F	Tiffani C.				15.25/M						21.5/F	21.75/M
9.	F	Sarah C.			14.25/F						20.25/M	20.5/F	
10.	F	Courtney D.		13.5/F						19.75/F	20.25/M		
11.	F	Jennifer R.	12.75/F		14/F					19.75/F	20/M		
12.	F	Jennifer S.			14.25/F	14.75/F		17.5/F	17.75/M				
13.	F	Natalie S.		13.25/M	13.5/F			17.5/F	18/M				
14.	M	Seth R.		13.5/F	13.75/M			17.5/F	17.75/M				
15.	M	Cassel S.			13.75/M	14/F		17.5/F	18/M				
16.	M	Christopher P.			14/M	14/F		17.5/F	17.75/M				

phenomena in accordance with the investigator's research plan. Second, the derived data are analyzed with the aim of revealing general principles that can be traced as present in the data.

Data derivation methods. The videotaped observational materials of this study were turned into data in two parallel ways. First, a categorization system was developed to characterize the toddler's, mother's, and S2's actions at a molar level (see Table 2).

As can be seen from Table 2, the categorization system was set up explicitly to capture the nature of toddler–stranger interaction. The system of categories captures mostly the child's conduct. Only three categories (MBYE, S2BYE, OBYE) pertain to actions that are initiated by somebody other than the child. In the child-initiated categories, the nature of the action (TO= touches, GV= gives, OF= offers, etc.) and the target person involved in the action (S1= stranger 1, S2= stranger 2, M= mother, etc.) are linked within the same code. At any time in the observed material, only one code would be assigned (no temporally "parallel" codes were allowed). The duration of the actions derived by the coding system was not taken into account. Similar codes could occur in adjacent positions only on two occasions. First, they could happen if there was a clear pause between them (which itself would not be codable—for instance, -LS2-LS2- sequence describes the child's looking at S2, pausing by not looking at any specifiable object, and looking at S2 again). Second, they could occur when the content of

Table 2.   The Coding System for the Entry of Transcripts. (Codes of the Target Child's Actions)

Code	Description
TOS1 or TOS2	Touches stranger (S1 or S2) directly
GVS1 or GVS2	Gives stranger (S1 or S2) an object
SS10 or SS20	Shows stranger (S1 or S2) an object
OFS1 or OFS2	Offers stranger (S1 or S2) an object
UOS1 or UOS2	Uses other person to give the specified stranger an object, or take an object from the stranger
VOC	Vocalizes
APS1 or APS2	Approaches the specified stranger
APM, APF, or APO	Approaches mother, father, or another adult who is not S1 or S2
IMS1 or IMS2	Imitates the specified stranger
LAS1 or LAS2	Lifts arm toward the specified stranger
MAS1 or MAS2	Moves away from the stranger
SNS1 or SNS2	Sits near the stranger
SOS1 or SOS2	Sits on stranger's lap
INTS1 or INTS2	Interacts with the stranger (book, game, toy)
AOS1 or AOS2	Accepts object from stranger
CRY	Cries
FUSS	Fusses
OOS	Out of sight of S1
OBS1 or OBS2	Follows instructions (obeys) stranger
INTM or INTF or INTO	Interacts (via toy, book, game) with mother, father, or other adult who is not S1 or S2
TM or TF or TO	Touches mother, father, or other adult who is not S1 or S2
THS1 or THS2	Throws object toward stranger
OTH	Other action (individual play within the visual fields of S1, S2, and parent)
LS1 or LS2	Looks at stranger
SMS1 or SMS2	Smiles at stranger
LM or LF or LO	Looks at mother, father, or other adult (not S1 or S2)
MBYE	Mother tells child to say bye/wave
S2BYE	S2 asks the child to say bye/wave
OBYE	Other (not S1 or S2) asks child to say bye/wave

the similarly coded category changes. This was often the case with the code (OTH), used to designate the child's individual actions that were not directly related to the strangers. Thus, if the child acted with one object, and subsequently switched to another, code sequences -OTH-OTH- were derived from the observations.

The interobserver agreement while deriving the data from videotapes on the basis of this coding system was determined on the basis of recoding five videotaped sessions. The sequences of action codes, organized along the time dimension, coded by different observers (as well recoded as by the same observer—the first author) were compared. The percentage of agreement (similarly coded frequency/frequency of all assigned codes) was found to range from 72% to 92% for different videotaped episodes (not corrected for chance), averaging at 84%. The majority of disagreements between observers were due to omission of codes rather than to divergent code attribution.

The use of any predetermined categorization system in service of deriving data from observational materials has a number of limitations. First, the way the categorization system is set up determines the kind of data that can in principle be derived from the phenomena. Second, the categorized data may abstract from important minor details of the original material, thus possibly eliminating some essential features of the latter. Therefore, it proves useful to provide narrative analyses of the ongoing child–stranger interaction, where the basic kind of action is supplemented by mentioning its specifics.

The narrative analyses of the observational materials render data that are close to everyday description of events. The narrative used in the present data derivation involved bringing out from the richness of observational materials the cases of coordination of actions of the toddler, S2, and the mother in the setting, allowing for the description of their joint actions and changes in those. In the present report, only the dynamics of triadic interaction from S2's entry until the first establishment of contact between the child and S2 is reported.

Data analysis techniques. All analyses of the data were performed within individual children, since we were interested in the ways in which the particular child establishes contact with the strangers on different occasions. Aggregation of data across individuals is counterproductive in psychological research (see Thorngate, 1986). The individual cases were analyzed for the temporal form of action (see Gottmann, 1982), using the sequence-structure analysis described in detail elsewhere (Valsiner, 1986).

The sequence-structure analysis is a means of extracting recurrent sequences of symbols of different lengths from an original full sequence of symbols of some kind. It is an advancement over the traditional conditional probability analysis of behavioral sequences, as it preserves the original sequential order in units longer than two adjacent symbols. It is usable in cases where the investigator has some reason to expect that an event he or she is interested in is going to repeat itself, fully or partially, during the observation period. Its application to the coded interaction of toddlers and visiting adults is made appropriate by previous empirical findings (see Ross & Goldman, 1977b) that have revealed long recurrent episodes of child–stranger reciprocal play. However, sequence-structure analysis is not useful for identifying completely unique (i.e., nonrecurrent) organized sequences of symbols from the full string. It does not capture the dynamic aspect of relationship formation in all its specificity (see Valsiner, 1986, pp. 366–367). Qualitative (narrative) description of the process of relationship formation helps to overcome this limitation, even if (or—perhaps exactly because) it does not render abstract formalized data in place of the phenomena under study.

Results

All 47 episodes of toddlers' contacting of S2 were coded in accordance with the coding system described. The data reported in this paper are based on the action strings that started at the entry of S2 into the situation, and ended at the moment S2 indicated his or her decision to leave the situation. There was rather high variability in the length (in action units) within the sample—from the minimum length of 41 to the maximum length of 191. That variability was partially due to the circumstances in which the S2's presence in the situation took place—the length of time S2 spent in the situation could not be kept standard (it varied between 6 and 20 minutes). Furthermore, some toddlers were more active than others during the S2's visit, and the same child may be differentially variable in acting towards the S2 on different occasions (e.g., child No.15 displayed the range from 61 to 191 action units over the four times the procedure was carried out).

Did the toddlers pay differential attention to S1 and S2? The effectiveness of our home-based experimental procedure was checked by comparing the frequencies of the toddler's visual regard to the "target" person (S2) with that to the cameraperson (S1). The data on visual regard towards S1 and S2 for all toddlers and experimental sessions are provided in Table 3.

In all but one session, S2 received higher frequency of the toddler's visual regard than S1. In that divergent condition, the child's (No. 13, third session at 17.5 months) visual regard was rare in general (three times towards S1, two towards S2). In addition, on four other occasions the visual regard of both strangers was either equal (No. 6, Episode 1) or only slightly less for S1 in comparison with S2 (No. 1, Episode 2; No. 4, Episode 2; No. 16, Episode 1). On the other extreme, a number of cases were observed to include visual regard of S2 exclusively, during the period of S1's and S2's simultaneous presence in the room.

Aggregated frequencies of stranger (S2)-related actions. Further evidence about particular actions used by individual toddlers during dif-

Table 3. Frequencies of Visual Regard towards the Target Adult (Code LS2) and the Cameraperson (Code LS1) during Individual Episodes of Exposure to Both Visitors in the Home Setting

No.	Sex	Initials	Episode No.	Total f	Looks at S1 f	Looks at S2 f
1.	M	J.D.	1	46	11	35
			2	26	12	14
2.	F	J.W.	1	33	5	28
			2	11	0	11
3.	M	D.B.	1	16	0	16
			2	18	7	11
4.	M	S.S.	1	21	6	15
			2	14	3	11
5.	F	T.S.	1	10	0	10
			2	19	9	10
6.	M	M.P.	1	18	9	9
			2	14	4	10
7.	F	L.H.	1	14	0	14
			2	24	2	22
8.	F	T.C.	1	5	0	5
			2	15	5	10
			3	31	0	31
9.	F	S.C.	1	12	0	12
			2	22	2	20
			3	15	2	13
10.	F	C.D.	1	26	8	18
			2	60	15	45
			3	40	11	29
11.	F	J.R.	1	29	4	25
			2	19	2	17
			3	32	3	29
			4	16	0	16
12.	F	J.S.	1	40	9	31
			2	26	8	18
			3	16	5	11
			4	29	2	27
13.	F	N.S.	1	18	6	12
			2	19	2	17
			3	5	3	2
			4	25	5	20
14.	M	S.R.	1	22	4	18
			2	16	4	12
			3	9	2	7
			4	6	0	6
15.	M	C.S.	1	6	0	6
			2	24	4	20
			3	33	12	21
			4	45	6	39
16.	M	C.P.	1	16	7	9
			2	24	3	21
			3	6	0	6
			4	24	2	22

ferent episodes as parts of their relating to the novel adult is presented in Table 4.

In this table, frequencies of all actions that can be instrumental in establishing contact with S2 are presented for each particular episode of every child. As can be seen from Table 4, the by far the most frequent (811 occasions in total) action category observed in the sample was "look at S2" (LS2), followed by "approaches S2" (APS2—total frequency 193), "gives object to S2" (GVS2—total frequency 155), "moves away from S2" (MAS2—total frequency 150), "smiles at S2" (SMS2—total frequency 135), and other codes. A similar pattern is revealed in the number of episodes (out of all 47) in which different actions of the toddler were observed at least once. "Looking at S2" occurred invariably in all episodes, followed by "approach S2" (in 35 of the 47 episodes), "move away from S2" (in 33 episodes), "accept object from S2" (in 28 episodes), "give object to S2" (in 27 episodes), and "smile at S2" (in 23 episodes). Other action categories were observed less frequently in the whole corpus of coded data.

The general frequency distribution of toddlers' actions that is reported in Table 4 makes it possible to gain an overview of the basic action domains used by toddlers in general. The action categories can be subsumed under more general topics to illustrate that general picture. Two major thematically interesting points emerge from the frequency analyses.

First, categories that describe the toddlers' movement relative to the position of the S2 (APS2—"approaches S2"; MAS2—"moves away from S2") are essentially complementary, and could occur in the sample with frequencies tending towards similar frequencies. In fact, approaching (APS2) can be expected to be slightly more frequent (given that, subsequent to some approaches, the toddlers do not move away from the adult but continue acting in his or her vicinity). That indeed was the case—APS2 occurred in the sample 193 times and in 35 episodes (as contrasted with MAS2—150 times, in 33 episodes).

Second, all action categories that involve the use of objects in relating to the novel adult are of interest. The toddlers could use practically any transportable object in the environment as a means of contact establishment and reciprocal interaction. However, the nature of particular actions with the objects used for that purpose could vary. Thus, our coding system included categories of "gives an object to S2" (GVS2—155 times in 27 episodes), "shows an object to S2" (SS20—13 times in 4 episodes), "offers S2 an object" (but does not actually give—OFS2—6 times in 3 episodes), and "throws object towards S2" (THS2—10 times in 3 episodes). These action categories are the object-oriented analogues to the child's own approach to the adult. The children

Table 4. Frequencies of Toddlers' Actions that Involve the Target Stranger (S2)

No.	Initials	Episode no.	LS2	SM2	GV2	TH2	LA2	AO2	SN2	SO2	MA2	AP2	OF2	SS20	TOS2	Total length of episodes (codes)	Number of different codes within episode
1.	J.D.	1	35	11	0	0	0	0	0	0	7	13	0	0	3	160	5
		2	14	3	3	0	0	0	0	0	0	3	0	0	0	94	4
2.	J.W.	1	28	0	2	0	0	2	0	0	0	2	0	0	0	99	4
		2	11	0	7	0	0	0	0	0	4	6	0	0	3	69	4
3.	D.B.	1	16	0	0	0	0	4	0	0	0	0	0	0	3	110	3
		2	11	2	0	0	0	3	0	0	4	4	0	0	4	114	6
4.	S.S.	1	15	7	4	0	2	4	0	0	9	9	0	4	3	93	9
		2	11	0	3	0	0	3	0	0	4	4	0	0	0	77	5
5.	T.S.	1	10	0	0	0	0	0	0	0	2	0	0	0	0	41	2
		2	10	0	9	4	0	4	0	0	7	8	0	0	0	119	6
6.	M.P.	1	9	4	4	0	0	5	0	0	5	7	0	0	0	161	6
		2	10	0	0	0	0	0	0	0	3	3	0	0	0	62	3
7.	L.H.	1	14	0	0	0	0	0	0	0	0	0	0	0	0	42	1
		2	22	6	6	0	0	0	0	0	8	7	0	0	0	107	5
8.	T.C.	1	5	0	7	0	3	5	0	0	11	12	0	0	0	88	6
		2	10	0	3	0	0	4	0	0	2	10	0	0	0	119	5
		3	31	3	7	0	0	4	6	0	3	8	0	0	0	158	6
9.	S.C.	1	12	2	2	0	0	4	8	0	4	4	2	0	2	67	8
		2	20	2	0	0	0	5	0	0	2	0	0	0	0	70	4
		3	13	0	0	0	0	5	0	0	2	0	0	0	0	41	1
10.	C.D.	1	18	5	8	0	0	5	0	0	5	4	0	0	5	108	7
		2	45	10	0	0	0	0	0	0	2	5	0	0	0	174	4
		3	29	4	0	0	0	0	0	0	0	0	0	0	0	107	2

(continued)

Table 4. (Continued)

No.	Initials	Episode no.	L S 2	S M S 2	G V S 2	T H S 2	L A S 2	A O S 2	S N S 2	S O S 2	M A S 2	A P S 2	O F S 2	S S 2 0	T O S 2	Total length of episodes (codes)	Number of different codes within episode
11.	J.R.	1	25	0	7	0	0	3	0	0	5	5	0	0	0	98	5
		2	17	5	5	0	0	7	0	0	0	0	0	0	0	81	4
		3	29	7	11	0	0	7	0	0	8	11	0	0	0	125	6
		4	16	7	11	0	2	14	0	0	2	6	0	0	0	150	6
12.	J.S.	1	31	6	0	0	0	3	4	0	2	4	0	5	0	168	7
		2	18	0	0	0	2	0	0	0	3	0	0	0	6	148	3
		3	11	2	4	0	0	2	0	0	0	4	0	0	0	72	6
		4	27	2	0	0	3	0	0	0	0	2	0	0	0	135	4
13.	N.S.	1	12	0	0	0	0	3	0	0	3	3	0	0	6	83	4
		2	17	0	0	2	0	0	0	0	4	4	0	0	0	75	5
		3	2	0	3	0	0	0	0	2	3	5	0	0	6	64	5
		4	20	7	12	0	0	0	0	0	6	7	0	0	0	102	5
14.	S.R.	1	18	6	5	0	2	0	0	0	0	2	2	0	0	60	4
		2	12	7	12	0	6	4	0	0	0	2	2	0	4	84	8
		3	7	0	4	0	3	2	0	0	2	0	0	0	0	85	5
		4	6	0	3	0	3	3	0	0	3	8	0	0	0	88	6
15.	C.S.	1	6	0	0	0	0	6	0	0	0	0	0	0	0	61	2
		2	20	0	0	0	6	13	0	0	7	4	0	0	0	148	5
		3	21	4	0	0	0	0	0	0	0	0	0	0	0	94	2
		4	39	23	5	4	0	3	0	0	10	10	0	0	0	191	7
16.	C.P.	1	9	0	0	0	0	0	0	0	0	0	0	2	0	62	2
		2	21	0	4	0	0	0	0	0	2	2	0	2	0	90	5
		3	6	0	0	0	0	3	0	0	2	2	0	0	0	46	4
		4	22	0	4	0	2	6	0	0	5	3	2	0	0	173	7
No. of episodes where code present:			47	23	27	3	10	28	1	1	33	35	3	4	9		

are likewise in the recipient's role in contact with the stranger via objects. The action category "accepts object from S2" (AOS2—131 times in 28 episodes) represents that aspect of the children's object-mediated contact with the novel adult.

The general frequency distribution of toddlers' actions summed over all particular occasions can tell us very little about the actual processes of action and interaction through which toddlers interact with novel adults. Any account based on general frequencies has all the problems of inference that the acceptance of a statistical model of inductive inference carries with it. First, it overlooks the peculiarities of the particular cases, treating those as occasional perturbations that obscure the "true" account of the phenomenon that is usually represented by an average for the whole sample. In order to avoid this pitfall, frequency distributions for every single episode that we studied are reported in Table 4. Secondly, inference from general frequency distributions eliminates the specificity of actions within a particular observation in favor of aggregated frequencies. Our data from particular episodes reported in Table 4 reveal that a high variety of combinations of different actions were observed within particular episodes, and from one child to another. Thus, the number of different actions observed within an episode varied from one (Subject No. 9 in Episode 3 used only visual regard towards S2 as the only way to interact with her) to nine (Subject No. 4 in Episode 1)—out of maximum possible 13 action categories in Table 4.

Results of the sequence-structure analysis. The use of frequency distributions as data—even if these data preserve the specificity of a particular episode—is still insensitive to the *temporal order* that is present in the phenomena. Therefore, our data analysis proceeded to reveal the recurrent facet of that temporal order through the use of sequence-structure analysis as described above. The sequence-structure analysis was performed on the action code strings. The analysis revealed high variability in the maximum lengths of recurrent substrings—ranging from 2 to 9 in the whole sample. Within individual cases, the maximum range was observed in the case of child No. 12—from 3 to 9. Thus, the sequence-structure analysis indicated that the toddler-S2 interaction within the period from S2's entry to her or his exit took highly variable form, both within individual subjects and in between-children comparisons.

The particular repertoires of individual toddlers' recurrent action patterns on every occasion of meeting S2 in our experiment are presented in Appendix A. That appendix includes the repertoires of toddlers' recurrent action repertoires that involve the participating strangers (S2 or S1). These subsequences were obtained through a two-step procedure (see Valsiner, 1986, p. 365 for an example and an explanation). First, a list of recurrent subsequences from the original action string was extracted. Secondly, that list was "purified" by excluding from it those shorter subsequences that were constituents of longer extracted subsequences. The list of subsequences of children's actions that was obtained by this procedure also included purely self-oriented, or only self-and-mother-oriented subsequences. Only stranger-related subsequences were taken from the full list and those are presented in Appendix A. The criterion used to define what is meant by "stranger-related" in this context was straightforward—a subsequence on the general list had to have one or more stranger-related action codes within itself to be included. Furthermore, we include brief synopses of parents' descriptions of their children's actions while meeting novel persons in their own home and in public in the Appendix.

The observational data on recurrent action sequences in Appendix A point to the principle of flexibility in making contact with a novel person. Despite the fact that the list of S2-related actions which are used to establish interaction is rather short, items from that list can become combined into a vast variety of temporally ordered recurrent chains. Within that empirical variety, we can observe three general classes of toddlers' action strategies. First, toddlers may try to engage the adult visitor in reciprocal interaction while making overtures from a distance. This *distal class* of contacting strategies involves staying away from S2, looking and smiling at him or her episodically, among other action and visual referencing of the parent. Second, toddlers can employ *transitional* contacting strategies—where the child moves from individual play or mother regard to direct approach to the novel adult. That approach may be followed by touching the adult or giving him or her an object, with a subsequent moving away from the adult. In this case the child may become involved in recurrent routines of approaching, contacting, and leaving the adult, rather than staying near the novel person after the initial approach has been successfully finished. Finally, some recurrent action sequences belong to the *proximal* class— once the child has arrived in the vicinity of the novel person, he or she makes use of that proximity by using it for further. That may include direct object exchange with the adult (e.g., -GVS2-AOS2-), interspersed with visual regard to the mother (LM) and individual other action.

The particular temporal patterns of toddlers' actions reported in Appendix A are derived from the *whole* episodes during which S2 was present in the room. Therefore, the sequence-structure analysis indiscriminately lumps together child's actions that were observed in the beginning of the episodes (i.e., when the contact is being established for the *first* time), and those from the middle or end part of the episodes (when the toddler had, most probably, engaged the novel stranger in some form of reciprocal interaction). The insensitivity of the sequence-structure analysis to unique sequences of events makes that data analysis method only partially useful for our purposes. In order to get a better overview of the empirical reality of individual toddlers' contacting novel persons, presentation of narrative qualitative transcripts of the beginning of the toddlers' contact-making is obligatory.

A qualitative description of toddler-adult contact establishment. The following narrative descriptions of the four episodes during which our subject No. 16 (C.P.) was observed to establish contact with S2 illustrate the complexity of the particular events of that kind. Every particular episode described here is unique in its unfolding temporal structure. The structure of the environment is the basic resource which is used by the participants to establish the toddler-S2 contact.

Episode 1 took place when the child was 14 months old, and involved a male S2. Prior to the entry of S2, the mother and child are observed sitting on the livingroom floor (child on mother's lap). The mother is showing the child a book and reading it with him. The child partici-pates—helps to turn pages, responds to some questions, laughs. A knock at the door is heard. Mother: "Come in!" (S2 enters) "Hello!" S2: "Hi!" (comes to the mother and child and sits down on the floor, facing both). The mother and S2 introduce themselves to each other. Then the process of the child's contacting S2 unfolds in the first 8 minutes:

0.07–0.19: The mother continues to show book to the child, who looks at the book. S2 looks at the child and leans towards him.

0.19–0.24: The child looks at S2, S2 touches child's head, who turns away looks over the shoulder of S2 towards camera.

0.24–0.31: The child and S2 look at each other.

0.31–0.40: The child points towards an unspecifiable location on his right. Mother comments: "Do you want to get cookie for Tom?"

0.40–0.50: The child (with mother's help) rises from sitting on her lap, walks around, fusses. Mother comments "Want to get cookie? I'll walk with you." Stands up herself, holding child's hand. "Come on, let's get a cookie." The child fusses.

0.50–1.14: Mother releases child's hand, both walk towards the kitchen (through a small corridor). Child falls down onto floor while in the corridor, sits and fusses. Mother (from the kitchen) "Here we go, here is the cookie" (hands it to child who is sitting on the corridor floor). "Take it to Tom." S2 encourages child to return into the living room. Mother moves past the child towards the living room, encouraging the child to follow.

1.14–1.30: Mother returns to the corridor, picks up the child, brings him into the living room. When released, he toddles over to a small wooden chest full of toys, near the wall and in view of S2, while mother and S2 chat.

1.30–2.01: Child stands in front of the chest, looking at the toys in it, picking some up and putting them down, looking episodically back in the direction of where mother and S2 are conversing about the child.

2.01–2.39: Mother: "Bring the horsie, Christopher!" Child looks in mother's direction. Mother: "Where's your horsie? Where is your horse?" Child picks an object from a basket on top of things in the chest, manipulates it, lets it fall back into the basket, and looks in mother's direction again. Continues watching mother and S2 chat, then starts eating cookie that is in his left hand.

2.39–2.59: Child continues eating the cookie, while still standing on the chest, finally turns his attention to the basket on top of the chest again.

2.00–3.42: Mother: "Where is your lawn mower, Christopher? Can you bring it to Mommy?" Child touches different objects on top of the chest. Mother: "Bring it to Mommie!" Child selects an object. Mother: "That's right!" Mother chats with S2 while child manipulates the selected toy. Drops it in the chest. Mother: "What's in there? Where is your too-too-too?" Child manipulates something in the chest. Mother: "Too-too-too?" Child takes a toy out. Mother: "That clown. That's a clown." Child holds it up in his right hand. Mother: "Where does he go?" Child puts it back in the chest, looks in mother's direction again. Mother and S2 chat.

3.42–4.06: Child continues to stand at the chest, mouthes cookie (in left hand), then lifts up the toy (clown) with his right hand from the chest, and vocalizes. Demonstrates it in the direction of mother and S2. Mother: "Can you bring it to mommy?" Child puts the toy back in chest, but does not release it. Looks in the direction of mother and S2.

4.06–4.34: Mother: "Want a coke? Christopher, come here!" Child stands at the chest, looking in the direction of mother and S2. Turns back to the chest, takes the clown toy out again, puts it into his mouth (the clown has a nipple on the top), looks towards mother and S2, puts the clown back in chest again. Adjusts toys in chest.

4.34–4.48: Child looks in the direction of mother and S2. Mother: "Let's go to the porch and show Tom how you climb! Come on! Come on, let's go to the porch!" S2: "Come, show how you play!" Child keeps standing at the chest, looking in the direction of the adults. Then turns again toward the chest.

4.48–4.54:   S2 (to mother): "I don't think he likes me." Mother (to S2): "I don't think it's you. He's had a rough day, with anxiety."

4.54–5.11:   Child moves away from the chest, walks to the door where mother urges him: "Come, let's go to the porch! Hold on to balloon (offers balloon to him)." Child stops at the doorstep to adjacent room, mother is in that room urging him to follow, S2 is standing behind the child, still in the living room.

5.11–5.20:   S2 moves forward to stand on the left to child at the door, picks up the balloon from the floor, lifts it on child's head, and lets it fall back on the floor. The balloon rolls in mother's direction. Child watches, then turns away towards the left. S2 moves past the child.

5.20–5.26:   S2 offers finger to child, who does not take it but instead moves back towards the livingroom, raising left arm and showing cookie in the direction of S1 (camera).

5.26–5.41:   Child turns back into the next room where mother and S2 are; S2 is kneeling down at 2–3 meters from child, and tries to attract his attention. S2 throws the balloon towards child. Balloon lands at half a meter from child, who watches it. S2 leans over and takes the balloon, throws it up in air. Child moves towards S2, then turns back to the door.

5.41–5.46:   Child looks back at S1. S2 throws the balloon towards child again, who looks at it, and then turns again back towards the door. Touches the wall with right hand. Then looks towards S2 briefly.

5.56–6.08:   S2 leans towards child to get the balloon. Takes it, hands it to the child, saying: "Here, toss it to me!" Child watches. S2 bounces it on the floor a couple of times (child watches), then lets it bounce to the child (on the floor). Child turns away from the balloon, towards the wall.

6.08–6.16:   S2 takes a toy train-engine and rolls it over the floor towards child. The train makes "too-too" noise, S2 imitates it. Child squats down on the floor, looks towards S2 and the toy train, then back towards S1.

6.16–6.20:   S2 moves the noise-making train back and forth to the child; child faces the wall. Then S2 turns the train around into a position that would allow the child to take control over it and roll it back towards S2. S2 releases the train.

6.20–6.36:   Child starts pushing the train towards S2; it reaches half-way. Child is on the floor, looking in the direction of S2 and mother. Child pushes the train again, imitating "too-too."

6.36–6.48:   Child moves the train back and forth. Looks towards S2.

6.48–6.58:   S2 takes the train from mid-way and rolls it towards himself. Child sits on the floor, turned away from S2. S2 rolls the train back towards child, who watches. Mother picks up cookie from under the sitting child and puts it back in his left hand.

6.59–7.23:   S2 tries to approach with the train again, no effect, then starts playing xylophone. Child watches. S2 moves the xylophone close to the child.

7.23–7.46:   S2 gives xylophone stick into child's left hand, who starts to hit the xylophone with it. S2 rolls the xylophone more closer to child. Child plays, then hands the stick back to S2 who plays.

The established contact between the toddler and S2 continues for some more minutes, until (at 10.06) S2 announces his intention to leave.

Episode 2 took place a couple of days later, and involved a female S2. Prior to the S2's entry, the child is observed playing with toys, taken from a shelf (in a room different from the livingroom where Episode 1 took place). Mother comments on child's actions and organizes his play. The slide (present in the back of the room, near the window) is used in joint play—mother directs child's actions with toys to take place on the slide. The process of establishing contact with S2 unfolded as follows:

0.00–0.13:   Knock at the door. Mother: "Who's at the door?" Instructs the S2 to come into the room (does not go to open the front door). Mutual introductions. Mother presents the S2 to the child: "Christopher, this is Nina." Child stays behind the slide, looking at S2, briefly fusses. Mother comments: "She's not your babysitter." S2 kneels down at the sliding-part of the slide, looks at child, blows a kiss to the child. Mother: "Say—'Hi, Nina!' " Child pushes a toy down the slide; both mother and S2 show fascination.

0.13–0.25:   Mother and S2 put toys on the top of the slide, in front of the child, and draw his attention to those. Mother demonstrates how one of those can slide down the slide. Child leaves the position behind the slide and goes over to the mother, who is sitting on the floor facing the slide from the right, while S2 faces it from the left. Mother and S2 interact.

0.25–0.48:   Child hides his face in mother's lap. Mother chats with S2, talks to child about a toy truck she is holding in her hand (suggests that he put it out on the slide). Mother puts the truck on top of the slide while continuing to interact with S2. Child watches her doing that.

0.48–0.53:   Child goes to the slide, then turns back and toddles towards the mother. Mother: "Say 'hi' to Nina!" Child buries his face in mother's lap.

0.53–1.13: Mother lifts the child up and sets him to sit on her lap, facing S2. Child looks to the right, towards the window (away from S2), then points towards the top of the slide.

1.13–1.24: S2 starts moving a toy truck towards child (who is on mother's lap, facing S2) and back, asking, "What's this?" Then picks up the truck and sets it on top of slide, asking, "Can it come down here? Can you push it down here?" Child watches S2 doing that. S2 lets the truck slide down once, then hands it to child, asking "Can you do that?"

1.24–1.36: Child points in the direction of the top of the slide, S2— towards the truck in front of the child. Child gets up from mother's lap and briefly approaches the slide, then turns back to the mother's lap and hides his face in the lap.

1.36–1.46: Child is hiding his face in mother's lap. Mother finally picks child up and puts him to sit on her lap, facing S2.

1.46–1.57: S2 pushes the toy truck on floor towards child, asking, "You want your truck?" Child gets up from mother's lap, reaches for the truck, picks it up. Mother intervenes, guiding the child's hands with truck towards the top of the slide, commenting, "There! Can you push all those (i.e., all the toys that are now on top of the slide) down?" S2 helps to adjust toys on top of the slide. Child watches.

1.57–2.05: S2 adjusts toys on top of the slide; Mother asks, "Can you push them down?" Child watches, then points in S2's direction and vocalizes.

2.05–2.18: Child sits on mother's lap, looks and waves in S2's direction. Mother and S2 interact. Child gets up, moves towards a toy on the floor. Mother: "Get your train, Christopher."

2.18–2.25: Child takes a small toy from the floor, moves towards S2, and shows it to her on an outstreched right arm. S2: "Can you give that to me?" Child toddles over to the S2 and puts the toy on her outstretched palm. S2 takes the toy; child moves past her to the shelf with toys (on S2's right).

2.25–2.54: Child is standing at the shelf, throws toys down onto floor, takes toy train and shows to S2, who points to mother asking "Bring it to mommy." Child lets the train onto floor.

2.54–3.50: S2 initiates play using a toy on the shelf; child joins her in play. He plays in front of S2, showing things to her.

3.50–end of episode at 15.24: S2, the child, and mother continue to interact and play jointly.

The qualitative analysis of episodes 1 and 2 makes it possible to reveal a pattern of intricate coordination of actions of the members of the triad, depending the given state of affairs with the child's inclination to act close to the adults or in a location away from them. The role of the mother as the major organizer of the toddler's contacting of the visitor becomes obvious from the transcript. Of course, it should be remembered that this role was expected from the mother from the way the whole experimental setting was set up. Therefore, her organizer's role does not necessarily occur in these observations in the exact form that it might on other occasions. First, the very beginning of the visitors' entry is used by the mother to promote culturally expected conduct (greeting behavior) in the child, although the child subsequently does not follow that expectation. Secondly, the mother presents the benevolent nature of the visitor to the child—by urging him to give the visitor a cookie (Episode 1) and reassuring the (briefly fussing) child that *this* visitor "is *not* his babysitter" (Episode 2, 0.00–0.13). Besides, the mother also regulates the role of the visitor in the dyad—for example, actively denying his claim (Episode 1, 4.48–4.54) that the child does not like him by explaining the child's conduct by the circumstances of the given day. The mother attempts to get the child to contact the visitor by re-engaging the child in the triad directly (if the child had wandered away—Episode 1, 3.00–3.42) or trying to get the child to play with objects in the vicinity of both herself and the visitor (when the child leaves the triad by hiding in the mother's lap—Episode 2).

The child's role in the establishment of contact with the visitor can be seen to vary a great deal between Episodes 1 and 2. In the first episode, it takes a long time and much effort of the mother and the visitor to become involved in joint action—only at the second time (with the xylophone), when the visitor takes the lead and yields the turn in joint play to the child, would the child become immersed in reciprocal joint action. In contrast, in the second episode, the child himself is observed to go over to the visitor and involve her in mutual play (giving her a toy). On the one hand, the child's role in the triad involves resistance to the suggestions provided by the mother and the visitor. On the other hand—the child can at any time take the first step in establishing reciprocal interaction with the visitor. These two facets—resistance and initiative—are intricately linked, and constitute an early ontogenetic example of the ways in which social suggestion and individuals' "independent" action are interdependent within social contexts.

The action strategies of the visitor in these two episodes are linked to the contexts in which the action takes place. The visitor in the first episode has to "work hard" to involve the child in reciprocal play, succeeding only after two objects suggested by him to the child for turn-taking in joint play (balloon, train) have been only marginally effective. The adult's goal of establishing reciprocity in joint action is obvious from the course of events: when the child has not taken the balloon, the adult retrieves it and performs the next action with it himself (5.26–5.41), or when the toy train is acted with, it is turned around so that the child can take his turn (6.16–6.20). In contrast, the visitor in the second episode fits her actions to the scheme introduced by the mother (present already prior to S2's entry) of directing the child's actions with toys onto the top of the slide in the room. In sum, all the three partners in the triad play the "game" in a mutually sensitive way, trying to reach their goals through coordination of their actions with those of the other two. However, the leading role of the mother is unchallenged, while the mother assumes the leadership in making it possible (and probable) that her child meets the visitor.

Episode 3 took place when the child was 17.5 months old, and involved a female S2. Prior to the entry of S2, the mother and child are sitting on the floor, talking to each other in the context of joint book reading. Mother is promoting child's vocabulary; child is seen repeating approximate versions of words.

0.00–0.19:   Doorbell rings. Mother gets up from the floor, saying, "Let's go see who is at the door." Child keeps sitting. Mother: "Come with mommy?"—pulls child by arm upright and both walk to the door.

0.19–0.44:   At the door, S2 enters; mutual introductions. Mother takes child by hand, saying, "Come go show Pam your books"; all walk towards the livingroom. Child: "Car." Mother: "That's right, you can show her the car." Child: "Come." Mother: "You want to show Pam where to sit? You want Pam to sit there?"

0.44–0.53:   Child sits down in front of the slide; S2 sits down facing him. Mother to child: "Say: 'Sit down.'" Mother herself sits to the right from the child (S2's view), adjust child's overalls, Child "Tractor." Mother: "Tractor" (referring to a picture in the book).

0.53–1.09:   Child and mother continue joint bookreading, child sitting on the floor facing S2. Mother instructs the child to show to S2 different objects in the pictures (Mother: "Show Pam where goldbug is!") Child points to pictures, imitates sounds of animals in the pictures, but does not look at the S2.

1.09–1.21:   Child turns away from the book, creeps around S2 close to the shelf, looks at S2, then returns to the book.

1.21–3.00:   Mother–child joint bookreading continues. Child is facing S2 but not looking at her. S2 asks episodic questions about pictures in the book. Child gradually moves on towards S2's end of the book, talking to mother about objects in the book, but not looking at S2.

3.00–3.03: S2 initiates contact, pointing to an object in the picture, asking, "What is this?" Child: "Tuck."

3.03–3.35: Mother continues to lead the child's book-reading. Child continues to avoid looking at S2, but at 3.24 gives a brief glance towards her.

3.35–4.16: Child moves away from book towards shelf behind the S2. Takes a toy truck, moves it on floor away from S2, making noises like an engine. Mother points at another toy, but child pays no attention.

4.16–5.10: Child gets up, walks to a location behind mother, plays with cat. Mother and S2 interact.

5.10–5.21: Child goes to mother, lounges into her lap, then goes by the S2 to the shelf.

5.21–5.35: Looks at S2, takes a plastic helmet from the shelf and gives it to S2; then takes another plastic helmet from the shelf, shows it to S2, and looks at her. S2 puts her helmet on; child puts his helmet on and toddles away from S2 towards mother, and hands his helmet to the mother.

5.35–5.45: Mother takes child's helmet, puts it on. Child watches mother do that, then walks over to S2, takes the other helmet from her hands, and puts it on his own head.

5.45–6.00: Child walks away from S2 and mother, wearing the helmet. Goes to the window, takes off the helmet.

6.00–end of episode at 11.05: S2, toddler, and mother continue playing.

Episode 4 took place a week later (age 17.75 months) and involved a male S2. Prior to entry of S2, the mother and child are sitting on the floor in front of the slide, jointly acting with objects. Mother talks to the child, the child talks (vocalizes) back. Mother stands up and goes to answer the door, invites child with her. He, however, remains sitting in the previous place, playing with toys. S2 enters; mother and S2 introduce themselves to each other. Mother and S2 come into the room where the child is; the latter continues to play with toys on the floor.

0.03–0.13: Mother to child: "Can you say 'Hi' to Sammy?" S2: "Hi, Christopher!" Mother: "Can you share your raisins with Sammy?" S2 comments on how good raisins are.

0.13–0.20: Child continues to sit/squat on floor, eating raisins from a box, looking up towards mother and S2, who are standing in front of him and chatting. S2 kneels down on the floor.

0.20–0.32: Child points to a toy, says "Truck!" stands up, and goes to the toy. S2 comments on the toy. Child moves the toy truck back and forth between himself and S2; S2 helps, holding his end of the truck.

0.32–1.13: Child abandons truck, turns to the shelf with toys and takes a top (spinner) from it, and starts spinning the top in front of S2, briefly gazing in S2's direction while spinning it. Looks back at mother, continues to spin the top, then briefly looks at S2. Continues spinning the top.

1.13–1.24: S2 initiates play with the previous truck, moving it towards the child and back. Child looks at the truck immediately.

1.24–1.30: Child stands up with the top in his right hand, runs around S2 to a little table with toys (on the back of S2), and vocalizes. Picks up a little toy doll from the table.

1.30–1.38: Child goes back, approaches the S2 (from S2's right), and gives the small doll to S2, putting it in his right hand. M comments: "This is the driver." S2 proceeds to put the doll in the truck, turning away from the child. The child returns to the table with toys.

1.38 and on—Child brings different objects to S2, chats with him, S2 comments on child's toys. Child shows different toys to S2 and M. Child and S2 play together. S2-toddler joint play with various toys continues until the end of the episode at 15.11.

Qualitative analysis of episodes 3 and 4 reveals a basic developmental change over the 3 months that separate those two episodes from the first two. The child on both occasions at 17–18 months is observed to be more vocal, actively imitating adults' speech, and using speech himself as a part of contact-making efforts oriented towards the visitor (e.g., Episode 4, 0.20–0.32) and in initiatives towards the mother (same episode, 0.44–0.53). It is in the realm of the joint reference to the pictures in the book that child–visitor reciprocity is first approximated in Episode 3 (1.21–3.03), followed later by joint action without speech (play with helmets—5.21–5.35).

Similarly to the previous episodes, the mother was observed actively promoting the child's greeting behavior and facilitating the emergence of reciprocity between the child and the visitor. The visitors in both episodes join in the previously ongoing activity (Episode 3—joint book-reading; Episode 4—child's action with the truck). The coordination of triadic actions involved all three partners, while the leading role in the small group remained with the mother.

GENERAL CONCLUSIONS

The present chapter has dealt with the issue of microgenesis of toddlers' novel relationships with previously unknown adults in the children's home environments. We were interested in the ways in which children utilize the resources of their physical and social environments to attain the goal of establishing contact with a visiting adult. It was demonstrated that very little knowledge about the microgenesis of toddlers' social relationships has emerged in the context of empirical attachment research. The reason for that was shown to be theoretical—the empirical questions that contemporary researchers have derived from the attachment theory have not focused on the microgenetic side of the use of attachment in establishment of novel social contacts.

Our empirical investigation revealed a high variety of recurrent temporal forms in the interaction of the toddler and the visitor. That variety was in part due to the active use of the structure of the particular environments in the triadic transaction process between the child, novel adult, and the mother. Furthermore, the variety of observed temporal forms of children's contact-establishment strategies was also due to the *constructed* nature of these strategies—in every particular situation where a toddler meets an unfamiliar adult, he or she actively constructs a sequence of actions that can lead to the estblishment of contact with the adult. However, that constructive process is coordinated with active efforts of the parent, and of the novel adult—in this respect, toddlers' establishment of contact with novel persons is a socially coconstructed process (see also chapters by Winegar and by Lightfoot, in volume 2).

The narrative description of one child's observed episodes of contact establishment revealed a complex picture of triadic coordination of actions. The mother was observed to promote culturally appropriate conduct (greeting) in the child when the novel adult entered the situation. Furthermore, the mother was seen to promote the child's contact with the visitor by encouraging him to involve the visitor in exchange of objects and joint play. On his or her side, the visitor acted within a culturally appropriate role of being a friendly stranger, willing to interact with the child. Becoming involved in reciprocal interaction with the child, through object exchange or turn-taking in the action upon a shared object, were observed as first the objectives that the child and the adult were striving towards, and the mechanism that led them to further joint action once they had reached such reciprocity. The mother's selective facilitation of such reciprocity created conditions where the child would establish a relationship with a novel adult. Even a more direct promoter's role of the parent was observed during the departure episodes (analyzed elsewhere—Valsiner & Hill, in press), where both the mother and the visitor set up rather intense expectations for the child to show culturally appropriate conduct in that situation.

Toddlerhood is the time when children start to establish relationships with unfamiliar adults, relying heavily on the assistance from the parents and the environment. The latter is itself socially organized—the parents are the agents who have structured the home environment which the toddler can use in the process of relationship formation. The parents' personal interpretations of their cultural backgrounds (see Epilogue of volume 2) mediate between the wider culture shared by many and the personal ways by which parents act to organize their children's relationships with their physical and social environments. The latter involves frequent appearance of novel, previously unfamiliar, persons in the children's lives. In addition to the existing attachment ties between children and parents, establishment of new social relationships in toddlerhood takes place as a necessary mechanism for the developing child's adaptation to the ever-changing environmental conditions within which human beings are intricately but flexibly related to one another all through their lives.

REFERENCES

Ainsworth, M.D.S. (1967). *Infancy in Uganda*. Baltimore, MD: Johns Hopkins University Press.

Ainsworth, M.D.S., & Bell, S.M. (1970). Attachment, exploration and separation: illustrated by the behavior of one-year-olds in a strange situation. *Child Development, 41*, 49–67.

Ainsworth, M.D.S., Blehar, M.C., Waters, E., & Wall, S. (1978). *Patterns of attachment: A psychological study of the Strange Situation*. Hillsdale, NJ: Erlbaum.

Ainsworth, M.D.S., & Wittig, B.A. (1969). Attachment and exploratory behavior of one-year-olds in a strange situation. In B.M. Foss (Ed.), *Determinants of infant behavior* (Vol. 4). London: Methuen.

Anderson, J.W. (1972). Attachment behavior out of doors. In N.G. Blurton Jones (Ed.), *Ethological studies of child behavior* (pp. 199–215). Cambridge, England: Cambridge University Press.

Bates, J.E., Maslin, C.A., & Frankel, K.A. (1985). Attachment security, mother-child interaction, and temperament as predictors of behavior-problem ratings at age three years. *Monographs of the Society for Research in Child Development, 50* (1–2, Serial No. 209), 167–193.

Beckwith, L. (1972). Relationships between infants' social behavior and their mothers' behavior. *Child Development, 43*, 397–411.

Benedek, T. (1938). Adaptation to reality in early infancy. *The Psychoanalytic Quarterly, 7*, 200–215.

Berland, J. (1982). *No five fingers are alike*. Cambridge, MA: Harvard University Press.

Bischof, N. (1975). A systems approach toward the functional connections of attachment and fear. *Child Development, 46*, 801–817.

Blurton Jones, N.G., Ferreira, M.C.R., Brown, M.F., & Moore, L. (1980). Dimensions of attachment. Comparing a "trait" approach with a functional approach to studying children's attachments to their mothers. In S.A. Corson (Ed.), *Ethology and nonverbal communication in mental health* (pp. 143–165). Oxford, England: Pergamon Press.

Bowlby, J. (1944). Forty-four juvenile thieves: their characters and home-life. *International Journal of Psychoanalysis, 25,* 19–53, 107–128.

Bowlby, J. (1951). Maternal care and mental health. *Bulletin of the W.H.O., 3,* 355–534.

Bowlby, J. (1952). *Maternal care and mental health* (2nd ed.). Geneva, Switzerland: W.H.O.

Bowlby, J. (1958). The nature of the child's tie to his mother. *International Journal of Psychoanalysis, 39,* 350–373.

Bowlby, J. (1969). *Attachment and loss. Vol. 1. Attachment.* New York: Basic Books.

Bowlby, J. (1980a). *Attachment and loss. Vol. 3. Loss, sadness, and depression.* New York: Basic Books.

Bowlby, J. (1980b). By ethology out of psycho-analysis: An experiment in interbreeding. *Animal Behaviour, 28,* 649–656.

Bretherton, I. (1978). Making friends with one-year olds: an experimental study of infant–stranger interaction. *Merrill-Palmer Quarterly, 24,* 29–51.

Bretherton, I. (1985). Attachment theory: Retrospect and prospect. *Monographs of the Society for Research in Child Development, 50,* 1–2 (Serial No. 209), 3–35.

Bretherton, I., Stolberg, U., & Kreye, M. (1981). Engaging strangers in proximal interaction: infants' social initiative. *Developmental Psychology, 17,* 6, 746–755.

Bretherton, I., and Waters, E. (1985). Growing points of attachment: Theory and research. *Monographs of the Society for Research in Child Development, 50,* 1–2 (Serial No. 209).

Bretherton, I., & Ainsworth, M.D.S. (1974). The responses of one-year-olds to strangers in a strange situation. In M. Lewis and L.A. Rosenblum (Eds.), *The origins of fear.* New York: Wiley.

Cairns, R.B. (1972). Attachment and dependency: a psychobiological and social learning synthesis. In J.L. Gewirtz (Ed.), *Attachment and dependency.* Washington, DC: Winston.

Cairns, R.B. (1977). Beyond social attachment: The dynamics of interactional development. In T. Alloway, P. Pliner, & L. Krames (Eds.), *Advances in the study of communication and affect. Vol. 3. Attachment behavior* (pp. 1–24). New York: Plenum.

Clarke-Stewart, K.A. (1978). Recasting the lone stranger. In J. Glick & K.A. Clarke-Stewart (Eds.), *The development of social understanding* (pp. 109–176). New York: Gardner Press.

Eckerman, C.O., & Rheingold, H.L. (1974). Infants' exploratory responses to toys and people. *Developmental Psychology, 10,* 255–259.

Erickson, M.F., Sroufe, L.A., & Egeland, B. (1985). The relationship between quality of attachment and behavior problems in preschool in a high-risk sample. *Monographs of the Society for Research on Child Development, 50,* (1-2, Serial No. 209), 147-166.

Fein, G.G. (1975). Children's sensitivity to social contexts at 18 months of age. *Developmental Psychology, 11,* 853-854.

Feiring, C. (1983). Behavioral styles in infancy and adulthood: the work of Karen Horney and attachment theorists collaterally considered. *Journal of the American Academy of Child Psychiatry, 22,* 1, 1-7.

Feiring, C., Lewis, M., & Starr, M. (1984). Indirect effects and infants' reaction to strangers. *Developmental Psychology, 20,* 485-491.

Goodnow, J.J. (in press). Children's household work: its nature and functions. *Psychological Review.*

Gottmann, J.M. (1982). Temporal form: Toward a new language for describing relationships. *Journal of Marriage and the Family, 44,* 4, 943-964.

Grossmann, K.E., Grossmann, K., Huber, F., & Wartner, W. (1981). German children's behavior towards their mothers at 12 months and their fathers at 18 months in Ainsworth's Strange Situation. *International Journal of Behavioural Development, 4,* 157-181.

Harkness, S., & Super, C. (1983). The cultural construction of child development: a framework for the socialization of affect. *Ethos, 11,* 221-231.

Hay, D.F. (1977). Following their companions as a form of exploration for human infants. *Child Development, 48,* 1624-1628.

Heymer, A. (1980). Bayaka-Pygmäen (Zentralafrika)—Freundlicher Fremdkontakt und Fremdenablehnung (Fremdenfurcht) von Kleinkindern. *Homo, 31,* 3-4, 241-251.

Hill, P.E., & Valsiner, J. (1984, April). *Contacting a visitor in home settings: Toddlers' strategies of entry into social contact with unfamiliar adults.* Paper presented at the International Conference on Infant Studies, New York.

Ignjatovic-Savic, N. (1986, September). *Cognitive aspects of attachment.* Paper presented at the 2nd European Conference of the International Society for the Study of Behavioral Development, Rome.

Kennell, J.H., Voos, D.K., & Klaus, M.H. (1979). Parent–infant bonding. In J. Osofsky (Ed.), *Handbook of infant development* (pp. 786-798). New York: Wiley.

Kennell, J.H., & Klaus, M.H. (1984). Mother-infant bonding: Weighing the evidence. *Developmental Review, 4,* 275-282.

Kindermann, T., & Valsiner, J. (in press). Strategies for empirical research in context-inclusive developmental psychology. In J. Valsiner (Ed.), *Cultural context and child development: Towards a culture-inclusive developmental psychology.* Göttingen: Hogrefe.

Klaus, M.H., & Kennell, J.H. (1976). *Maternal–infant bonding.* St. Louis, MO: Mosby.

Klinnert, M.D., Emde, R.N., & Butterfield, P. (1983, April). *The infant's use of emotional signals from a friendly adult with mother present.* Paper presented at the meeting of the Society for Research on Child Development, Detroit, MI.

Lamb, M., Thompson, R.A., Gardner, W., & Charnov, E.L. (1985). *Infant-mother attachment*. Hillsdale, NJ: Erlbaum.

Leis, N.B. (1982). The not-so-supernatural power of Ijaw children. In S. Ottenberg (Ed.), *African religious groups and beliefs* (pp. 151–169). Meerut, India: Folklore Institute.

Levitt, M.J. (1980). Contingent feedback, familiarization, and infant affect: How a stranger becomes a friend. *Developmental Psychology, 16,* 5, 425–432.

Lewis, M., & Feiring, C. (1981). Direct and indirect interactions in social relationships. In L.P. Lipsitt (Ed.), *Advances in infancy research* (Vol. 1, pp. 129–161). Norwood, NJ: Ablex Publishing Corp.

Maccoby, E., & Jacklin, C.N. (1973). Sex, activity, and proximity seeking: sex differences in the year-old child. *Child Development, 44,* 34–42.

Miller, G.A., Galanter, E., & Pribram, K.H. (1960). *Plans and the structure of behavior.* New York: Holt, Rinehardt, & Winston.

Myers, B.J. (1984a). Mother–infant bonding: The status of this critical-period hypothesis. *Developmental Review, 4,* 240–274.

Myers, B.J. (1984b). Mother–infant bonding: Rejoinder to Kennell and Klaus. *Developmental Review, 4,* 283–288.

Rheingold, H.L. (1969). The social and socializing infant. In D.A. Goslin (Ed.), *Handbook of socialization theory and research* (pp. 779–790). Chicago, IL: Rand-McNally.

Rheingold, H.L. (1985). Development as the acquisition of familiarity. *Annual Review of Psychology, 36,* 1–17.

Rheingold, H.L., & Eckerman, C.O. (1969). The infant's free entry into a new environment. *Journal of Experimental Child Psychology, 8,* 271–283.

Rheingold, H.L., & Eckerman, C.O. (1970). The infant separates himself from his mother. *Science, 168,* 78–83.

Ross, H.S. (1975). The effects of increasing familiarity on infants' reactions to adult strangers. *Journal of Experimental Child Psychology, 20,* 226–239.

Ross, H.S., & Goldman, B.D. (1977a). Infants' sociability toward strangers. *Child Development, 48,* 638–642.

Ross, H.S., & Goldman, B.D. (1977b). Establishing new social relations in infancy. In T. Alloway, P. Pliner, & L. Krames (Eds.), *Advances in the study of communication and affect. Vol. 3. Attachment behavior* (pp. 61–79). New York: Plenum.

Ross, H.S., Rheingold, H.L., & Eckerman, C.O. (1972). Approach and exploration of a novel alternative by 12-month-old infants. *Journal of Experimental Child Psychology, 13,* 85–93.

Sagi, A., & Koren, N. (1985). *The Strange Situation procedure in cross-national research: A test of validity.* Paper presented at the 8th Biennial Meetings of the International Society for the Study of Behavioural Development, Tours, France.

Sagi, A., & Lamb, M.E. (1985). *Is there a congruence between strange situation assessments made by trained vs. naive observers? A test of external validity.* Paper presented at the 8th Biennial Meetings of the International Society for the Study of Behavioural Development, Tours, France.

Sorce, J.F., & Emde, R.N. (1981). Mother's presence is not enough: effect of emotional availability on infant exploration. *Developmental Psychology, 17,* 6, 737–745.

Sroufe, L.A. (1979). The coherence of individual development. *American Psychologist, 34,* 834–841.

Sroufe, L.A., & Fleeson, J. (1986). Attachment and the construction of relationships. In W.W. Hartup & Z. Rubin (Eds.), *Relationships and development* (pp. 51–71). Hillsdale, NJ: Erlbaum.

Sroufe, L.A., Waters, E., & Matas, L. (1974). Contextual determinants of infant affective response. In M. Lewis & L. Rosenblum (Eds.), *The origins of fear* (pp. 49–72). New York: Wiley.

Stern, D.N., & Bender, E.P. (1974). An ethological study of children approaching a strange adult: Sex differences. In R.C. Friedman, R.M. Richert, & R. Wiele (Eds.), *Sex differences in behavior.* New York: Krieger.

Suess, G., Escher-Graeub, D., & Grossmann, K.E. (1985). *Different patterns of adaptation in preschool: Relations to early attachment classifications.* Paper at the 8th Biennial meeting of the International Society for the Study of Behavioural Development, Tours, France.

Super, C., & Harkness, S. (1986). The development niche: a conceptualization at the interface of child and culture. *International Journal of Behavioral Development, 9,* 545–569.

Takahashi, K. (1982). Attachment behaviors to a female stranger among Japanese 2-year olds. *Journal of Genetic Psychology, 140,* 292–307.

Thompson, R.A., Lamb, M.E., & Estes, D. (1982). Stability of infant-mother attachment and its relationship to chainging life circumstances in an unselected middle-class sample. *Child Development, 53,* 144–148.

Thorngate, W. (1986). The production, detection, and explanation of behavioral patterns. In J. Valsiner (Ed.), *The individual subject and scientific psychology* (pp. 71–93). New York: Plenum.

Valsiner, J. (1986). Sequence-structure analysis: Study of serial order within unique sequences of psychological phenomena. In J. Valsiner (Ed.), *The individual subject and scientific psychology* (pp. 347–389). New York: Plenum.

Valsiner, J. (1987). *Culture and the development of children's action.* Chichester, England: Wiley.

Valsiner, J., & Hill, P.E. (in press). Socialization of children for social courtesy: American parents' canalization of toddlers' waving of "bye-bye." In J. Valsiner (Ed.), *Cultural context and child development: Towards a culture-inclusive developmental psychology.* Göttingen: Hogrefe.

Van IJzendoorn, M.H., Tavecchio, L.W.C., Goossens, F.A., Vergeer, M.M., & Swaan, J. (1983). How B is B4? Attachment and security of Dutch children in Ainsworth's Strange Situation and at home. *Psychological Reports, 52,* 683–691.

Waters, E., & Deane, K.E. (1982). Infant-mother attachment: Theories, models, recent data, and some tasks for comparative developmental analysis. In

L.W. Hoffman, R. Gandelman, & H.R. Schiffman (Eds.), *Parenting: Its causes and consequences* (pp. 19–54). Hillsdale, NY: Erlbaum.

Waters, E., & Deane, K.E. (1985). Defining and assessing individual differences in attachment relationships: Q-methodology and the organization of behavior in infancy and early childhood. *Monographs of the Society for Research in Child Development, 50,* 1–2 (serial No. 209), 41–65.

Wills, D.D. (1977). *Culture's cradle: Social structural and interactional aspects of Senegalese socialization.* Unpublished Ph.D. dissertation in Anthropology, University of Texas at Austin.

Wolfenstein, M. (1955). French parents take their children to the park. In M: Mead & M. Wolfenstein (Eds.), *Childhood in contemporary cultures* (pp. 99–117). Chicago, IL: University of Chicago Press.

APPENDIX A

Results of the Sequence-Structure Analysis (Content of Repertoires of Individual Toddlers' Recurrent Stranger-Contacting Action Patterns).

No. Initials	Parental Report and Recurrent Stranger-Oriented Action Patterns
1. J.D.	PARENTAL REPORT: In home—with stranger, becomes quiet, and stays near the parent; outside, not as shy, approaches, warms up quickly

Session 1:
-OTH-LS1-LM-APS2-LS2-OTH-
-LS2-LM-LS2-OTH-LS2-
-SMS2-LM-LS2-LM-LS2-
-OTH-OTH-APS2-LS2-
-LM-OTH-LS2-SMS2-
-LS2-LM-LS2-SMS2-
-OTH-LS2-APS2-
-APS2-LS2-MAS2-
-APS1-SMS1-OTH-
-APS1-LS1-OTH-
-SMS2-LS2-OTH-
-OTH-SMS2-LS2-
-OTH-LS2-OTH-
-MAS1-APS2-
-LS2-LS1-
-APS2-SMS2-

Session 2:
-LS2-OTH-LS1-OTH-
-OTH-LS1-OTH-LM-
-OTH-OTH-LS1-OTH-
-INTM-LS2-OTH-
-INTS2-OTH-INTS2-
-LS2-LS1-OTH-
-OTH-LS1-OTH-
-OTH-LS2-OTH-
-LS2-OTH-LS2-
-LS2-INTM-
-LM-LS1-
-LS1-LS2-

| 2. J.W. | PARENTAL REPORT: In home—acts shy, hides behind mother's legs, and holds onto her clothes. If not pressed, eventually approaches the novel person |

Session 1:
-VOC-LS2-OTH-LS2-
-OTH-LS2-VOC-LS2-
-VOC-OTH-LS2-OTH-
-LS2-OTH-LS2-LM-
-LS2-VOC-OTH-
-LS2-LS1-LS2-
-LS2-LM-LS2-
-LS1-LM-
-INTS2-AOS2-
-LS2-APS2-
-TO-LS2-

Session 2:
-VOC-VOC-GVS2-
-OTH-VOC-LS2-
-LS2-OTH-VOC-
-APS2-GVS2-MAS2-
-OTH-APS2-GVS2-
-GVS2-VOC-
-GVS2-LS2-
-LS2-VOC-
-LS2-APS2-
-OTH-LS2-

3. D.B.   PARENTAL REPORT: In home—looks, smiles, hides face on mother's shoulder or lap. Withdraws initially if stranger reaches out to take him. Warms up quickly. Outside—smiles readily and jabbers. If stranger tries to touch him, looks at mother, may whimper and reach for her.

Session 1:
-VOC-OTH-VOC-LS2-
-LS2-OTH-LS2-OTH-
-OTH-VOC-LS2-OTH-
-LS2-OTH-VOC-
-LS2-TOS2-OTH-
-LS2-VOC-

Session 2:
-LS2-OTH-LS2-
-LS1-VOC-LS1-
-LS2-VOC-OTH-
-MAS2-APM-
-INTS2-VOC-
-LM-APS2-
-OTH-APS2-
-TOS2-VOC-
-LM-LS2-

4. S.S   PARENTAL REPORT: In home—very friendly, smiles. Outside—friendly, smiles.

Session 1:
-SMS2-APS2-TOS2-MAS2-OTH-
-OTH-LS2-APS2-
-LS2-OTH-SSO2-
-OTH-APM-APS2-
-APS2-GVS2-
-MAS2-APF-
-LS2-LAS2-
-APF-LS2-
-LS1-APS1-
-LS2-LS1-
-GVS2-LS2-
-AOS2-MAS2-
-SSO2-OTH-
-LS2-SMS2-
-MAS2-LS1-
-APS2-MAS2-

Session 2:
-VOC-LS2-OTH-
-INTM-VOC-LS2-
-MAS2-APM-
-MAS2-OTH-
-LS1-SMS1-

5. T.S.   Session 1:
-OTH-LS2-OTH-LS2-OTH-
-LS2-TM-

Session 2:
-GVS2-LS2-LM-OTH-
-OTH-LS2-TM-LS1-
-AOS2-MAS2-APM-
-APM-OTH-APS2-
-OTH-LS2-OTH-
-TM-LS1-OTH-
-LS2-LM-APM-
-MAS2-OTH-
-INTS2-LM-
-THS2-INTS2-
-INTS2-LS1-
-GVS2-MAS2-
-APM-APS2-
-APS2-GVS2-
-LM-LS2-

6. M.P. PARENTAL REPORT: In home—stares at stranger from distance, continues to play, but also acknowledges the stranger's presence. Eventually tries to get stranger's attention for interaction. Outside—stares, smiles, tries to get attention by being "cute" or vocalizing

Session 1:	Session 2:
-OTH-OTH-APS2-	-OTH-LS2-LS1-
-TM-VOC-LS1-	-VOC-LS2-VOC-
-LS1-VOC-OTH-	-MAS2-OTH-
-VOC-LS1-VOC-	-VOC-MAS2-
-OTH-VOC-OOS-	-LS2-OTH-
-AOS2-GVS2-	
-APS2-VOC-	
-INTS2-VOC-	
-MAS2-APF-	
-VOC-LS2-	
-OOS-CRY-	
-LS2-OTH-	

7. L.H. PARENTAL REPORT: In home—depends on mood. Sometimes very receptive, walks up to stranger. Outside—depends on mood and how receptive the stranger is to her

Session 1:	Session 2:
-LS2-OTH-FUSS-LS2-	-OTH-LS2-OTH-LS2-OTH-LS2-OTH-
-OTH-LS2-FUSS-	-APS2-GVS2-MAS2-APS2-GVS2-MAS2-
-LS2-FUSS-LS2-	-MAS2-APS2-GVS2-MAS2-APM-APS2-
-LS2-FUSS-OTH-	-LS2-OTH-SMS2-OTH-
-TM-FUSS-OTH-	-TM-OTH-LS2-OTH-
-FUSS-LS2-FUSS-	-LS2-OOS-OTH-
-LS2-TM-	-LS2-TM-
-TM-LS2-	-SMS2-TM-

8. T.C. PARENTAL REPORT: Both in home and outside very friendly to strangers

Session 1:	Session 2:
-APS2-GVS2-MAS2-APS2-AOS2-	-OTH-LS1-LM-LS2-APM-
-OTH-APM-APS2-	-APS2-VOC-MAS2-
-LAS1-OTH-OTH-	-VOC-APS2-VOC-
-LS2-APS2-TOS2-	-APS2-AOS2-MAS2-
-MAS2-APM-	-OTH-VOC-APS2-
-OTH-APS2-	-VOC-APS2-GVS2-
-TOS2-MAS2-	-MAS2-OOS-
-MAS2-APF-	-LS2-VOC-
	-VOC-MAS2-
	-INTS2-VOC-
	-LS1-VOC-

Session 3:

-VOC-OTH-VOC-LS2-OTH-	-LS2-APM-
LS2-OTH-	-LM-LS2-
-LS2-OTH-VOC-LM-	-APM-LS2-
-OTH-VOC-LS2-VOC-	-OBS2-VOC-
-OTH-APS2-GVS2-LS2-	-LS2-INTS2-
-LS2-OTH-VOC-LS2-	-VOC-MAS2-
-LS2-APS2-LS2-	-AOS2-VOC-

-LS2-OTH-OTH-   -LS2-AOS2-
-APS2-GVS2-INTS2-   -INTS2-OTH-
-VOC-GVS2-   -LS2-LM-
-INTS2-VOC-   -VOC-SMS2-
-APM-APS2-   -LS2-VOC-

9. S.C. PARENTAL REPORT: In home—selectively wary. Watches quietly for a few minutes, then cries. Outside—never wary, flirts

Session 1:   Session 2:
-OTH-LS2-OTH-   -LS2-MBYE-LS2-
-AOS2-OTH-LS2-   -LS2-OTH-LS2-
-OTH-LS2-VOC-   -OTH-LS2-OTH-
-LS2-OTH-LS2-   -LS2-AOS2-LS2-
-OTH-LS2-LM-   -LS2-AOS2-OTH-
-OTH-MAS2-   -OTH-LS2-AOS2-
-MAS2-APM-   -OTH-OTH-LS2-
-TM-APS2-   -S2BYE-LS2-
                       -LS2-LS1-

Session 3:
-TF-LS2-OTH-LS2-
-LS2-OTH-LS2-LS2-

10. C.D. PARENTAL REPORT: In home—stands away a few minutes, may go to mother, put head down on her lap, smile at stranger. A few minutes later, takes something to the stranger. The same is the case outside. Does not like the stranger to "rush" at her

Session 1:   Session 2:
-APS2-LS2-OTH-LS1-   -LM-LS2-LS1-LM-LS2-LS1-LM-LS2-
-GVS2-AOS2-INTS2-   -OTH-LS2-INTS2-LS2-LS2-
-OTH-LS2-SMS2-   -APS2-LS2-OTH-LS2-LS2-
-LS2-OTH-LS2-   -LS2-LS1-OOS-VOC-OTH-
-SMS2-LS1-LS2-   -OTH-LS2-SMS2-OTH-
-LS1-OTH-   -LS2-SMS2-OTH-LS2-
-MAS2-APM-   -LS2-LS2-LS1-VOC-
-LS2-GVS2-   -LM-LS2-OTH-OTH-
-LS2-MAS2-   -VOC-OTH-LS2-
-LS2-TOS2-   -LS1-VOC-LS2-
-APM-LS2-   -OTH-APS2-LS2-
-LS2-LM-   -APM-TM-LS2-
                                  -LS1-OTH-VOC-
                                  -INTM-LS2-
                                  -LS2-VOC-
Session 3:   -SMS2-LS2-
-LS2-LM-OTH-LM-LS2-VOC-OTH-   -TM-APS2-
-LM-LS2-VOC-OTH-LM-
-OTH-LM-LS2-SMS2-VOC-
-LS2-OTH-LM-LS2-
-VOC-OTH-LS2-OTH-
-LS2-VOC-OTH-LS2-
-LS2-OTH-LS2-LS2-
-LS2-OTH-VOC-LS2-

11. J.R.   PARENTAL REPORT: In home—shy, clings to parents. Outside—smiles at strangers, no fear unless the stranger becomes too friendly

Session 1:
-MAS2-APM-LS2-APS2-MAS2-
APM-
-LS2-LM-LS2-OTH-
-GVS2-LS2-OTH-LS2-
-OTH-LS2-OTH-
-LS2-TM-APS2-
-AOS2-GVS2-LS2-
-OTH-LS2-FUSS-
-VOC-LS2-
-LS2-GVS2-
-TM-LS2-
-OTH-GVS2-

Session 2:
-LS2-TM-LM-OTH-
-OTH-LM-LS2-
-OTH-LS2-SMS2-
-TM-LS2-OTH-
-LS2-OTH-LS2-
-CRY-TM-LS2-
-AOS2-OTH-
-OTH-GVS2-
-GVS2-AOS2-

Session 3:
-LS2-SMS2-LS2-
-APS2-GVS2-LS2-
-LS2-SMS2-OTH-
-INTM-LS2-SMS2-
-OTH-APS2-GVS2-
-APM-TM-LS2-
-APS2-AOS2-AOS2-
-LS2-APS2-GVS2-
-MAS2-APM-TM-
-APS2-GVS2-MAS2-
-LM-LS2-OTH-
-AOS2-VOC-
-MAS2-LS2-
-LS2-APS2-
-AOS2-MAS2-
-APM-LS2-
-LS2-LS2-
-LS2-LM-
-LS2-LS1-
-OTH-LS2-

Session 4:
-AOS2-OBS2-OTH-
-OBS2-THS2-AOS2-
-LS2-SMS2-OTH-
-OBS2-GVS2-
-THS2-OTH-
-OTH-THS2-
-GVS2-OBS2-
-LS2-OBS2-
-INTS2-LS2-
-AOS2-OTH-
-OBS2-AOS2-
-AOS2-INTM-
-LS2-AOS2-
-OTH-APS2-
-OTH-LS2-
-LM-LS2

12. J.S.   PARENTAL REPORT: In home—has met no strangers. Outside—waves at strangers, warms up to strangers immediately when visiting some other home

Session 1:
-VOC-LS1-OTH-LS2-OTH-LS2-
-OTH-VOC-OTH-LS1-OTH-
-LS2-OTH-LS2-OTH-
-OTH-LS2-OTH-VOC-
-OTH-LS2-LS2-
-LS2-LS2-OTH-
-LS2-OTH-OTH-
-OTH-LS2-SMS2-
-SMS2-OTH-LS2-
-INTS2-OTH-VOC-

Session 2:
-OTH-LS1-OTH-OTH-OTH-LS2-
OTH-VOC-OTH-
-OTH-VOC-LS2-OTH-OTH-LS2-
-OTH-LS2-OTH-LS1-
-OTH-VOC-LS1-
-LS1-VOC-OTH-
-MAS2-OTH-

-OTH-INTS2-OTH-
-LS2-VOC-OTH-
-LS2-OTH-SS20-
-VOC-LS2-
-SS20-VOC-
-AOS2-SMS2-
-OTH-APS2-
-SNS2-OTH-
-SNS2-LS2-

Session 3:
-VOC-TOS2-TOS2-OTH-
-AOS-OTH-GVS2-
-LS2-LM-LS1-
-OTH-GVS2-VOC-
-LS2-VOC-
-OTH-APS2-
-LS2-OTH-
-OTH-LS2-

Session 4:
-OTH-VOC-OTH-LS2-OTH-VOC-
-LS2-OTH-LS2-LM-
-LS2-OTH-VOC-OTH-
-VOC-LS2-OTH-VOC-
-OTH-VOC-LS2-
-OBS2-LS2-
-FUSS-LS2-
-LS2-LS1-
-LS2-VOC-
-LS2-OBS2-
-TM-LS2-

13. N.S.   PARENTAL REPORT: More likely to approach a stranger outside home than in home

Session 1:
-OTH-LS2-OTH-LS2-
-OTH-OTH-APM-LS2-
-OTH-APS2-OTH-
-VOC-LS1-
-LS1-OTH-
-LS2-LM-

Session 2:
-TOS2-LS2-MAS2-OTH-
-LS2-OTH-VOC-LS2-
-LS2-APS2-TOS2-LS2-
-LS1-APM-TM-LS2-
-MAS2-OTH-OTH-
-VOC-TOS2-
-LM-LS2-
-OTH-LS2-

Session 3:
-TOS2-VOC-OTH-
-TOS2-VOC-LS1-
-INTS2-VOC-OTH-
-VOC-OTH-TOS2-
-LM-TOS2-
-LS2-OTH-
-MAS2-APS2-

Session 4:
-MAS2-OTH-LS1-
-LS2-OTH-LS2-
-OTH-LS2-SMS2-
-LS2-LS2-OTH-
-GVS2-OTH-LS2-
-OTH-SMS2-GVS2-
-APM-LS1-
-LS1-APM-
-INTS2-MAS2-
-GVS2-INTS2-
-OTH-APS2-
-SMS2-OTH-
-LS2-GVS2-
-GVS2-LS2-
-MAS2-APS2-
-SMS2-MAS2-

14. S.R.   PARENTAL REPORT: In home—clings to mother, approaches the stranger, and plays after 10 minutes. Outside—shy, would not go to a stranger

Session 1:
-SMS2-OTH-LS2-SMS2-OTH-

Session 2:
-OTH-LS2-OTH-LS2-

-LS2-GVS2-LS2-
-LS2-OTH-LS1-
-OTH-LS2-OTH-
-LS2-GVS2-OTH-
-LS1-OTH-

-AOS2-OTH-AOS2-
-OTH-OTH-GVS2-
-GVS2-OTH-OTH-
-GVS2-INTS2-
-OTH-LS1-
-AOS2-GVS2-
-TOS2-SMS2-
-GVS2-GVS2-
-LS2-VOC-
-LS2-SMS2-
-LM-LS2-
-SMS2-OTH-
-APS2-GVS2-
-LS1-LS2-

Session 3:
-VOC-OBS2-LM-VOC-
-OTH-MAS2-OTH-
-VOC-LS2-
-OTH-LS2-
-LS1-OTH-
-FUSS-LAS2-
-LAS2-VOC-
-LAS2-OBS2-
-GVS2-INTS2-
-OTH-GVS2-

Session 4:
-OTH-APS2-APM-OTH-
-OTH-APS2-GVS2-
-LM-LS2-
-APS2-OTH-
-AOS2-OTH-
-MAS2-OTH-

15. M C.S. PARENTAL REPORT: Friendly with strangers who play with him, anywhere. If the stranger is apprehensive, cries and goes to the parent

Session 1:
-OTH-LM-LS2-OTH-
-VOC-AOS2-INTS2-
-INTS2-VOC-
-OBS2-INTS2-
-INTS2-IMS2-
-OTH-LS2-

Session 2:
-LS2-OTH-LM-LS2-OTH-
-OTH-LS2-AOS2-OTH-
-OTH-AOS2-OTH-
-INTS2-AOS2-OTH-
-OTH-OTH-LS2-
-AOS2-OTH-VOC-
-OTH-VOC-LAS2-
-LS2-OTH-VOC-
-OTH-LS2-OTH-
-VOC-LM-LS2-
-LM-LS2-LS1-
-LAS2-OTH-
-OTH-INTS2-
-LAS2-MAS2-
-APS2-LAS2-
-LS1-OTH-
-MAS2-LS2-

Session 3:
-LS2-LS1-LS2-LS1-LS2-
-OTH-LS2-LS1-LS2-
-LS1-SMS1-LM-OTH-
-OTH-LS1-VOC-

Session 4:
-VOC-OTH-VOC-LS2-LM-OTH-
-LS2-APS2-LS2-MAS2-
-LS2-SMS2-LM-LS2-
-SMS2-LS2-SMS2-

-VOC-LS2-OTH-
-OTH-LS2-LM-
-LM-OTH-LS2-
-OTH-LS2-OTH-
-LS2-SMS2-OTH-
-LS2-VOC-
-LM-LS2-

-VOC-OTH-APS2-
-LS2-MAS2-SMS2-
-APS2-SNS2-LS2-
-LS2-MAS2-OTH-
-LS2-SMS2-LS2-
-LM-LS2-SMS2-
-MAS2-APS1-VOC-
-SMS2-OOS-
-THS2-LS2-
-GVS2-LS2-
-VOC-SMS2-
-GVS2-VOC-
-SMS2-GVS2-
-INTS2-SMS2-
-SMS2-AOS2-
-OTH-APS2-
-LS1-LS2-
-LS2-VOC-
-SMS2-VOC-
-APS2-OTH-
-LS2-OTH-
-OTH-LS2-
-LS1-VOC-
-OTH-LS1-

16. M C.P. PARENTAL REPORT: In home—cries, clings to mother if thinks that the mother is leaving. Outside—smiles if spoken to, seems oblivious of others

Session 1:
-OTH-LS1-LM-OTH-
-OTH-LS2-OTH-OTH-
-OTH-LS2-LS1-
-SS20-VOC-

Session 2:
-LS2-OTH-LS2-OTH-
-OTH-LS2-OTH-LS2-
-OTH-LS2-VOC-
-OTH-LS2-LM-
-LS2-OTH-INTS2-
-LS1-OTH-
-OBS2-OTH-
-VOC-LS2-
-LS2-OBS2-
-LM-LS2-

Session 3:
-INTM-VOC-LS2-
-VOC-APS2-
-LS2-OTH-
-LS2-APM-

Session 4:

-OTH-VOC-OTH-VOC-OTH-LS2-
-LS2-OTH-VOC-OTH-VOC-OTH-
-MAS2-OTH-VOC-OTH-
-VOC-LS2-OTH-VOC-
-VOC-MAS2-OTH-LS2-
-VOC-OTH-GVS2-LS2-
-OTH-LS2-VOC-OTH-
-LS2-VOC-OTH-LS2-
-IMS2-OTH-VOC-

-VOC-LS2-VOC-
-GVS2-LS2-OTH-
-OTH-LS2-OTH-
-LS2-OTH-LS2-
-VOC-AOS2-
-AOS2-VOC-
-AOS2-OTH-
-VOC-INTS2-

CHAPTER 6

Early Childhood Attachment and Later Problem Solving: A Vygotskian Perspective*

René van der Veer and Marinus H. van IJzendoorn

Department of Education
Section W.E.P.
University of Leiden
Leiden, The Netherlands

INTRODUCTION

A classical dilemma of developmental psychology concerns the relationship between societal and individual development. Until recently most psychologists tended to ignore society's role in child development, depicting the developmental process as a "lone venture" for the child (Bruner, 1984). There is growing concern with this attitude, however, resulting in critical analyses and studies. Riegel was among the first American psychologists to oppose this "lone venture approach." He criticized developmental psychologists for studying developmental processes without studying the historical conditions and changes under which they take place. In his opinion the child should be seen as developing in a developing society. Ignoring this fact means neglecting the crucial, formative role of society (van IJzendoorn & van der Veer, 1984). Recently, researchers such as Bronfenbrenner (1983), Hinde, Perret-Clermont, and Stevenson-Hinde (1985), and Harré, Clarke, and De Carlo (1985) have ventilated similar concerns.

---

* Preparation of this chapter was supported in part by the Nationaal Comité voor Kinderpostzegels. We gratefully acknowledge the assistance of Sita van Vliet-Visser in collecting and coding data.

Bronfenbrenner (1983) tried to explain the complex issues at stake by comparing the developing child in a developing society to a person walking in a train. The person can walk backward (regress) and forward (progress) in the cars of the (developmental) train, but the train itself will inevitably pass through a changing environment. As with other metaphors, this one is not without its drawbacks, however, as has been pointed out by Engeström (1986). One of its weak points is that no one seems to be driving the train, implying that children do not actively construct their environment and are but passive passengers of life. This certainly is not true, as has been amply demonstrated in various child studies (Trevarthen, 1977; Brazelton, Koslowski, & Main, 1974).

In order to understand the complex dialectic between child development and societal development, most researchers have focused on the social relationships the child engages in. This seems to be the place par excellence where child and culture meet. There is, to be sure, a limitation in this approach, because the influence of society can be exerted also through cultural objects and means, such as toys and books, and through culturally structured environments (Valsiner, 1987). Following a purely "interpersonal" approach one would, therefore, underestimate the role of social and cultural factors in child development (van der Veer & van IJzendoorn, 1985). Nevertheless, the emphasis on an interpersonal approach can be defended, because children are introduced to cultural objects and means mostly through personal relationships. In particular for infants and small children, then, it seems a plausible choice to study the societal "background" of development through studying social relationships.

Most children in Western societies grow up in a nuclear family, forming attachments with one or more blood relatives. As they grow older, the network of attachments expands to include other persons outside the family. It is generally supposed that these long-lasting attachments to a small number of significant persons are of great importance for the child's developmental trajectory. In nontechnical language this means that the love and friendship of a few important others are crucial for the child's development and will partly determine its course. For this reason Hinde et al. (1985) have pleaded the necessity for a science about long-term dyadic and triadic relationships. These authors concentrate on the interplay between the child's social interactions and relationships on the one hand, and his or her cognitive development on the other hand, emphasizing that it is in practice wellnigh impossible to separate the cognitive aspects of development from other aspects.

As we are going to talk about adult–child relationships in this chapter, and in particular, about mother–child relationships, we will ignore the influence of relationships with siblings and peers. It is important to note that these relationships are quite significant for child development (Newcombe & Brady, 1982). They will not be studied here, however, to avoid excessive complication of already very intricate phenomena.

SOME METHODOLOGICAL REMARKS

It is quite hard to conceptualize the way social relationships structure the child's development. Hartup (1985, p. 66) has tried to elucidate this question, suggesting that relationships serve three functions in the social and cognitive development of the child. First, they are the contexts in which basic competencies emerge. Second, relationships are resources that furnish the child with the security and skills needed. Third, relationships are forerunners of other relationships. Taking this point of view, one avoids making the mistake of exclusively concentrating on the cognitive effects of social relationships, seeing the adult partner of the dyad solely as the more capable one. The caregiver is, apart from being a cognitive agent, a potential source of emotional warmth and feelings of security as well. Hartup (1985) has also pointed out some aspects of the complex dialectic between ontogeny and relationships— among other things, the fact that two persons are developing within these relationships, not one. In adult–child relationships one of the developmental trajectories is rapid, and the other slow. But even though the adult's trajectory may be slower than that of the child's, it has implications for the relationship that exists between them. The situation is complicated even more by the fact that both mother and child can have more relationships. Referring back to Bronfenbrenner's metaphor, one might say that mother and child walk at different speeds through the developmental train and, moreover, continually stumble across other people who further or hinder their progress. Clearly, in this complex situation it is hard to answer causal questions. Hartup even gives up and states that to ask these questions with respect to the development of relationships and the development of cognition is to ask the "chicken and egg" question. The development of cognition is as much the result of developing relationships as it is the cause of their future course. Accepting Hartup's position would imply that we are in no position to question Samuel Butler's aphorism that "a hen is but an egg's way of making another egg."

An even more complicated picture is sketched by Hinde et al. (1985, XV). They state that, in social relationships, the nature of the interactions depends upon the natures of the participant individuals, while the characteristics that individuals display depend in part on the nature of the interaction and relationship in which they are involved. Moreover, in the longer term the characteristics that they can display are influenced by the interactions and relationships they have experienced. Further, the nature of relationships depends on those of the constituent interactions, but the nature of those interactions depends on the participants' perceptions of the nature of the relationship. The nature of any relationship is affected by that of the social group in which it is embedded, etc.. Reasoning in this way they come to the situation delineated in Figure 1. Hinde and his colleagues conclude that the child psychologist evidently must come to terms with a whole series of dialectics between successive levels of social phenomena. At the same time he must realize that each level does not represent a fixed state but a process in continuous creation through the agency of dialectics.

Taking into account this intricate state of affairs, it is not to be expected that isolated empirical or theoretical studies will soon lead to an all-embracing theory about the role of social relationships in child development. It will rather take years of diligent work by many researchers to find the missing pieces of the puzzle, and, of course, now and then a brilliant researcher will stand up and tell us that we are solving the wrong puzzle. It will be quite difficult to clarify the role of social relationships in child development, but in our opinion it is not a hopeless task. There are ways to tackle some of the "chicken

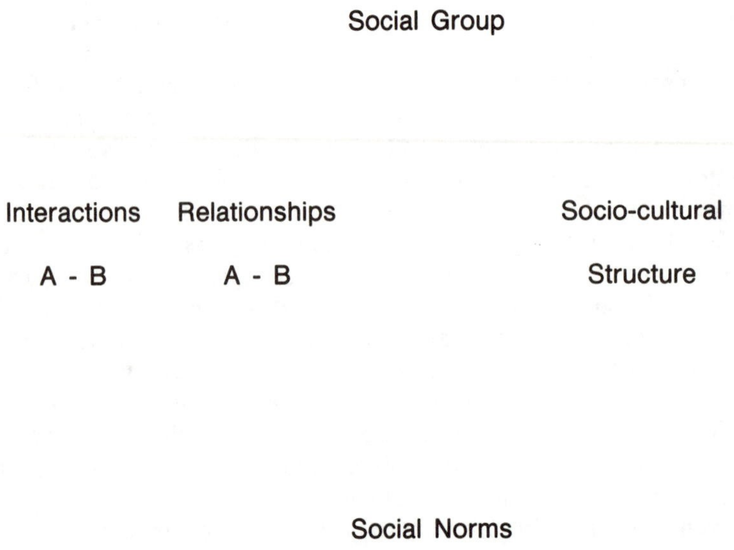

Social Group

| Interactions | Relationships | | Socio-cultural |
| A - B | A - B | | Structure |

Social Norms

Figure 1. The dialectics between successive levels of social complexity (From Hinde, Perret-Clermont, & Stevenson-Hinde, 1985, p. xv).

and egg" problems, and under these circumstances solutions like Samuel Butler's can be proven implausible.

The traditional approach is to combine experimental or intervention studies with correlational studies. Bryant (1985) argues that both have their advantages and disadvantages. In his opinion intervention studies are capable of showing the fact that A (for example, a tutorial strategy followed by a mother) causes B (for example, enhanced cognitive performance of her child). But there is a basic problem about such studies, and this is the danger of artificiality. That is why Bryant argues that the experimental approach should be combined with (longitudinal) correlational studies, which constitute a better approach to find real-life effects. It is unclear, however, how this approach would solve our problems. The interpretation of correlational findings is, as we will see, fraught with difficulties. Moreover, Bryant's treatment of the intervention study seems to imply that the concept of direct linear causality (A $\rightarrow$ B) is applicable to processes of child development. This is doubtful, in view of the complexities sketched above. A tutorial strategy may facilitate or maintain the child's developing cognitive abilities, but it does not cause these abilities. The wish to find causal effects does not seem to be compatible with the dialectics of child development. More specifically, it seems to imply that the child's development is nothing more than the sum total of influences undergone by that child. This view would deny the active role of the child in structuring his or her own environment. An active role which has been defended by such diverse psychologists as Piaget and Vygotsky.

In the present study we will explore some of the connections between social relationships and child development from a less traditional perspective. The frameworks we will use are Vygotsky's cultural-historical theory and the attachment theory developed by Bowlby and Ainsworth. It is our feeling that the long-term influence of early childhood attachments for cognitive development has not yet been demonstrated convincingly. Finding such influence would considerably strengthen attachment theory. On the other hand, we feel that the cultural-historical approach lacks an appropriate perspective on the relevance of non-cognitive adult–child interactions. As we have argued in the introduction, the adult is not only a cognitive agent but also a potential source of love and protection. Both factors may influence the child's cognitive development.

ATTACHMENT

The main points of attachment theory about the influence of early-childhood attachments on cognitive development can be summarized as follows. The qualities of mother–child interaction can be assessed using the classification scheme developed by Ainsworth and Wittig (1969) for assessing the security of attachment between the mother and the child. In secure relationships mother and child seem to be sensitively tuned to one another in terms of proximity-maintenance and in terms of their emotions and communication. Secure attachments then, should be excellent contexts for mediating the regulation of the child's cognitive actions (Hartup, 1985, p. 79). Several findings seem to confirm this hypothesis (Matas, Arend, & Sroufe, 1978; Bretherton, Bates, Benigni, Camaioni, & Volterra, 1979). Securely attached mother–child dyads, for example, seem to include more enthusiastic and compliant children in problem-solving tasks who also exhibit fewer frustration-related behavior. Longitudinal research also demonstrated the fact that these children at 2.5 (Hazen & Durrett, 1982) and 5 years of age (Arend, Gove, & Sroufe, 1979) are more inclined to explore the surroundings than anxiously attached children. Finally, they are also more eager to learn and show more inquisitiveness (Waters, Wippman, & Sroufe, 1979). Hartup (1985) argues that the cognitive advantage of securely attached mother–child dyads is mainly to be found in the domain of regulative activities rather than other cognitive functions. Such advantages need not be reflected in global measures of intelligence such as IQ tests (but see van IJzendoorn & van Vliet-Visser, 1988), nor need they lead to higher chances of achieving success with a task. But they might result in a different patterning of specific abilities, in different emotional accompaniments of cognitive performance, and in different mother–child dialogues in problem solving tasks. Long-term effects of these cognitive differences were found in Arend (1984) and Rahe (1984).

A key concept in attachment theory seems to be that of "sensitivity" or "sensitive responsiveness" (Ainsworth, Bell, & Stayton, 1974). The caregiver has to respond sensitively in order for a secure relationship to be able to evolve. *Sensitivity* may be defined as a caregiver's tendency to provide contingent, appropriate, and consistent responses to an infant's signals or needs. Sensitive responses to an infant's signals will foster his or her feelings of security and competence: If every signal is adequately received and responded to, the infant develops a feeling of mastery over the environment and of trust in the persons who react to the signals. To react sensitively, the adult has to perceive the infant's signal or need, interpret it correctly, select an appropriate response, and implement it effectively (Lamb & Easterbrooks, 1981). Both understimulation (e.g., forcing the child prematurely to act independently, denying love) and overstimulation (e.g., overprotective behavior depriving the child of the possibility of independent explorations) should be avoided (Belsky, Rovine & Taylor, 1984). This does not necessarily mean that an attachment relationship should be without frictions or even conflicts. Studies with nonhuman and human infants have shown that mothers will normally demand certain activities from their children when they feel it is appropriate to do so (Plooij & van der Rijt-Plooij, 1983). Perceiving that the infant is ready to perform the activity, they will demand from him or her to act, even if the infant is at first quite reluctant to engage in his or her "zone of proximal development" (see below).

We thus see that the caregiver–child attachment will function as a context for the child's cognitive development. The first interactional patterns between caregiver and child will have largely an emotional, affective nature. These interactions will develop into an affective relationship, the quality of which can be assessed by different means. Gradually the caregiver and child will start jointly performing increasingly difficult tasks, and the child will start independently exploring his or her environments. This means that the caregiver–child interactions will be cognitively more demanding. The affective interchanges will recede to the background while continuing to form an important context of the child's cognitive development.

COGNITION

The picture sketched above fits nicely with the concept of social interaction developed within the cultural-historical tradition. Researchers working in this tradition claim that a large part of cognitive development evolves in social interaction with a more able partner. Child and caregiver continually participate in joint activities, and these activities are thought to be crucial for cognitive development. The adult partner in a relationship should be very well aware of the child's current abilities and should try to lure the child into joint activities slightly above his or her level of independent performance. This should help creating the so-called *zone of proximal development* defined by Vygotsky as "the divergence between the mental age, or level of actual development, which is determined with the help of independently solved tasks, and the level which is reached by the child solving tasks not independently but in collaboration" (Vygotsky, 1982, p. 247). Vygotsky was rather vague about the type of collaboration children need. He mentioned that the only good kind of instruction should march ahead of development and lead it (Vygotsky, 1982, p. 252), but this mainly referred to instruction in schools and he did not provide any detailed analyses of adult–child interactions. A basic idea behind the concept of the zone of proximal development is that the origin of all higher cognitive processes is to be found in joint activities (van der Veer & Valsiner, 1986). At first they take place at the interpersonal level and only later, through internalization, they turn into intrapersonal capabilities (Vygotsky, 1983, p. 145). Many researchers, both in the West and in the East, have been inspired by these rather global but perceptive insights resulting in various different post-Vygotskian interpretations.

For our purpose the most relevant work has been done by Bruner (1983, 1984), Wood (1980; Wood, Wood, & Middleton, 1978; Wood, Bruner, & Ross, 1976) and Wertsch (1985a; b). Bruner has elaborated the concept of the zone of proximal development by introducing the notion of "scaffolding." He also pointed out the importance of "formats," that is, standard situations in which the interactions (e.g., play, problem solving) between caregiver and child invariably take place. Finally, Bruner demonstrated the importance of preverbal adult–child interactions for cognitive and language development. Thereby, he extended the period of supposed importance of adult–child interactions considerably to include infancy. Vygotsky tended to neglect these early joint activities (van der Veer & van IJzendoorn, 1985; van der Veer, 1986). Bruner's extension is also of importance for the connection with attachment theory. The reason is that the affective components of adult–child interactions are much more prominent in this period of life. By emphasizing the importance of this period for cognitive development and by analyzing emotionally-colored activities such as play and games, he turned our attention to the affective concomitants of interactions.

The work of Wood and his colleagues (Wood, Bruner, & Ross, 1976; Wood, Wood, & Middleton, 1978; Wood, 1980) is especially important because he has introduced a way of looking at the concept of sensitive responsiveness in the cognitive domain. Wood's idea was that mothers ideally should follow the so-called "contingency strategy" when trying to solve a problem together with their child. This strategy implies that the level of the mother's intervention in the child's problem-solving process should closely follow the child's successes and failures. If the child makes a mistake, the mother should provide instructions or suggestions just one level lower than she did before. An important characteristic of this strategy is that the mother adjusts her assistance in a very special way: she increases her demands as the child is doing well. This means that the mother is continually trying to get her child to perform at a higher level, thereby promoting independent problem solving. Effective instruction, thus conceived, consists in continually confronting the child with problems of controlled complexity, setting goals or making requests which lie beyond the child's current level of attainment but not so far beyond that he is unable to "unpack" or comprehend the suggestion or instruction being made (Wood, Wood, & Middleton, 1978). Wood (1980) was able to show that children of mothers who followed this tutorial strategy were better able to solve the task without help afterwards. What is more, he demonstrated that teachers especially trained to follow the contingency strategy produced the same results. Children who had been solving problems with these teachers performed better than other children. This means that Wood and his colleagues were able to show that the mother's tutorial strategy contributed significantly to the independent problem-solving behavior of the children. The result is significant and should be kept in mind when analyzing the mother–child interactions in the present study. It implies that one should attempt to analyze mother–child interactions by retaining the sequential nature of these interactions. Only then can be seen which of the mother's interventions follow the child's actions. This reciprocal process will not be revealed by correlational findings but requires a sequential analysis.

Wertsch (1985a, 1985b) has done much to clarify the semiotic background of mother–child interactions reasoning from a Vygotskian point of view. He focused on the means mothers have at their disposal to create a perspective on problem situations shared by the child. When jointly solving a problem, mother and child frequently have different perspectives of the problem solving situation. It is the adult's responsibility to adapt flexibly to the child's perspective and to create a temporarily shared reality. In practice mothers follow, according to Wertsch, the strategy of accepting the perspective of their child if it is necessary for mutual understanding, but at the same time they repeatedly try to return to their own perspective of the situation. Not only do they quite probably think that their perspective is the more correct one, they also check whether the child is prepared to accept the adult view of the situation. When the mother realizes that her child is not capable of seeing the situation in another way than his or her own, she temporarily abandons her perspective. Mothers follow a quite flexible strategy in this respect. It is important to note that this strategy is essentially the same as the one advocated by Wood. When things go well, the mother starts demanding more; when things go wrong, she is satisfied for the time being and adjusts to the child's level. This, then, seems to exemplify sensitive responsiveness in the cognitive domain.

SENSITIVE RESPONSIVENESS

It is still unclear whether the concepts of affective sensitivity and cognitive sensitivity can be taken together under the heading of "general sensitivity." This would mean that the basic processes of sensitive responsiveness are the same for both the affective and the cognitive domain. From the outline given above, certain similarities seem obvious. In both domains careful monitoring of the child's current abilities, signals, or state of mind is required. In both domains the caregiver should adjust to the child's point of view in order to reach common understanding. Finally, in both domains the caregiver will make demands on the child if he or she feels the child is ready for it. Despite these similarities one can imagine that some caregivers are more sensitive in one domain than in the other. In fact, evidence for the existence of two independent dimensions of sensitivity, one for affective behaviors and one for instructional behaviors, has been found by us in an earlier study (van IJzendoorn, van der Veer, & van Vliet-Visser, 1987; van der Veer & van IJzendoorn, 1987). In this study both the mother's affective (e.g., smiling, distance from child, encouragement) and cognitive (e.g., hints, feedback, instruction) behaviors during a joint problem solving task were rated. It turned out that these behaviors varied independently (formed two orthogonal factors in a factor analysis), thus suggesting that some mothers may provide a very good emotional climate while not being very adequate instructors, and vice versa. This would mean that, despite the structural similarities between the concepts pointing to an "umbrella" concept of sensitivity, in practice behavior may be specific for one or the other domain.

In the above it has been argued that the long-term influence of early childhood attachments has not yet been convincingly demonstrated. A more adequate conception of the importance of the intellectual interplay between caregiver and child may be needed. At the same time it was argued that researchers working in the Vygotskian line lack a perspective on the importance of affective caregiver–child interactions. The relevance of sensitive emotional behavior seems grossly underestimated in this school of thought (as is the case for any theory of cognitive development). These are reasons for trying to combine certain findings of attachment theory and cultural-historical theory. Concepts of sensitivity as outlined above could play an important role in this attempt. Keeping the idea of sensitive responsiveness in mind, we will try to explore in the present study some of the connections between affective and cognitive aspects of joint task performance. It goes without saying that we should not forget that the distinction between affective and cognitive behaviors is made by the researchers, and that in practice these behaviors will hardly ever be found in "pure" form. As Hinde et al. (1985, p. xvi) have put it, "we shall be forced to bear in mind that the concepts we use—relationships, cognition, emotion, stage, and so on—are at the same time essential tools for understanding and blinkers that constrain our vision."

THE STUDY

In the present study some of the long-term repercussions of early childhood attachments will be explored. In particular, we are interested in the possible relevance of mother–child attachments for later joint actions of mother and child. To classify the early childhood attachment relationships, use was made of the well-known Strange Situation procedure. This resulted in the equally well-known categories of securely attached, and resistantly and avoidantly attached dyads. Three years later, the same mother–child pairs were asked to solve a cognitive task together, and both their verbal interchanges and their behaviors were analyzed. We wondered whether there would still be differences between the respective attachment groups in this situation of joint problem solving. In keeping with what was said in the paragraphs above, it was decided to study both the cognitive and the affective utterances and behaviors of mothers and children. The focus was thus not only on clearly cognitive aspects, like advice given by the mother, but also on encouraging remarks, etc. In this way any long-term differences for different attachment groups for both intellectual and emotional interchanges could be seen.

In agreement with the contingency strategy outlined by Wood and Wertsch (see above), special attention was given to the mothers' interventions following their children's behavior. Such a strategy seemed to be in keeping with the general Vygotskian framework which emphasizes the initial asymmetrical cooperation between adult and child. It is the adult who ideally adjusts his or her tutorial interventions to the child's efforts. Of course, inevitably, his or her actions will in their turn influence the child and promote some general atmosphere (van IJzendoorn et al. 1987; van der Veer & van IJzendoorn, 1987). In this chapter, however, the focus is on the question of whether adults generally follow a sensitive (contingency) strategy and whether such strategies are related to the attachment background. In addition we looked for emotional actions undertaken by the mother in reply to the child's efforts. Here also, the main interest was in the problem of the adults' sensitive responsiveness—in other words, the way adults react to children's actions in the emotional domain.

We will make use of different ways of analyzing the findings. In the first place, some traditional correlational results will be presented. It will be argued that these results are difficult to interpret and not sufficient for our purpose. The reason is that correlational analyses are performed within groups and, therefore, speak only about the structure of these groups. They do not reveal anything about particular individuals within groups (Valsiner, 1986), nor do they tell us anything about the sequential structure of the data. In view of the goal stated above—to study mothers' interventions following children's actions—it was decided to add a sequential analysis. The sequential analysis fits the questions raised in this chapter particularly well, because the original temporal structure of the mother–child interactions is retained in the data. This analysis, therefore, allows interpretations about temporal contingencies and enables us to study maternal strategies in joint problem-solving situations.

Design

At 24 months of age (range: 23 to 25 months), 77 children and their mothers were observed in the Strange Situation. Sixty-five of the mother–child pairs participated in a follow-up study 3 years later. The children completed an individual IQ test, and mother–child pairs completed a problem solving task. The whole process was videotaped. In the follow-up study, the mean age of the children was 64 months (range: 57 to 72 months).

Sixteen percent of the original subjects did not participate in the follow-up study. Respondents and nonrespondents were compared on the following variables: attachment classification, attachment behaviors, social economic status, and sex. No significant differences were found. Therefore, it was concluded that the nonrespondents did not constitute a specific selection from the original sample. Details about the original selection and the way it was selected can be found in Goossens (1986).

Procedure

The Strange Situation. The Strange Situation is essentially focused upon the relationship between caregiver and child (Ainsworth, Blehar, Waters, & Wall, 1978). It consists of eight episodes, the last seven of which should ideally last 3 minutes each. The first one is variable and usually takes less than 30 seconds. After some final instructions in this first episode, caregiver and child are left in the playroom (Episode 2). In Episode 3, a stranger enters who, after 3 min, signals to the mother to leave (Episode 4). In Episode 5 the mother returns, to leave again in Episode 6. The stranger re-enters the room in the seventh episode, and in the last episode the mother returns once again. The whole procedure took place in a laboratory at the university. To assess the quality of the relationship, the interaction between mother and child

is scored on six 7-point rating scales, which take into account the frequency, intensity, and latency of specified behavioral components. The scales are for proximity and contact seeking, maintenance of contact, resistance, avoidance, search behavior, and distance interaction. The frequency of crying and explorations is observed. The patterns of scores on the first four scales in the reunion episodes (5 and 8) leads to the classification of mother–child pairs in anxiously avoidant attachment (A), secure attachment (B), or anxiously resistant attachment (C). These three main groups may be further subdivided into various subgroups (A1, A2, B1, B2, B3, B4, C1, C2). The securely attached group shows minimal resistant or avoidant behavior; children from secure dyads are somewhat upset when their mother has left, but her return has an immediate calming effect. The children from the A and C dyads deviate from this pattern. Some children avoid their returning mother (A), whereas other children behave ambivalently, seeking contact but resisting the mother as well (C). The subcategories B1 and B4 have been called "marginal" groups, because their position in the classification system is not altogether clear (Ainsworth et al., 1978). Children from the B1 dyads show some resemblance to children from A-dyads, because of their tendency to slightly avoid the mother. Children from the B4 group have been called anxiously dependent (van IJzendoorn, Goossens, Kroonenberg, & Tavecchio, 1985; Sagi, Lamb, Lewkowicz, Shoham, Dvir, & Estes, 1985). These children are very upset in the Strange Situation: they cry a great deal and show little exploration or playing behavior. However, they greet their returning mother less ambivalently than do children from C dyads. Two observers independently scored 22 randomly selected videotaped Strange Situations. The interrater reliability, computed with Pearson's r, was good; for proximity in the two reunion episodes, .77 and .91, respectively; for maintaining contact, .95 and .97; for resistance, .88 and .92; for avoidance, .86 and .91. On the basis of these interactive scales, the children were classified as A, B, or C group children. The interrater agreement for this step was 95.5%; for the subcategories it was 91.5%. The scores on these scales and the classifications were derived from Goossens (1986). The interrater reliability for the scales in the other episodes and for "search" and "crying" ranged from .73 to .97. Agreement for exploratory manipulation was 78%. These scales and the behavioral patterns were scored by the second author. The stability and validity of the procedures for 24-month-old children is described elsewhere (Goossens, Van IJzendoorn, Tavecchio, & Kroonenberg, 1986; Goossens, 1986).

The problem solving task. Mother–child pairs were asked to come to the laboratory and to solve the so-called Butterdish problem. The mother was requested to assist her child (if necessary) as she and her child were accustomed to. The whole problem-solving process was videotaped. The Butterdish is a series of round boxes of different sizes which fit together only when turned upside down (because of the protruding bottom of each box). The task for the child is to fit the boxes together in such a way as to form one compact box (having the size of the largest box). The maximum amount of problem solving time was fixed at 10 minutes. The actual amount of time needed was, however, much less. Mean time for reaching the solution was 139 seconds.

Protocol analysis. On the basis of the videotapes the dialogues between mother and child were transcribed. These protocols were then analyzed using various categories to score the verbal output of both mother and child. The utterances of the child were scored into the following categories: 1—Asking for feedback. All utterances of the child in which she or he asks for approval or disapproval of her or his actions by the mother. Examples could be utterances like "Is this wrong?", "This is okay, isn't it?", etc.; 2—Asking for advice. In this category were scored all requests for a general strategy, or questions about how to proceed in the next step of the process. The child might say, for instance, "What should I do now?" or "Where do I start?"; 3—Positive comments on the child's own actions; 4—Negative comments on the child's own actions; 5—Rest category of utterances not falling into the first four categories and of utterances which could not be deciphered. In addition the total frequency of the child's utterances was computed.

The mother's utterances fell into seven categories: 1—Positive evaluation; 2—Negative evaluation; 3—Neutral evaluation. All utterances in which the mother evaluated the actions of her child fall into these three categories; 4—Strategical advice. This category contains all the mother's suggestions concerning the most preferable way to proceed in this task to find the solution. The mother attempts to formulate a long-term strategy (either algorithm-like or heuristic-like) for her child. An example would be "Start with the smallest box and then try to fit the next smallest one, etc." (algorithm), or "Put aside all the boxes you already tried" (heuristic); 5—Direct advice. This category concerns all suggestions made by the mother about the best way to proceed in the phase immediately following the child's last action. The mother gives next-step or short-term hints and prompts to her child; 6—Egocentric talk. The mother comments on her own actions while trying to solve (a part of) the problem. In doing so she does not address her child; 7—Rest category of utterances not falling into the first six categories or utterances which could not be deciphered. In addition the mother's total number of utterances was computed.

Two raters independently scored all mother–child dialogues. The mean interrater-reliability was .92 (range: .65 to .99).

Behavioral analysis. The protocol analysis was based on the utterances of mothers and children. Of course, their interaction during joint problem solving does not solely consist of verbal utterances: both partners can display various nonverbal behaviors like pointing, looking, showing, etc. Therefore, using the videotapes, a system was developed to score the nonverbal interactions too. The categories used to score the verbal interactions were for the most part retained. This led to the following possible categories for the child's behavior: nonverbal request for help (the child is looking puzzled at the mother), asking for feedback, asking for advice, positive comment on own task performance, and negative comment on own task performance (for a description of these categories, see the paragraph above). The maternal behavior was scored into the following categories: no instruction (the mother is not paying attention to the child or is silently watching), global feedback (the mother gives feedback to the child without specifying any steps to be taken, e.g., yes, all right, try again, you can do it, etc.), strategical advice, giving and taking of the materials (the mother structures the task for the child by taking away irrelevant materials and supplying the right materials), demonstration (the mother shows the child how part of the task should be solved), and solving the task (the mother tries to solve the problem without the intention of showing her child how the task should be solved). All behaviors were scored using 3-sec intervals.

ANALYSIS AND RESULTS

All utterances made by mothers and children were scored into the abovementioned categories. Because of the skewness of the resulting frequency distributions, it was decided to analyze the data using non-parametric statistical methodology.

Analysis of Correlation Matrices

The first thing one would like to know is whether the utterances of both partners in the dialogue are in some meaningful way interrelated. It seems evident that the mothers and children in problem solving tasks are communicating in the real sense of the word, and that their dialogue in no way resembles that of the proverbial cocktail party. A correlational analysis of the protocol data seems to confirm this idea (see the first part of Table 1).

The computation of Spearman rank-order correlations gives rise to the following considerations. The category "Asking for advice" is clearly related to various types of utterances made by the mothers. It seems that, if the children frequently ask for advice, the mothers will react by frequent evaluations of the children's actions and by indeed giving either strategical or direct advice. The correlations between the children's asking for advice and the mother's giving of advice are quite strong.

Table 1. Correlations Between Maternal Behaviors and Children's Behavior for all Subjects (n=64), and for the Various Subgroups.

Child	Positive evaluation	Neutral evaluation	Negative evaluation	Strategical advice	Direct advice
		Mother Total group (n=64)			
Asking feedback	.20	.07	.12	. .24* [1]	.11
Asking advice	.24*	.23*	.26*	.45** [2]	.32**
Positive comments on own actions	.25*	.27*	.17	.24*	.09
Negative comments on own actions	-.03	.22*	.03	.10	-.07
		B2/B3 (n=19)			
Asking feedback	.19	-.22	-.16	.08	.23
Asking advice	.07	.22	.14	.67*	.60
Positive comments on own actions	.14	.10	.04	.42*	-.07
Negative comments on own actions	-.02	.13	-.09	.14	-.16
		A/C (n=13)			
Asking feedback	.21	-.06	.27	.32	-.05
Asking advice	.26	.52*	.09	.07	.31
Positive comments on own actions	.40	.12	.04	.25	.15
Negative comments on own actions	.15	.35	.17	-.20	-.16
		B4 (n=14)			
Asking feedback	.30	.26	.42	.53*	.03
Asking advice	.53*	.24	.46*	.54*	-.20
Positive comments on own actions	.50*	.49*	.46	.42	.03
Negative comments on own actions	-.02	-.03	.06	.27	.08
		B1 (n=18)			
Asking feedback	.11	.16	.32	.20	.09
Asking advice	.20	.15	.39	.43*	.44*
Positive comments on own actions	.20	.41*	.40*	-.11	.14
Negative comments on own comments	-.09	.28	.06	.28	-.12

1. * indicates a level of significance of p ≤.05
2. ** indicates a level of significance of p ≤.01

This could mean that mothers react to their children's questions by providing much assistance. Of course, one should be cautious here. It might be that mothers giving much advice actually promote the asking of many questions. The correlations do not allow for any conclusions regarding the sequential chains in this situation. Whether the child's questions elicit the mother's tutorial behavior, or whether her instructions stimulate the child to ask for more advice, can only (partially) be solved by a sequential analysis (see below). On further inspection of the first part of Table 1, it becomes clear that the children's positive comments on their own actions are positively related to both neutral and positive evaluative comments made by their mothers. This would seem an obvious result if we suppose that both the children's positive comments and the mothers' positive evaluative remarks are probably related to a smooth task performance. Again, the plausibility of this assumption can only be demonstrated in a detailed sequential analysis of the child's actions and the mother–child dialogue. The children's negative comments on their own actions are positively related to neutral evaluative comments made by their mothers. This result can be interpreted in various ways. A plausible explanation would be that mothers do not wish to discourage their suboptimally performing children. They therefore restrict themselves to neutral comments.

From this correlational analysis it may be concluded that the mothers and children of our study generally interact in a meaningful and sensitive way when jointly solving an unknown problem. Referring back to the first part of our study, we can now ask the question of whether these interactional patterns are related to the attachment classifications established 3 years earlier. Is the emotional bond between mother and child, as established through the Strange Situation procedure, related to the nature of their cognitive interplay 3 years later? Let us remark first that such relations, when found, are quite hard to interpret. Indeed, they could reflect some stable aspects of the relationship between mother and child. But another possibility is that mother and/or child continue to show some characteristics which were built up in or influenced by their first attachment relation. In van IJzendoorn et al. (1987), we tried to solve some of these problems.

To analyze the cognitive interaction in our problem solving task for different attachment classes, we computed the Spearman rank-order correlations for four subgroups of mother–child pairs. Because the group of C dyads consisted of only four pairs, it was decided to combine the A and C groups. The normative B2 and B3 groups were also combined. This resulted in the following four attachment classes: A+C; B1; B2+B3; and B4. In Table 1 the correlation matrices for the different attachment classes can be found. The question arises of whether the correlational patterns for the various subgroups are clearly different and, if so, whether these differences can be meaningfully interpreted. It would be particularly interesting if the differences were related to the assessments of the interaction made in the Strange Situation 3 years before.

Let us start with the normative group of B2 and B3 dyads (see the second part of Table 1). Significant relations were found between the children's asking for advice and the mothers' supplying of strategical and direct advice. Also, the children's positive comments on their own actions are positively related to the mothers' long-term instructions. Apparently, when the children are at a loss what to do and ask their mothers for advice, it is often given to them. The mothers, on the other hand, do not instruct their children if the latter are not explicitly asking for it (see the sequential analysis below). This would seem to be a reasonable picture for two partners well attuned to each other. In fact, in all groups, except the A/C group of avoidantly and resistantly attached dyads, a strong correlation between the mothers' long-term strategical advice and the children's positive comments on their own task behavior was found. The A/C group presented a remarkable picture, because only one significant correlation was found (see the third part of Table 1). The children's asking for advice was positively related to the mothers' neutral evaluations. One is tempted to conclude that mothers and children are not really well attuned to one another in this task. Their verbal utterances are not strongly related to each other, which suggests that Piaget's apt qualification "collective monologue" may be applied in our situation as well. One should be careful, however, because independent behavior need not always point to an inferior quality of interaction (see below).

We will refrain from discussing the correlational results for the B1 and B4 groups; their interactions resemble the B2/3 group much more than the A/C group. By now it has become clear that the correlation matrices do not permit strong conclusions with respect to the temporal order of the mother–child interactions. As the sequential nature of these interactions is one of our main interests, we now turn to another type of analysis which could be more fitting for our goal.

Sequential Analysis

One way to get a more detailed picture of the interactional nature of mother–child dialogues is to analyze the actual sequence of the behaviors. Considering every behavior by one of the partners of a dyad as a turn in the ongoing dialogue, it becomes possible to compute the probability of occurrence of any turn as a function of the preceding turn(s). These probabilities are, of course, actually inductively found

Table 2. Mothers' Instructional Reactions to Children's Behaviors (n=64; 3 Lags, 2659 Turns, 715 Behaviors)

	Children's behavior												
	Request for feedback			Asking for advice			Positive comment			Negative comment			Total lag 1
Lag / Mother:	1	2	3	1	2	3	1	2	3	1	2	3	
No instruction	56 (-)	63 (-)	52 (-2.0)	20 (-2.4)	21 (-2.1)	22 (-)	149 (2.5)	130 (-)	131 (-)	50 (-)	49 (-)	54 (-)	275
Global feedback	53 (-)	51 (-)	56 (2.1)	12 (-2.3)	17 (-)	18 (-)	86 (-)	79 (-)	67 (-)	35 (-)	30 (-)	21 (-)	186
Global instruction	29 (-)	24 (-)	21 (-)	24 (3.8)	18 (2.3)	13 (-)	22 (-2.8)	29 (-)	24 (-)	15 (-)	13 (-)	14 (-)	90
Concrete advice	40 (-)	40 (-)	41 (-)	20 (-)	17 (-)	18 (-)	48 (-)	50 (-)	50 (-)	20 (-)	25 (-)	24 (-)	128
Does it herself	7 (-)	8 (-)	9 (-)	13 (4.0)	15 (3.8)	15 (3.2)	10 (-)	17 (-)	19 (-)	6 (-)	6 (-)	10 (-)	36
Total	185			89			315			126			715
%	25.9%			12.4%			44.1%			17.6%			

frequencies (e.g., "conditional frequencies" turned into percentages). Thus, if the child asks for advice in turn n, it is possible to compute the probability of occurrence of any behavior by either child or mother in turn n+1, n+2, n+3, etc. In Table 2 the frequencies of all maternal behaviors are presented as a function of the immediately preceding child behavior. Thus far we have concentrated on the purely verbal part of the mother–child interaction. However, both in the emotional and cognitive domain nonverbal behaviors may play an important role. That is why we now take into consideration several task-related behaviors (verbal as well as nonverbal), and analyze the sequential patterns of these behaviors. Because sequential analysis is based upon probabilities, we had to combine some observational categories to get reliable results. Therefore, we combined two categories of child behavior, e.g., nonverbal requests for feedback and asking for feedback. Both behaviors are global ways of getting information about the problem-solving process. We also combined three categories of maternal behavior which are focused upon concrete instructions and advice, giving concrete advices, taking and giving material, and demonstrating part of the solution to the child. In this way, we are able to present all data from 3-sec interval observations in 4 (child) × 5 (mother) categories. Single cases were connected through one, two, or three "missing data" codes, depending upon the number of lags analyzed, to prevent confounding of cases and lags (see Skinner, 1986, for a similar multiple cases approach of sequential analysis). In Table 2 the standardized residuals or z-values, computed on the basis of the conditional frequencies, are also shown for all subjects. Positive standardized residuals indicate that the frequency of the particular behavior was higher than expected (expectations being based on the assumption that all behaviors following a particular child behavior should have the same chance of occurring). Negative standardized residuals indicate that the particular behavior follows (far) less than expected.

Standardized residuals for three lags are given, because sometimes the child's behavior will influence maternal instruction only after several 3-sec intervals. First, the frequencies of the first lag will be considered. It is remarkable how often children have positive comments on their own performance: almost half of their behaviors consist of these positive comments, whereas only small part of their contribution to the dialogue consists of negative comments. For mothers the category "no instruction" is prevalent, whereas only small part of their assistance consist of solving the problem themselves. It is also remarkable that only during about a quarter of the turns do children show behaviors that are relevant to the problem solving process, e.g., 715 of 2659 turns. This could be the result of the restricted domain of our observational system, but it is also conceivable that kindergarten children are unable to concentrate intensively on one task for a long period of time.

Second, standardized residuals for the three lags will be considered. Beginning with (verbal and nonverbal) requests for feedback, we notice that there is no maternal behavior connected with this behavior of the child in the first two lags. Only in the third lag do requests for feedback predict more global maternal feedback and less instructional aloofness of the mother than one would expect on the basis of the marginal frequencies. It is only after a delay that mothers relinquish their passive attitude and assist the child's problem solving with global feedback. We found a correspondence between asking for feedback and strategical advice in the correlational analysis, but here no immediate connection is to be seen. Mothers seem to need some time in order to decide whether their child is able to solve the problem alone before intervening on a rather global level. If, however, the child asks for concrete advice instead of global feedback, maternal reactions are faster and much more concrete. Already in the first lag, mothers show more involvement in the problem solving process, and it seems as if global feedback is considered inadequate for reacting to the child's request for advice. Global instructions prevail, as well as active participation in problem solving. These maternal reactions to the children's asking for advice are also visible in the second lag, and active maternal involvement is present in all three lags. If the child asks for advice, mothers' reactions are prompt and persistent. The results of the correlational analysis are therefore confirmed and specified. As we have seen above, asking for advice was correlated with maternal evaluations and strategical and direct advice. Asking for advice was correlated with most maternal behaviors, and we also see that asking for advice is sequentially connected most frequently with maternal reactions. Asking for advice, therefore, appears to be the most salient child behavior in a problem-solving process, eliciting prompt and persistent maternal instructions. Sometimes mothers will do (part of) the job themselves after the children's request for advice, thereby actually demonstrating difficult steps of the problem and allowing their children to observe how the task can be solved.

Positive or negative comments by the children on their own performance do not elicit much maternal reactions. Positive comments lead to less instruction by the mother, in particular to less global instruction. The child appears to correctly evaluate his or her task performance, and the mother refrains from intervening when the child shows he or she can handle the problem alone. Here, the results of the sequential and the correlational analysis diverge. We have seen that positive comments correlated with maternal evaluations and strategical advice, but this outcome is not corroborated by the sequential analysis. Negative comments do not appear to be connected in any predictable way to maternal reactions. Mothers do not seem to take negative comments as an indication that their children need some help, and they appear to wait until requests for feedback or advice have been formulated more explicitly. These interactional patterns hold true for the aggregated "dyad" in our study. As in the correlational analysis, the question can be asked whether these patterns are related in some meaningful way to the attachment classifications established 3 years earlier. The sequential patterns for the four attachment groups are presented in Table 3. Of course, the results presented in this table are somewhat less reliable than those for the whole group because of the diminished number of turns in each group.

In Table 3, only the results for the first lag are presented. Frequencies for the second and third lag did not differ very strongly from those for the first lag. Below, we shall comment on significant standardized residuals for the second and third lag. First, the frequencies will be commented upon. Looking at the securely attached reference group, B2/3, we may conclude that the children from this group comment most frequently in a positive way on their performance. Negative comments are far less frequent. Children from B2/3 dyads seem to be most optimistic and self-confident about solving the problem. Together with the children from the other B groups, they also appear to ask less often for advice, but to request for feedback—verbally or nonverbally— more often than the anxiously attached A/C group. To see if these differences in the children's behavior result in different instructional behavior of the mothers, we have to look at the standardized residuals in Table 3. It is remarkable that three categories of children's behavior, i.e., requests for feedback, positive comments, and negative comments, do not appear to predictably elicit maternal instructional behavior. The diminished number of observations is, of course, of some importance here, but we already presented some correlational findings above which pointed in the same direction. As with the correlational analysis, only asking for advice is connected with maternal behavior in the first lag. However, these connections are restricted to the securely attached dyads: in the anxiously attached dyads, the A/C group, there is no sequential pattern whatsoever to be found in the data for the first lag. Mothers and children in the A/C group do not seem to interact meaningfully from the perspective of our observational system: asking for advice does not enhance the chance that mother will give some kind of advice or instruction in the first lag. In the securely attached dyads, however, asking for advice leads to more frequent global instruction and to the mothers doing some part of the task themselves. This last result, though,

Table 3. Mothers' Instructional Reactions to Children's Behaviors in the Four Attachment Classes (Lag 1)

	Children's behavior															
	Request for feedback				Asking for advice				Positive comment				Negative comment			
Mother:	A/C	B1	B2/3	B4	A/C	B1	B2/3	B4	A/C	B1	B2/3	B4	A/C	B1	B2/3	B4
No instruction	11	25	14	6	6	6	6	2	32	38	49	28	11	17	9	13
	(-)	(-)	(-)	(-)	(-)	(-)	(-)	(-)	(-)	(-)	(-)	(-)	(-)	(-)	(-)	(-)
Global feedback	8	16	14	15	6	4	1	1	18	26	23	17	7	11	7	10
	(-)	(-)	(-)	(-)	(-)	(-)	(-)	(-)	(-)	(-)	(-)	(-)	(-)	(-)	(-)	(-)
Global instruction	6	11	5	7	4	7	7	7	3	7	11	13	3	5	2	5
	(-)	(-)	(-)	(-)	(-)	(2.0)	(2.2)	(2.1)	(-)	(-)	(-)	(-)	(-)	(-)	(-)	(-)
Concrete advice	4	18	10	6	6	5	5	3	13	9	15	10	5	11	1	3
	(-)	(-)	(-)	(-)	(-)	(-)	(-)	(-)	(-)	(-)	(-)	(-)	(-)	(-)	(-)	(-)
Does it herself	2	1	3	1	3	3	5	2	4	2	4	0	2	1	2	1
	(-)	(-)	(-)	(-)	(-)	(2.5)	(2.5)	(2.5)	(-)	(-)	(-)	(-)	(-)	(-)	(-)	(-)
Total	31	71	46	35	25	25	24	15	70	82	102	68	28	45	21	32
%	20%	32%	24%	23%	16%	11%	12%	10%	46%	37%	53%	45%	18%	20%	11%	21%

is based upon small frequencies and thus has to be considered less reliable. Mothers in the securely attached group appear to react meaningfully to their children when the latter have difficulties solving the problem independently: they give instructions or show how to solve the problem by demonstrating part of the solution. The impression of a collective monologue in the anxiously attached dyads, and a genuine dialogue in the securely attached dyads, is confirmed in the next two lags. Especially in the reference group B2/3 of very securely attached dyads, asking for advice after the first lag is followed by more instruction (standardized residual, sr=−2.3) and by mothers doing more of the task themselves; this is, therefore, a continuation of maternal reactions in the first lag. In the third lag, there remains more instruction than expected (sr=−2.1), but now the child is getting more concrete advice (sr=2.4). This seems to be a sensitive strategy: after having given global instructions and trying to solve some part of the problem by themselves, the mothers of the B2/3 group turn to giving concrete advice in the third lag. Apparently, they wish the child to solve the rest of the task with the help of their advice. In the other—marginally secure—dyads (B1 and B4), this sequential pattern is less pertinent. In the B1 group, there is no connection between maternal and child behavior in the last two lags, whereas in the B4 group mothers are solving the problem themselves in the second (sr=2.1) and third (sr=2.3) lag, which seems to be a less sensitive strategy compared to giving concrete advices as the B2/3 mothers do. In the anxiously attached A/C group, mothers react to the children's asking for advice with global instruction in the second lag (sr=2.2), but not in the third lag. They do not react promptly and they do not appear to persist in their reactions. We are, therefore, inclined to think that children from the A/C group are operating in a more difficult task environment than the "ideal" reference group B2/3. In the B2/3 group, and to a lesser extent also in the B1 and B4 groups, chances were rather high that the mother would indeed supply the requested instructions. Not so for the A/C group, where the chances that the mother will give adequate instructions do not seem to depend on any previous action undertaken by the child. In general, one can say that in these dyads the mothers' reactions are distributed among categories by chance and cannot be predicted on the basis of the child's actions in the previous lag. In this respect, the sequential analysis confirms the correlational structure of the data, in which almost no significant and interpretable correlations were found for the A/C group. Finding no clear sequential pattern in problem-solving interactions of the A/C group might mean that the mother is not closely monitoring the child's actions and, therefore, acts more or less independently. A more favorable but less plausible interpretation would be that she is well aware of her child's actions but deliberately ignores questions for help, approval, etc., perhaps in an effort to promote independent problem solving.

We conclude this paragraph by looking at differences between boys and girls. In Table 4 the results of the sequential analysis for girls and boys, respectively, are presented.

For girls, not much sequential structure can be found. Negative or positive comments on their own actions do not elicit any reaction from their mother; the same holds true for requests for feedback. Only asking for advice stimulates maternal reactions: in general the mother gives more instruction, more global instructions, and tends to do the task herself more often than expected by chance. Generally speaking, one finds more interactional structure for mother–boy dyads than for mother–girl dyads. Whereas girls' positive comments elicit no consistent maternal reaction, boys experience consistent instruction: they get less global instructions, and more "no instructions," that is, less instructions generally, than would be expected by chance. These reactions seem adequate responses to the self-confident behavior of the boys and may stimulate their autonomous problem-solving capability. Boys also get more consistent and prompt reactions to their verbal and nonverbal requests for feedback. Mothers give more instructions generally and, in particular, more concrete advice. They appear to react about the same to the boys as in the case of girls' asking for advice. The differences between boys and girls are even more apparent for the second and third lags. For mother–girl dyads, no sequential structure was found.

Table 4. Mothers' Instructional Reactions to Behaviors of Girls and Boys Separately (Lag 1)

Mother:	Children's behavior							
	Request for feedback		Asking for advice		Positive comments		Negative comments	
	girls	boys	girls	boys	girls	boys	girls	boys
No in-	34	22	9	11	64	85	27	23
struction	(-)	(-2.5)	(-2.0)	(-)	(-)	(2.2)	(-)	(-)
Global	21	32	7	5	41	45	19	16
feedback	(-)	(-)	(-)	(-)	(-)	(-)	(-)	(-)
Global	13	16	12	12	14	14	6	9
instruction	(-)	(-)	(2.5)	(2.5)	(-)	(-2.1)	(-)	(-)
Concrete	15	25	12	8	22	26	16	4
advice	(-)	(2.1)	(-)	(-)	(-)	(-)	(-)	(-)
Does it	5	2	6	7	5	5	5	1
herself	(-)	(-)	(2.0)	(4.0)	(-)	(-)	(-)	(-)
Total	88	97	46	43	146	175	73	53
%	25%	26%	13%	12%	41%	48%	21%	14%

For mother–boy dyads, the following pattern seems to arise: in the second lag, only asking for advice elicits a predictable response; the mother tends to do some part of the task herself (sr=4.3). The same connection can be discerned in the third lag (sr=3.9). However, in the third lag, requests for feedback also lead to systematic reactions: mothers give more instructions in general (sr=−2.1), and react with global feedback more often, than was to be expected by chance (sr=2.1). Finally, boys' positive comments on their own performance stimulate the mothers to give "no instruction" (sr=2.1). In sum, in all three lags maternal reactions to boys appear to be more prompt and consistent, that is, more sensitive compared to their reactions to girls. These results are intriguing and difficult to account for at the same time. It appears that a statistical explanation can be ruled out—although the number of turns for boys is slightly higher than for girls (1332 vs. 1119), this difference in itself is unlikely to account for the sex differences found in the sequential analysis. There was also no confounding of attachment classification and sex in the sample. This implies that the finding is real and that we have to look for theoretical explanations.

DISCUSSION AND CONCLUSIONS

The present study started as an attempt to explore some of the long-term repercussions of early childhood attachments. In particular, we were interested in the possible influence of attachment class on mothers' and children's later joint problem solving. Different methods to analyze the mother–child interactions were used. Generally speaking, the classical method of correlational analysis of mother–child interactions was found to be the least useful. The value of this method, the validity of which has been questioned by Valsiner (1986), seems rather limited, at least for the type of phenomena studied here. More informative were the sequential analyses of the mother–child interactions. In particular, the sequential analysis of both the verbal and nonverbal aspects of the interactions yielded some interesting results. Sequential analysis thus seems to be a potentially effective tool when studying this type of phenomena. A possibly more detailed understanding of the phenomena studied might have been reached by leaving the perspective of looking for between-group differences and diving into the individual mother–child interactions. This would also have brought us closer to the concept of sensitive responsiveness, as was outlined in the first paragraphs of this chapter. However, as we were interested in between-group differences, in particular the difference between securely and anxiously attached dyads, we used the concept of sensitivity in a less restricted and more "loose" way.

Some interesting findings concerning early childhood attachments and later joint problem solving indeed were found. We will concentrate here on the differences found between dyads originally classified as either securely attached (B2/3) or anxiously attached (A/C). For securely attached dyads, the picture was as follows. When the children from the B2/3 group asked for advice, their mothers replied by giving such advice, i.e., global instruction, or by doing part of the task themselves. They, therefore, reacted meaningfully to their children's initiatives. As argued before, these replies made by the mother might be called sensitive in the "loose" sense of the word. The situation was different for the group of anxiously attached dyads. There, asking for advice was not characteristically met by prompt and consistent maternal reactions. Mothers were not likely to give the advice the children were asking for, at least not in the first lag. No pattern whatsoever could be found in our sequential analysis for the first lag. For the next two lags, meaningful patterns in the securely attached groups were detected, but only one link between maternal and child behavior in the anxiously attached group. One is tempted to conclude, therefore, that, 3 years after the original classification, there still are differences in interactional patterns between these groups. The dyads originally classified as insecurely attached still appear to interact in a climate which seems less supportive.

These findings are relevant for the two frameworks we have described in this chapter—cultural-historical theory and attachment theory. As has been said before, cultural-historical theory lacks an adequate perspective on early childhood affective interactions. It could benefit from attachment theory which has described in detail how the emotional bond between caregiver and child develops, starting from the earliest contact-eliciting child behaviors like smiling, crying, and proximity seeking. The reciprocal, interactional nature of this bonding process has become firmly established. It is our opinion that cultural-historical theory—starting from the same interactional perspective—can easily and should incorporate this attachment perspective. This would provide it with the much needed conceptualization of affective interactions. Elsewhere (van der Veer & van IJzendoorn, 1987), we have argued that both frameworks are compatible in this respect. The primitive contact seeking behaviors (e.g., smiling and crying) could be thought of as Vygotskian lower psychological processes which become interpreted in culturally bound ways (van IJzendoorn, 1986). Thus, findings and concepts from attachment theory can be a valuable contribution to cultural-historical theory. The latter's historically strong focus on verbal interaction is attenuated, and the former's emphasis on affective preverbal interaction gets its due attention.

Attachment theory, on the other hand, may benefit from concepts and methodology developed within the cultural-historical framework. The claim of attachment theorists that the quality of emotional bonds is crucial for both the child's emotional and cognitive development can be corroborrated only using the right means for assessment of emotional and cognitive development. The notion of the zone of proximal development and the idea of a contingency strategy seem to be valuable means in this respect. Moreover, as we have argued before, they seem to match closely the concept of sensitive responsiveness developed within the attachment approach.

The combination of cultural-historical theory and attachment theory thus seems to give us at least the outlines of a comprehensive theory of child development. Attachment theory is particularly appropriate for describing the evolvement and development of the first emotional relationship(s) of the child. Virtually all caregiver–infant interactions are heavily affect-laden. Gradually the character of the interactions will change, however, and the affective aspect—though still strongly present—will become less prominent. The almost purely affective dialogue will gradually turn into a more cognitive dialogue. The emotional bond will not disappear, of course, and will form the context for all non-emotional interactions. Children from a securely attached dyad, for instance, will feel emotionally secure when coping with difficult cognitive problems. Quite probably this will affect their behavior in these tasks. In this chapter we have found evidence that patterns of interactions of dyads originally classified through the Strange Situation procedure still differ in a problem-solving task 3 years later. Apparently, although the bond between mother and child will be gradually transformed (and sometimes redefined by one or both of the partners), there still is some stability in their interactions. This stability showed up in our sequential analysis, suggesting a continuity between affective early childhood interactions and later joint problem solving.

However, we should be cautious. The differences between the various attachment groups are not overwhelmingly clear, and other, independent, classifications (e.g., sex) also result in some significant differences. This means to the present authors that one should look for other factors apart from quality of attachment on the dyadic level. As we argued elsewhere (van IJzendoorn, van der Veer, & van Vliet-Visser, 1987), when analyzing mother–child interactions one should realize that the child is part of a developing network of social relationships. A qualitatively good attachment network could provide the developing child with a degree and quality of support which makes it hazardous to make any definite statements about the child's current or future cognitive and emotional development based upon dyadic data. Paraphrasing Hinde et al. (1985, p. xvi), we might say that the dyadic concept of attachment is at the same time a potentially useful tool for understanding and a blinker that constrains our vision.

REFERENCES

Ainsworth, M.S.D., Bell, S.M., & Stayton, D.J. (1974). Infant–mother attachment and social development: "Socialization" as a product of reciprocal responsiveness to signals. In M.P.M. Richards (Ed.), *The integration of a child into a social world* (pp. 99–135). London: Cambridge University Press.

Ainsworth, M.S.D., Blehar, M.C., Waters, E., & Wall, S. (1978). *Patterns of attachment. A psychological study of the strange situation.* Hillsdale, NJ: Erlbaum.

Ainsworth, M.S.D., & Wittig, B.A. (1969). Attachment and exploratory behavior of one-year-olds in a strange situation. In B. Foss (Ed.), *Determinants of infant behavior* (pp. 111–136). New York: Wiley.

Arend, R. (1984). *Preschooler's competence in a barrier situation: patterns of adaptation and their precursors in infancy.* Unpublished doctoral dissertation, University of Minnesota.

Arend, R., Gove, F.L., & Sroufe, A.L. (1979). Continuity of individual adaptation from infancy to kindergarten: A predictive study of ego-resiliency and curiosity in preschoolers. *Child Development, 50,* 950–959.

Belsky, J., Rovine, M., & Taylor, P. (1984). The Pennsylvania infant and family development project III: The origins of the individual differences in infant-mother attachment. Maternal and infant contributions. *Child Development, 55,* 718–728.

Brazelton, T.B., Koslowski, B., & Main, M. (1974). The origins of reciprocity: The early mother-infant interactions, in M. Lewis & L.A. Rosenblum (Eds.). *The effect of the infant on its caregiver* (pp. 49–77). London: Wiley.

Bretherton, J., Bates, E., Benigni, L., Camaioni, L., & Volterra, V. (1979). Relationships between cognition, communication, and quality of attachment. In E. Bates, L. Benigni, J. Bretherton, L. Camaioni, & V. Volterra (Eds.), *The emergence of symbols: Cognition and communication in infancy* (pp. 223–269). New York: Academic Press.

Bronfenbrenner, U. (1983). The context of development and the development of context. In R.M. Lerner (Ed.), *Developmental psychology: Historical and philosophical perspectives.* Hillsdale, NJ: Erlbaum.

Bruner, J. (1983). *Child's talk. Learning to use language.* New York: Norton.

Bruner, J. (1984). Vygotsky's zone of proximal development: the hidden agenda. In B. Rogoff & J.V. Wertsch (Eds.), *Children's learning in the "zone of proximal development"* (pp. 93–97). San Francisco, CA: Jossey Bass.

Bryant, P. (1985). Parents, children, and cognitive development. In R.A. Hinde, A.N. Perret-Clermont, & J. Stevenson-Hinde (Eds.), *Social relationships and cognitive development* (pp. 239–249). Oxford, England: Clarendon Press.

Engeström, Y. (1986). The zone of proximal development as the basic category of educational psychology. *The Quarterly Newsletter of the Laboratory of Comparative Human Cognition, 8,* 23–42.

Goossens, F.A. (1986). *The quality of the attachment relationship of two-year-old children of working and non-working mothers and some associated factors.* Unpublished dissertation. University of Leiden, The Netherlands.

Goossens, F.A., Van IJzendoorn, M.H., Tavecchio, L.W.C., & Kroonenberg, P.M. (1986). Stability of attachment across time and context in a Dutch sample. *Psychological Reports, 58,* 23–32.

Harré, R., Clarke, D., & De Carlo, N. (1985). *Motives and mechanisms. An introduction to the psychology of action.* London: Methuen.

Hartup, W.W. (1985). Relationships and their significance in cognitive development. In R.A. Hinde, A.N. Perret-Clermont, & J. Stevenson-Hinde (Eds.), *Social relationships and cognitive development* (pp. 68–81). Oxford, England: Clarendon Press.

Hazen, N.L. & Durrett, M.E. (1982). Relationships of security of attachment to exploration and cognitive mapping abilities in 2-year olds. *Developmental Psychology, 18,* 751–759.

Hinde, R.A., Perret-Clermont, A.N., & Stevenson-Hinde, J. (1985). *Social relationships and cognitive development.* Oxford, England: Clarendon Press.

Lamb, M.E., & Easterbrooks, M.A. (1981). Individual differences in parental sensitivity: Origins, components, and consequences. In M.E. Lamb & L.R. Sherrod (Eds.), *Infant social cognition: Empirical and theoretical considerations* (pp. 127–154). Hillsdale, NJ: Erlbaum.

Matas, L., Arend, R.A., & Sroufe, L.A. (1978). Continuity of adaptation in the second year: The relationship between quality of attachment and later competence. *Child Development, 49,* 547–556.

Newcomb, A.F., & Brady, J.E. (1982). Mutuality in boys' friendship relations. *Child Development, 53,* 392–395.

Plooij, F.X., & Van der Rijt-Plooij, H.H.C. (1983). Ethologische studies van privatie, deprivatie en escalatie [Ethological studies of privation, deprivation, and escalation]. *Pedagogisch Tijdschrift, 8,* 418–428.

Rahe, D.F. (1984). *Interaction patterns between children and mothers on teaching tasks at age 42 months: antecedents in attachment history, intellectual correlates and consequences on children's socio-emotional functioning.* Unpublished doctoral dissertation. University of Minnesota.

Sagi, A.A., Lamb, M.E., Lewkowicz, K.S., Shoham, R., Dvir, R., & Estes, D. (1985). Security of infant–mother, –father, and –metapelet attachments among kibbutz-reared Israeli children. In I. Bretherton & E. Waters (Eds.), Growing points of attachment theory and research. *Monographs of the Society for Research in Child Development, 50,* 257–275.

Skinner, E.A. (1986). The origins of young children's perceived control: Mother contingent and sensitive behavior. *International Journal of Behavioral Development, 9,* 359–382.

Trevarthen, C. (1977). Descriptive analysis of infant communicative behavior. In H.R. Schaffer (Ed.), *Studies in mother-infant interaction* (pp. 227–270). London: Academic Press.

Valsiner, J. (1986). Between groups and individuals: Psychologists' and lay-persons' interpretations of correlational findings. In J. Valsiner (Ed.), *The role of the individual subject in scientific psychology* (pp. 113–151). New York: Plenum.

Valsiner, J. (1987). *Culture and the development of children's action: A cultural-historical theory of developmental psychology.* Chichester, England: Wiley.

van der Veer, R. (1986). Vygotsky's developmental psychology. *Psychological Reports, 59,* 527–536.

van der Veer, R., & van IJzendoorn, M.H. (1985). Vygotsky's theory of the higher psychological processes: Some criticisms. *Human Development, 28,* 1–9.

van der Veer, R., & van IJzendoorn, M.H. (1987). La teoría de Vygotski y la necesidad de conceptualizar las relaciones emocionales. In A. Alvarez (Ed.), *Psicología y educación.* Madrid: Visor Libros.

Van der Veer, R., & Valsiner, J. (in press). Lev Vygotsky and Pierre Janet. On the origin of the concept of sociogenesis. *Developmental Review.*

van IJzendoorn, M.H. (1986). The cross-cultural validity of the Strange Situation from a Vygotskian perspective. *The Behavioral and Brain Sciences, 16,* 558–559.

van IJzendoorn, M.H., Goossens, F.A., Kroonenberg, P.M., & Tavecchio, L.W.C. (1985). Dependent attachment: B4 children in the strange situation. *Psychological Reports, 57,* 439–451.

van IJzendoorn, M.H., & Van der Veer, R. (1984). *Main currents of critical psychology: Vygotsky, Holzkamp, Riegel.* New York: Irvington.

van IJzendoorn, M.H., Van der Veer, R., & Van Vliet-Visser, S. (1987). Attachment three years later. Relationships between quality of mother-infant attachment and cognitive-emotional development in kindergarten. In L.W.C. Tavecchio & M.H. Van IJzendoorn (Eds.), *Attachment in social networks. Contributions to attachment theory* (pp. 185–225). Amsterdam, Netherlands: Elsevier Science Publishers (North-Holland).

van IJzendoorn, M.H., & Van Vliet-Visser, S. (1988). Attachment and intelligence. The relationship between quality of attachment in infancy and IQ in kindergarten. *Journal of Genetic Psychology.*

Vygotsky, L.S. (1982). *Sobranie sočinenij 2. Problemy obščej psichologii. [Collected Works 2. Problems of General Psychology]* (in Russian) Moscow: Pedagogika.

Vygotsky, L.S. (1983). *Sobranie sočinenij 3. Problemy razvitija psichiki. [Collected Works 3. Problems of the Development of Mind]* (in Russian) Moscow: Pedagogika.

Waters, E., Wippman, J., & Sroufe, L.A. (1979). Attachment, positive effect, and competence in the peer group: Two studies in construct validation. *Child Development, 50,* 821–829.

Wertsch, J.V. (ed.), (1985a). *Culture, communication, and cognition: Vygotskian perspectives.* New York: Cambridge University Press.

Wertsch, J.V. (1985b). *The social formation of mind: A Vygotskian approach.* Cambridge, MA: Harvard University Press.

Wood, D. (1980). Teaching the young child: Some relationships between social interaction, language, and thought. In D.R. Olson (Ed.), *The social foundations of language and thought* (pp. 280–296). New York: Norton.

Wood, D., Bruner, J.S., & Ross, G. (1976). The role of tutoring in problem solving. *Journal of Child Psychology and Psychiatry, 17,* 89–100.

Wood, D., Wood, H., & Middleton, D. (1978). An experimental evaluation of four face-to-face teaching strategies. *International Journal of Behavioral Development, 1,* 131–147.

EPILOGUE

Relations of Cognition and Interaction in Parental Conduct

Jaan Valsiner

Department of Psychology
University of North Carolina

This first volume of *Child development within culturally structured environments* was devoted to issues of parental cognition and parent–child interaction. In general, these issues were viewed from a cultural-historical perspective by some of the contributors (Chapters 4 and 6), whereas others advanced dialectical (Chapter 2) and transactional (Chapters 1 and 5) views on parental cognition and conduct. The contemporary tradition of cognitive psychology to explain human reasoning processes by way of attribution of its different facets to distinguishable "heuristics" was likewise critically examined in this volume (Chapter 3).

Any effort to integrate cognitive aspects of parenting with their explications in the sphere of adult–child interaction is likely to encounter a number of theoretical obstacles that are inherited by contemporary psychology from its history. First, there is the long-cherished emphasis on the "objectivity" of "behavior," paired with frequent claims that "prediction and control" of "behavior" are "the task" of psychology. The roots of this emphasis can be traced back to the behavioristic belief system that has had a widespread influence in psychology over the last six decades. Second, an obstacle that is frequently encountered in cognitive developmental psychology of the present time is the non-developmental nature of most of the cognitive science. Cognitive explanations of psychological phenomena are mostly built up to characterize the status quo of these phenomena, rather than explain their transformation into novel states of affairs. Finally, psychologists have often become caught in trying to prove that "cognition" and "behavior" are consistent with each other. Since that seldom seems to be the case, psychology may be perceived at times to be "in crisis" because predictability from thoughts (represented in words) to deeds is low. These obstacles deserve further conceptual analysis, since no *empirical* effort to overcome them is likely to be productive.

WHERE IS "OBJECTIVITY OF BEHAVIOR" IN ADULT-CHILD TRANSACTION?

Developmental psychology of the recent two decades has been filled with efforts to study adult–child interaction, with the help of observational methods. Mere registration of behavior, however, constitutes no explanation. In this respect, the behavioristic belief system that conquered psychology from 1913 onwards has accomplished a curious epistemological trick—the emphasis on the objectivity of behavioral *observations* has become extended, so that its halo effect covers also behavioristic *explanations* and legitimizes their "objectivity." The subjectivity of experience that served as the primary datum for introspectionist psychology was transformed into a conjunction of objective observations and subjectivistic theorizing. *Both* of the latter became designated as "objective," on the basis of belief triggered by the apparent reality of the former. Behavioristic world view in psychology has hidden the subjective nature of psychologists' theorizing behind the "objectivity" of the "behavioral data."

Research on adult–child interaction in recent decades bears the mark of similar epistemological difficulty. The possibility of observing "what adults and children are doing while interacting" has rendered empirical investigation of interaction an interesting activity of child psychologists, albeit with rare efforts to make theoretical sense of the principles according to which adult–child interaction is organized. Theoretical problems cannot be solved through inductive inference from empirical investigations. However, that simple rule is rarely clearly understood by contemporary child psychologists. As a result, the seeming "objectivity" of the multitude of observational studies of adult–child interaction covers the weakness of the area—lack of general conceptualizations of that interaction process.

How, then, can the adult–child interaction process be conceptualized? The usual way it is done, implicitly or explicitly, is to view it as a uni- or bidirectional "exchange" of (or stimulation by) "behaviors." The behavioristic scheme is rather obvious—the child "sends" behavioral "stimuli" to the adult via the vocal and visual communication channels, and the adult "responds" by similar stimulation. Since the "behaviors" that are involved can be observed "objectively" (usually, that means that a behavior classification system is devised and used by some "independent" observers in a sufficiently concurrent way), it is assumed that the "exchange" of these behaviors is as "objective" as these behavioral units themselves.

It is obvious from the present volume that such a "behavior exchange" theory of adult–child interaction misses a major point—*the role of a particular behavioral phenomenon in the process of interaction is not given by its own nature, but may acquire different functions under different circumstances.* Thus, the function of an adult smile while meeting a new person is quite different from a similar smile used within an aggressive encounter. Likewise, a look by the toddler towards a visiting adult in the first minute of their encounter is different from a look (similar in form) the same toddler gives to the same adult 10 minutes later, when both are involved in joint play (see Chapter 5). Human interaction involves behavior, not in its "objective" sense that behavioristic heritage would attribute to it, but in the function of *instrument* that is used by the interacting persons in a goal-oriented manner. The instrumental role of behavior in the web of goal-oriented interaction makes it imperative to analyze the link of behavior and cognition. The term *conduct* is suggested here to be resurrected into the vocabulary of developmental psychology, to denote behavior that is intertwined with the cognitive sphere of the person.

Conduct of partners in adult–child interaction is necessarily context-bound, aside from being goal-oriented. It unites the "higher" and "lower" psychological processes (in Vygotsky's sense) within the ongoing interaction process. Observable "behavior" is therefore only a limited part of conduct, as it is intricately tied with the affective psychological basis (as Van der Veer & Van IJzendoorn argue in Chapter 6), or with the system of "zones" of child development (see Ignjatovic-Savic et al. in Chapter 4), or with the motivation to establish new, even if temporary, social relationships (Hill & Valsiner, Chapter 5). Conduct exists objectively in the interaction process (that is—at every moment of time when we interact with others, our conduct is objective), but its study in psychology becomes "objective" only when our theories of interaction become adequately linked with empirical observations of conduct. These latter observations, on their own, are never "objective" in the positivistic sense, since they capture only the "tip of the iceberg" of the conduct as a whole. In general, objectivity in science is not a starting point from which we can start to construct theories, but an end point where (originally equally subjective) theories and empirical investigations meet to construct adequate knowledge about the world.

COGNITIVE SCIENCE AND THE STUDY OF CHILD DEVELOPMENT

Research on human conduct (rather than behavior) makes it possible to (re)introduce the cognitive side into our general picture of child development. It is no longer important to merely observe how parents act with their children, in one or another situation. It becomes relevant to explicate the ways in which parents reason about their acting upon their children, and how they conceptualize their childrearing in terms of goals and means to reach those goals. Furthermore, parents may reorganize their particular ways of thinking about childrearing in conjunction with events that take place in their interaction with the children. Parental reasoning about the prevention of childhood injuries (Gärling & Gärling, Chapter 3) is probably the domain in which the feedback between thinking and preventive actions is of the most applied value. It is therefore not surprising that the authors find some widely popular concepts of contemporary cognitive psychology, like "heuristics," to be only partially valuable in accounting for parental reasoning.

The major strength at times present in contemporary cognitive psychology that child development research can borrow is perhaps in an emphasis on the process orientation. Cognition is a process, and can be studied as a process—rather than a static and nontemporal entity. This process orientation, however, does not usually include openness towards allowing reorganization in the cognitive mechanisms that carry the process. That limitation is of crucial relevance for the study of child development, where a developmental researcher presumes qualitative transformation of the cognitive processes as the child develops. Similar qualitative change can be expected in parental cognition. Holden and Ritchie's (Chapter 2) introduction of dialectical logic into the study of parental reasoning processes constitutes a step towards overcoming the nondevelopmental limitation of contemporary cognitive perspectives.

INCONSISTENCY OF COGNITION AND CONDUCT

Finally, child development entails necessary inconsistency between parental reasoning about childrearing, their actions, and their outcomes. Children usually develop in ways different from the predictions by parents and child psychologists. Parents are often inconsistent between their words and deeds, and children have ample opportunities to experience it; and—they do become similarly inconsistent. For the widespread world view that many psychologists follow and which entails a belief in the inherent goodness of consistency and predictability, empirical evidence to the contrary is epistemologically upsetting. If there is little cognition-to-action consistency in psychologists' data obtained from parents, the question of how can we ever explain the actual processes that guide child development may suggest itself as an insurmountable obstacle. The reasons for such inconsistency become apparent from the systemic analysis of family transactions described by Stratton (Chapter 1). It is the complex causal system of multiple actions and lines of reasoning of different family members that organizes their thinking and acting in respect to the child. Simple causality (A causes B) is a severely simplified model for understanding parental cognition and action in a family context. Complex causal cyclicity, instead, is the rule. It can give rise to episodic, and at times paradoxical, psychological outcomes. Sometimes, the causal system may generate consistency between parental reasoning and acting, but at other times it is not the case.

Perhaps a way out of the impasse of cognition–conduct inconsistency is to set up the function of cognition from the perspective of the cognizing organism. For the parent (who reasons about childrearing, claims some results of that reasoning, and then carries out actions that contradict these results), cognitive functioning is *not necessarily* a way that leads towards more accurate understanding of the child. Aside from the function of understanding children better, there exist many other functions that the parent's cognition can cater for. Parents, like anybody else, are vulnerable to reasoning in order to "defend their egos" (or at least legitimize some of their conduct). Denial, projection, and any other of the multitude of ego-defense mechanisms that psychoanalytic thinkers have described, can be revealed in parental reasoning. *Both* consistency and inconsistency between parental reasoning and acting can be highly adaptive, dependent upon the circumstances in which these occur. Cognition is a means to assist conduct, as much as conduct helps cognition, in the curious interplay of agents in the social organization of child development within environmental contexts.

SOCIAL CO-CONSTRUCTION OF CHILD DEVELOPMENT

The contributions to the present volume lead to the relevance of conceptualizing child development as it is gradually constructed by the developing child himself or herself, and by the persons who give care to the child. Some leads for such, *co-constructionist* perspective on child development are provided in the second volume of this book. Contributors to Volume 2 continue along the lines of creating novel theoretical approaches and relating those to empirical phenomena, so that the social and cognitive sides of child development become integrated into one framework. Again, it is tempting to attach the label "Vygotskian" to that enterprise, but perhaps a word of caution is worthwhile in that respect. By calling something by the name of a classic thinker we actually do not explain anything, but rather help the reader to classify the given writing to a class of writings that is associated with him or her. The contributors to this, and the second, volume of *Child development within culturally structured environments* proceed along their individually specific paths towards a goal that hopefully amounts to better understanding of development. On their way, they may be indebted to different theorists of the past or present, but in fact they may follow nobody but themselves, since in the end it is the *novel* rather than the familiar that should emerge from a scientific enterprise.

Author Index

A

Abelson, R.P., 67, 75, *83*

Ainsworth, M.D.S., 34, *52, 58,* 91, *150,* 163, 166, 167, 168, 170, 171, *201, 202,* 220, 227, *243*

Ajzen, I., 61, 64, 6б, *80*

Alvarez, W.F., 20 *26*

Anders, T.F., 16, *29*

Anderson, B.J., 106, 107, *153*

Anderson, J.W., 163, *201*

Arend, R., 220, *243, 244*

Aronfreed, J., 34, 35, *52*

Ashton, G.C., 18, 19, *27*

Atkinson, J.W., 61, 64, *82*

Azuma, H., 38, 39, *52, 53, 58*

B

Bakeman, R., 118, *150*

Baker, S.P., 61, *80*

Bakhtin, M., 89, *150*

Bannister, D., 22, *26*

Basseches, M., 41, *52*

Bates, J.E., 165, *201,* 220, *243*

Baumrind, D., 34, 35, 36, 47, *52*

Bayley, N., 34, 37, *53,* 104, *150*

Beail, N., 19, *26*

Becker, W.C., 6, *26,*

Beckwith, L., 172, *201*

Bell, R.Q., 8, *26,* 34, 37, 42, *53,* 65, *80*

Bell, S.M., 34, 42, *52,* 171, *201,* 220, *243*

Belsky, J., 34, 42, *53,* 220, *243*

Bender, E.P., 168, *205*

Benedek, T., 164, *201*

Benedict, R., 38, *53*

Benigni, L., 220, *243*

Berland, J., 161, *201*

Bettelheim, B., 42, *53*

Bever, T.G., 86, *87*

Biel, A., 63, *83*

Birch, H.G., 16, 21, *28, 29*

Birns, B., 19, *29*

Bischof, N., 166, *201*

Björklid, P., 62, *80*

Black, A.E., 34, 35, 36, *52*

Blackburn, T.C., 39, *58*

Blades, M., *83*

Blehar, M.C., 91, *150,* 167, 168, 170, 201, 227, *243*

Bloch, M.N., 62, *80*

Block, J., 36, *53*

Blurton, 166, *201*

Boguslavskaia, Z.M., 97, *150*

Bowlby, J., 163, 164, 165, 166, 173, 174, 175, *202*

Bradley, R., 34, *53, 54*

Brady, J.E., 217, *244*

Brazelton, T.B., 216, *243*

Bretherton, I., 166, 167, 170, 172, *202,* 220, *243*

Brinker, R.P., 23, *26*

Brody, G.H., 36, *53*

Bronfenbrenner, V., 20, *26,* 85, *87,* 215, 216, *243*

Brooks-Gunn, J., 34, *56*

Brossard, A., 95, 96, *152*

Broussard, E.R., 16, *26*

Brown, A.L., 98, *151*

Brown, J.V., 98, 118, *150*

Brown, M.F., 166, *201*

Bruner, J., 92, 149, *151,* 222, *243, 246*

Brunner, J., *243*

Bryant, P., 219, *244*

Budwig, N.A., 98, *153*

Butterfield, P., 173, *203*

253

Subject Index

A

Accidents
  protection from, 68–70
  scenarios of, 73–75, 77–78
Action (activity)
  choices of, 19
  "free", 104–105
  individual, 90
  joint (adult–child), 85, 95, 100–101,
    110–111, 175–178, 191–199
Adaptation
  transactional, 1, 7–9, 41–42
Assimilation and accommodation, 9, 41
Attachment
  and cognitive development, 219–225
  and social relationships, 162–163, 216
  empirical research on, 165–166
  "measurement" of, 167–169
  static essence vs. process view,
    166–167
  theory, 86–87, 163–164, 240–243
    and relationships formation, 173–175
  types of, 87, 178, 230–240

B

Behavior
  "objectivity" of, 247–249
Beliefs
  nested, 12–13
  parents about children, 13–20, 68–69

C

Causality
  linear versus systemic, 23–25
  schema(ta) of, 66–67
Child-rearing
  dialectics in, 44–46

  in Japan, 38–40
Cognition, 247–248
  and communication, 89, 91–95
  and conduct
    inconsistency between, 250–251
    interdependency of, 14
  parental, 32–37
    study of, 49–51
  and study of child development, 250
  reflexivity in, 1
Culture, 1
  and beliefs, 15–16, 18–20
  comparisons across cultures, 2
  and development, 97–100, 216–217
  values, 6–7

D

Development
  child
    collective organization of, 162
    constructivist ideas, 251–252
    and society, 215–216
Dialectics (*see also* Child-rearing), 2,
    40–41

E

Environment
  adult-made, 92
  and accident prevention, 3, 69–71,
    78–80
  and children, 13–20, 62–64, 216–217

F

Family, 5–7, 9–13

G

Goals
  structure of, 177

259